IMAGES
of America

SEBRING

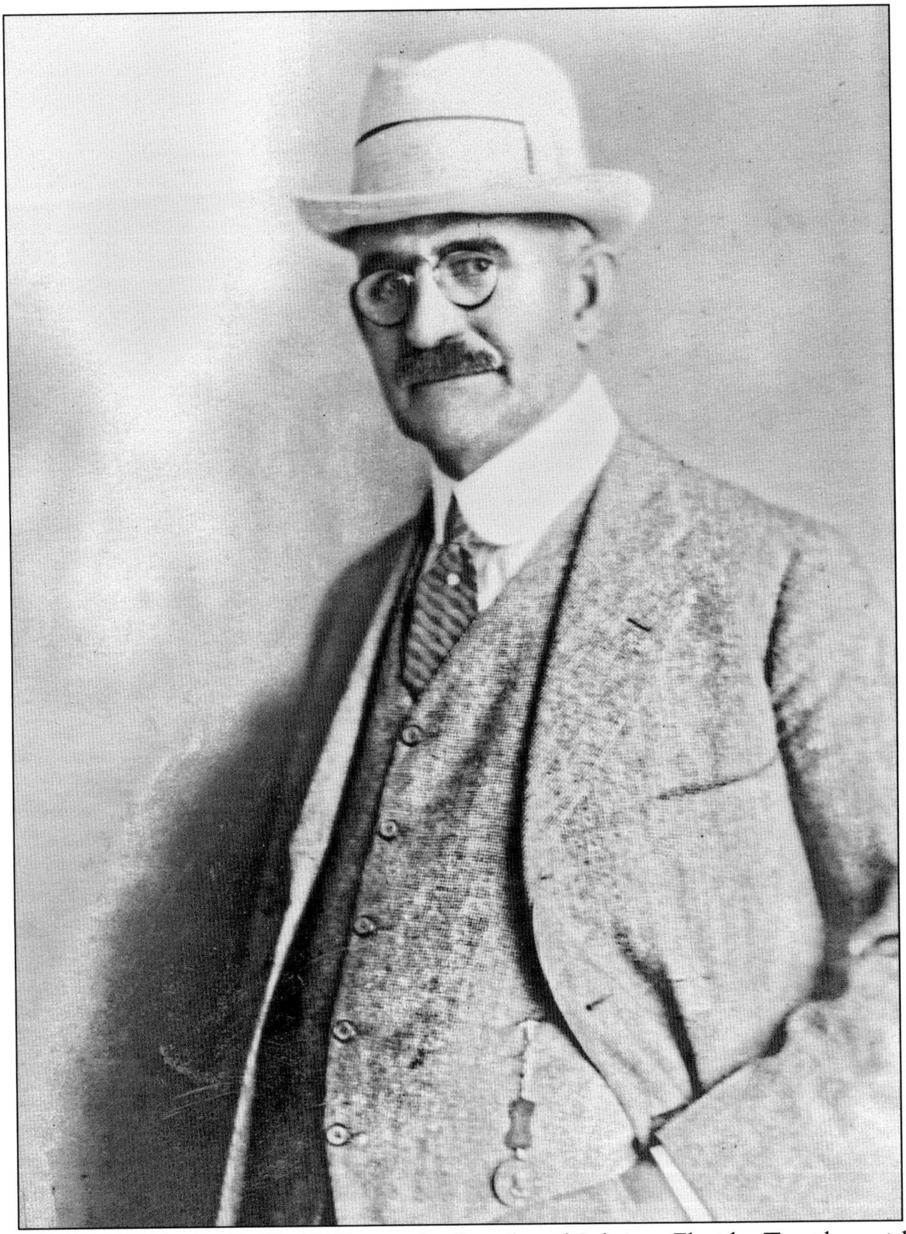

George Eugene Sebring (1859–1927) was the founder of Sebring, Florida. Together with his son and partner H. Orvel Sebring, they watched the young town grow into a model planned community and winter oasis for northern residents. The elder Sebring never held local office and was seldom heard to speak in public; his vision and works instead became his enviable legacy. (Courtesy Sebring Historical Society.)

ON THE COVER: Participants in the July 4, 1926, Sebring Fire Department "Miss Flame" beauty pageant are shown on the department's newest truck, purchased that year. Among the participants were Lois Starbuck and Virginia Woods, third and fourth from left. The truck appears to be in the municipal pier parking lot, approximately where today's public library is located, with the Masonic Temple (1921) visible in the distance. (Courtesy Sebring Historical Society.)

IMAGES
of America

SEBRING

Susan Priest MacDonald,
Randall M. MacDonald,
and the Sebring Historical Society

ARCADIA
PUBLISHING

ISBN 978-0-7385-5301-6

Published by Arcadia Publishing
Charleston, South Carolina

Printed in the United States of America

Library of Congress Catalog Card Number: 2007929690

For all general information contact Arcadia Publishing at:
Telephone 843-853-2070
Fax 843-853-0044
E-mail sales@arcadiapublishing.com
For customer service and orders:
Toll-Free 1-888-313-2665

Visit us on the Internet at www.arcadiapublishing.com

Lovingly dedicated to the memory of Thomas Mitchell Priest and to Betty Jo Priest, for whom Sebring holds treasured memories; and to Lillian Grace Marsh Thro, our niece.

Contents

Acknowledgments

The conclusion of *The Fifty Years of Sebring, 1912–1962* summarizes a challenge to historians: "All histories share two characteristics: they omit far more than they tell, and they are unending." Our purpose in these pages is to provide a glimpse of life in early Sebring. To the extent we have succeeded, we owe a great deal to the generosity of others.

This project would not have materialized without the steadfast assistance and guidance of Sebring Historical Society archivist Carole Goad. Her wide-ranging knowledge of Sebring's people, places, and events is impressive, and her friendship and affable spirit are greatly appreciated. Volunteers Jackie Koza, Gary Harnage, and Elizabeth Walker provided helpful assistance in our research, and it has been a pleasure to work on this project with the Sebring Historical Society.

The invaluable assistance of Allen C. Altvater III deserves special recognition. Allen has done much to preserve the history of Sebring by updating and publishing works his grandfather Allen C. Altvater authored. For allowing us to reproduce photographs from the Allen C. Altvater Collection and for help identifying Sebring sites, we extend our gratitude. Others who provided assistance include Marie Williams Daniels, David Klatt, Sarah E. MacDonald, Betty Jo Priest, Thelma Pyle, Mike Sawyer, and Mandy Sheets. Arcadia Publishing has been wonderful to work with, from our initial conversations with Ingrid Powell, to the cheerful guidance of Kate Crawford and Lauren Bobier.

Special appreciation goes to Patricia Mays Hollenberg, a treasured friend for 37 years, and to Constance Marsh MacDonald and Malcolm M. MacDonald.

This project has been of intense personal interest. Susan Priest MacDonald is a proud 1976 graduate of Sebring High School, living in Sebring from 1969 until 1978, and her family remained in town until 2004. At the time of their marriage, she and Randall M. MacDonald learned that his grandmother Ruth Newcomb Greene MacDonald vacationed in Sebring as a young woman, visiting Kenilworth Lodge to golf. Sebring holds a special place for us, just as it does for so many others, and we look forward to seeing what comes next as the history of Sebring continues.

INTRODUCTION

In 1911, no modern roads led to Lake Jackson, south of Avon Park, Florida, and few families had settled in this raw wilderness known for bountiful fishing and game some 30 miles from the nearest railroad depot in Wauchula. Yet entrepreneur George E. Sebring was drawn to this locale and saw in its beauty the promise of a new town. Sebring had done this before; as one of four brothers in the pottery manufacturing business, he had helped found Sebring, Ohio, in 1898 as a planned industrial community in support of the family businesses, and eventually, it became known as the "Pottery Capital of the World." Sebring traveled extensively and, by 1909, was spending winters in Daytona Beach. His interests turned to citrus production, and he envisaged another Sebring that would attract new residents to the largely unsettled south central Florida peninsula.

Sebring purchased some 9,000 acres on the shore of Lake Jackson from Wauchula realtor A. G. Smith, and his new town—known for a brief period as Lakeview Park—was designed and surveyed between October 1911 and April 1912 by A. C. Nydeggar of Winter Haven and Lakeland's J. W. Turner. Turner is credited with determining the final position of the Circle, which fast became the center of the community, joined by three roads in six places: Center Avenue, Commerce Avenue, and Ridgewood Drive. George E. Sebring's partner in this new venture was his eldest son, H. Orvel Sebring. Together they applied years of business acumen and connections throughout the Midwest to attract new landowners, businesses, and other makings of a new community. By 1912, they formed two companies to develop and promote the town: the Sebring Development Company and the Sebring Real Estate Company, with the goal of establishing a self-sustaining community in short order. These efforts were successful; as potential landowners arrived, they liked what they saw, bought land, and helped to nurture Sebring. What of George E. Sebring's interest in citrus? According to local practice, every new dwelling had a citrus tree in the yard, and coincidentally, the entire region became known as a center of citrus production.

By virtue of its location along the Atlantic Coast Line Railroad line, establishment of Sebring as county seat of Highlands County a year after it was formed in 1921, and with amplified growth of central Florida's Ridge area, Sebring emerged as a novel tourist and golfing destination. The best-known hotels were Kenilworth Lodge (1916), Tropical Hotel (1922), the Nan-Ces-O-Wee Hotel (1923), and Harder Hall (1927), and guests enjoyed the recreational activities sponsored by the Sebring Tourist Club. A point-by-point description of Sebring appeared in *The Sebring White Way* as the Harder Hall project was underway, providing a snapshot of the developing city. Printed as one long column, the description reads as follows:

> Sebring has: Pep. A Band. One dairy. Two banks. Ten hotels. Whiteways. Ice factory. Six doctors. Six garages. Two railways. Confectionary. Masonic lodge. Cabinet works. Eight attorneys. Taxicab service. One paint store. 5 and 10¢ store. One music store. Oddfellows lodge. Baseball grounds. Two lumber mills. One kindergarten. Two barber shops. One jewelry store. Transfer company. Two electric shops. Ten filling stations. Knights of Pythias. Boat & Canoe club. Five grocery stores. Eastern Star lodge. Realtor

associations. Two civil engineers. Seven eating places. Two millinery shops. Ornamental Nursery. High school athletics. Two hardware stores. Two furniture stores. Western Union office. Three packing houses. Nine contracting firms. Municipal golf course. Four dry goods stores. American Legion Post. Three plumbing shops. High school orchestra. About 4,500 fine folks. Chamber of Commerce. Accredited high school. Good daily newspaper. Moving picture theatre. Parks and playgrounds. A fertilizer warehouse. Woman's Club building. Five insurance agencies. Two model beauty shops. One cement block factory. Automobile fire apparatus. Two photographic studios. Spanish War Veterans Post. Three dry cleaning houses. Parent-Teachers association. One pool and billiard parlor. Two ladies furnishing shops. Wholesale and retail bakery. Seven church denominations. Two men's furnishing shops. A number of citrus nurseries. Painting and decorating firms. Two gasoline and oil agencies. Thirty-four miles asphalt streets. Two railway commercial agencies. American Railway Express Company. Rows of orange trees over mile long. Boulevard around lake, 10 miles long. Municipal Golf course and club house. Numerous apartment and boarding houses. Telephone service with 700 subscribers. Local baseball club and basketball club. Two large grove caretaking companies. Rolling hills and many fresh water lakes. Numerous real estate offices or firms. Light and power plant. Sparkling clear water free from mineral taint. Four million-dollar developments. One 30 million dollar development.

The Florida land bust and Depression exacted a toll on the local economy, but the creation of Highlands Hammock State Park and the arrival of Hendricks Field—a World War II Army Air Force training base—brought thousands of new residents to Sebring, increasingly known as the "Hub of the Peninsula." The Twelve Hours of Sebring automobile endurance race has been held annually since 1952; for many worldwide motor sports enthusiasts, this is the Sebring they know.

M. W. "Milt" Baker and John F. Newcomb were among the earliest residents in Sebring; Baker arrived with his family in October 1911, and Newcomb, a retired Salvation Army officer, arrived with his family the next month. Thanks to these pioneers, much is known about daily life from the beginning of Sebring's history. Baker was a shutterbug who recorded the earliest images of Sebring while running the first grocery, and Newcomb maintained exquisitely detailed diaries of Sebring's people and events until his family relocated in 1916. Through Baker's camera lens and Newcomb's discourse, we witness the clearing of Circle Park, the first religious services, early settlers, and the construction of homes, businesses, and accommodations for tourists.

Allen C. Altvater was also instrumental in recording and publishing Sebring's history from his arrival in 1915 and subsequent roles in all aspects of local governance and community involvement through 1994. Ted Shoemaker beautifully photographed scores of local scenes beginning in the 1940s. Rev. Robert J. Walker's poignant memories of growing up in Sebring are essential reading for any student of local mid-20th-century life. The Sebring Historical Society was chartered in 1968 and serves as an exemplar for local historical associations. Their collections and displays are edifying and enjoyable, and the society welcomes all those interested in the history of the city.

Drawn primarily from the collections of the Sebring Historical Society, these vintage photographs evoke a time long past when enthusiasm for the new settlement reached its apogee and when families relocating from more established areas carved a community out of the wilderness. Cultural and technological progresses have transformed the rural community into a thriving modern city, which today retains its small town atmosphere—the City on the Circle.

One

Sebring Pioneers

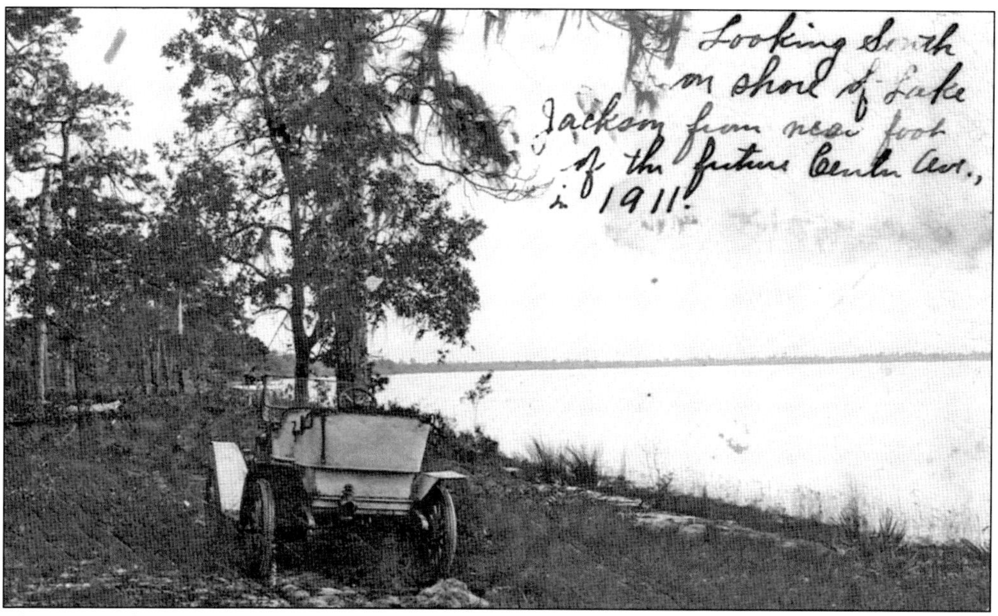

The first residents of what became Sebring arrived in October 1911. Among the earliest photographs is this view of Lake Jackson, taken where Center Avenue soon met Dreamland Road, known shortly thereafter as Lakeview Drive. The first sawmill was located here; in 1914, George E. Sebring constructed his second home on this spot; and today it is the site of the Sebring Public Library. (Courtesy Sebring Historical Society.)

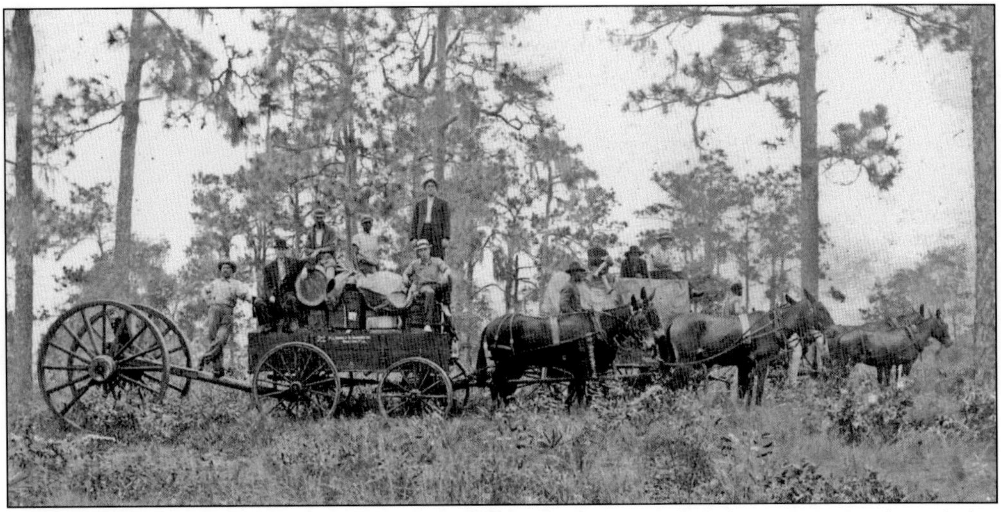

The Sebring area was only sparsely populated before the arrival of the pioneer settlers. A few homesteaders were scattered south of Lake Jackson, many miles from Avon Park, Wauchula, and other modest population centers. These homesteaders watched as wagonloads of supplies and furniture arrived with optimistic souls who had left behind greater comforts. These wagons from Bartow arrived in October 1911. (Courtesy Sebring Historical Society.)

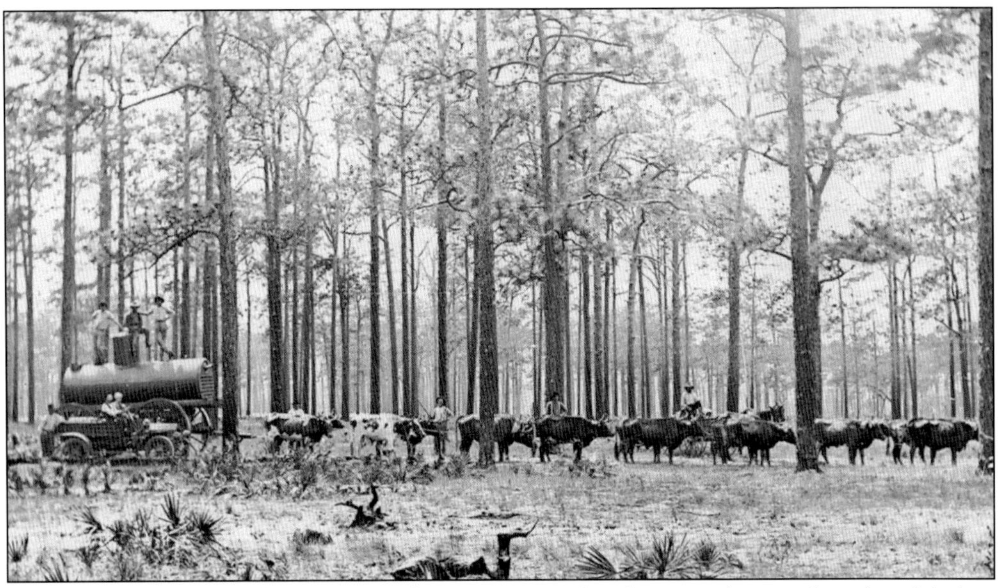

Establishment of a sawmill demonstrated progress; it employed new residents and produced shelter. The sawmill was initially located on the shore of Lake Jackson. This proved unsatisfactory when enthusiastic sawyers accidentally removed some of the lakeside trees meant to remain. This Milt Baker photograph shows the sawmill boiler being transported on an enormous wagon. (Courtesy Sebring Historical Society.)

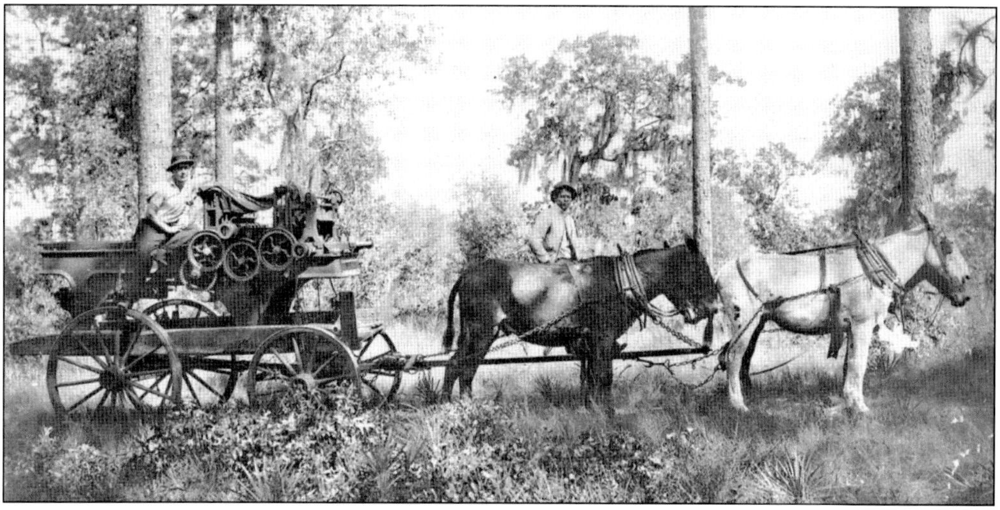

The sawmill planer is shown arriving at the Sebring town site in October 1911. Mill foreman Joe Jones is seated atop the planer. Mule and oxen teams were used to convey heavy loads in the soft Florida sand. Adam McPherson and his sons Turner and Will from Auburndale managed the mule teams and were instrumental in transporting logs to the sawmill. (Courtesy Sebring Historical Society.)

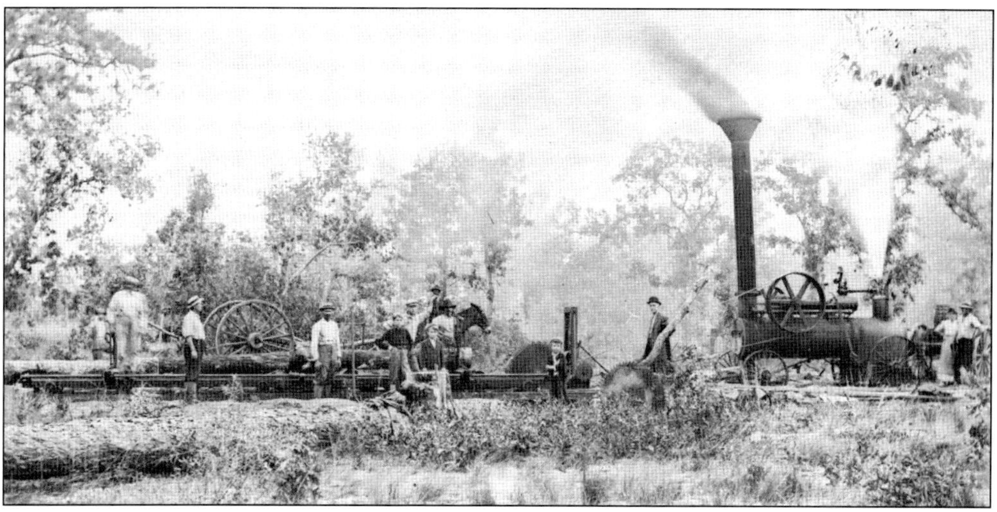

This October 1911 photograph shows the sawmill at its second location, south of the Circle. By October 15, it was being dismantled for the move to Dinner Lake; the planer was moved on November 30. At the far left is manager Aaron Withers, sawyer Jack Whaley is sixth from the left, preacher L. O. Dowds is eighth from the left, and Mr. and Mrs. Joe Jones are at far right. They were the first married couple in Lakeview Park. (Courtesy Sebring Historical Society.)

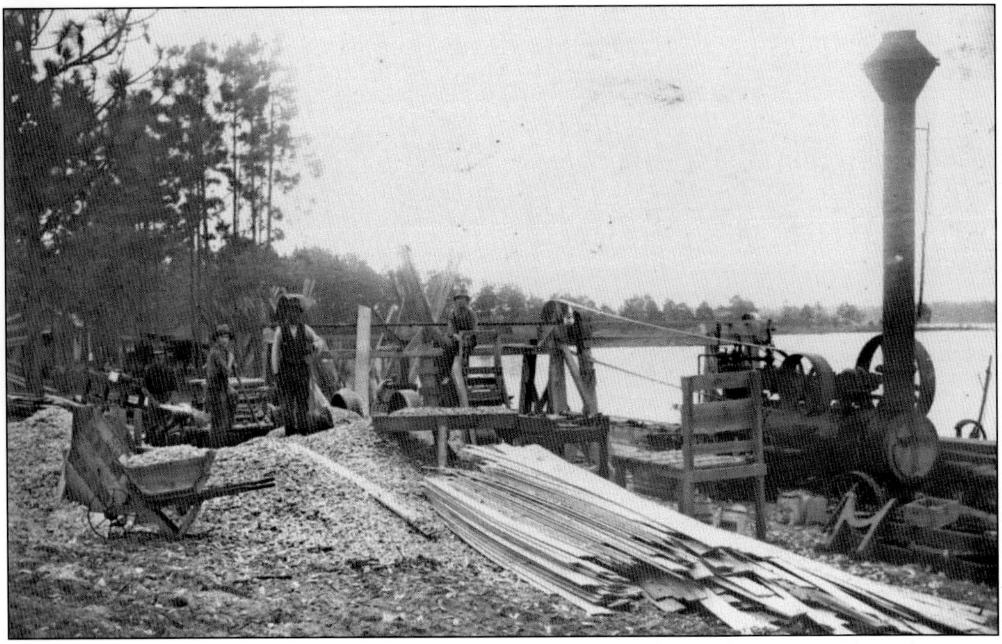

The third sawmill site, shown here, was on the southwest shore of Dinner Lake. This 1912 view hints at the ambitious growth of the new community; buildings and homes were springing up, and wood shavings from the mill were used to cover the new streets. (Courtesy Sebring Historical Society.)

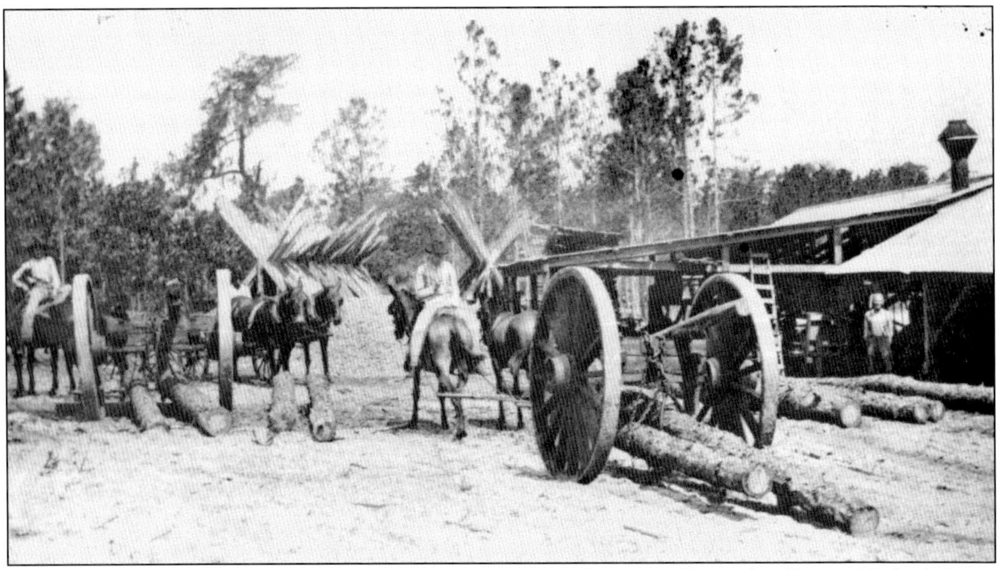

Dinner Lake was outside the proposed city limits when the sawmill was finally established there, but it was an active site in June 1912. Among the mill workers were manager Aaron Withers, foreman Joe Jones, head sawyer Jack Whaley, sawyers Jim Middleton and Mark Thornberry, and Ohio carpenters Bortz, Hazen, and Mitchell. In December, they were joined by homesteaders A. and O. Howard from Alabama. (Courtesy Sebring Historical Society.)

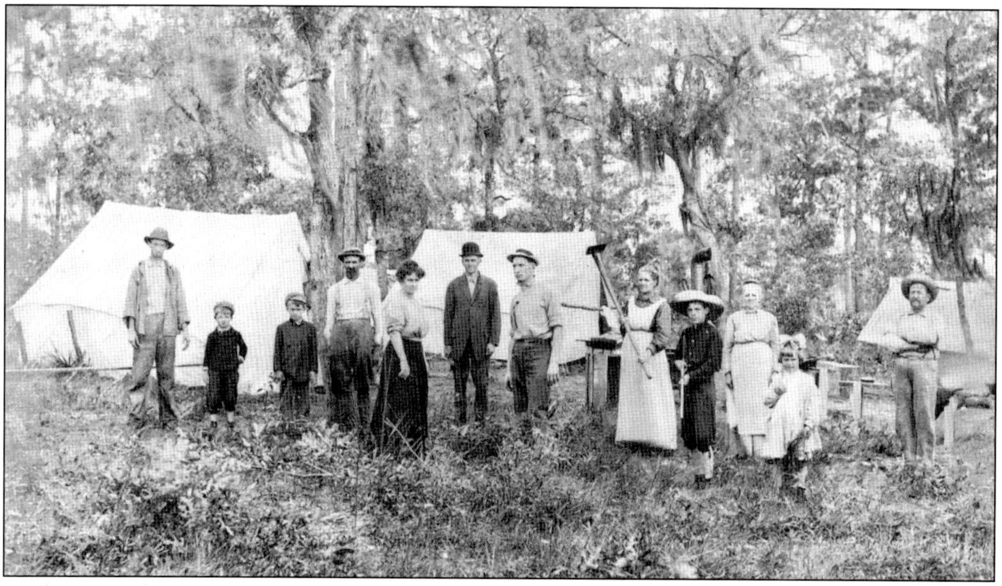

By the 1911 Christmas season, there were nine families—about three-dozen residents in all—living in Sebring. These pioneers led a hardscrabble existence. Besides their work, they had to cook, clean, and bathe, all with limited access to clean drinking water. Christmas dinner at the Schlosser homestead on the south shore of Lake Jackson included razorback, bear, and deer, followed by an early evening swim near town. (Courtesy Sebring Historical Society.)

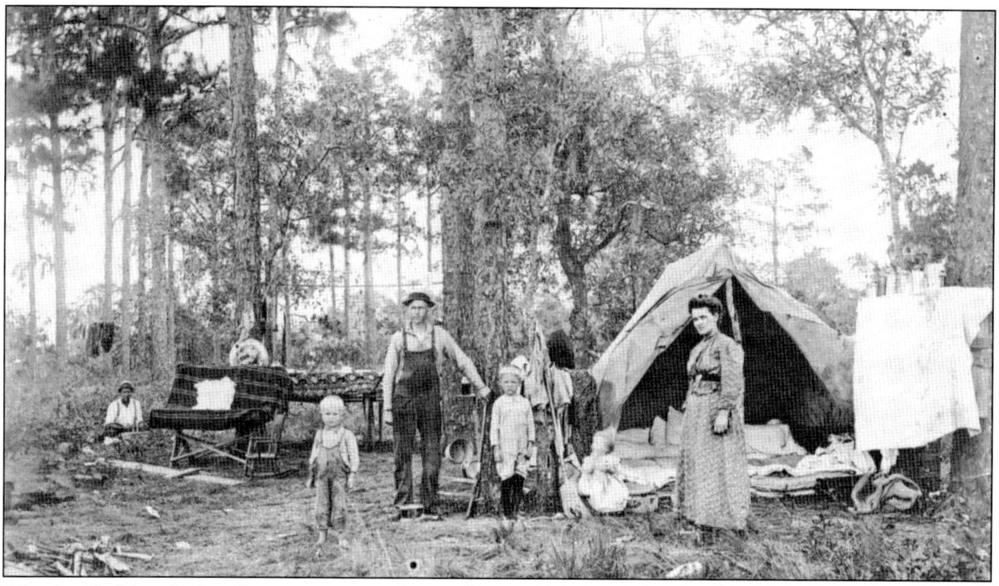

The L. O. Dowds family was among the earliest pioneers. Mr. Dowds was a retired Methodist minister in poor health, and the rigors of frontier life were likely too much to bear. The family left the community on January 9, 1912, bound for Sarasota. They sold some of their belongings to those who remained, including their flat bottom rowboat, with the stipulation that it not be used for Sunday fishing. (Courtesy Sebring Historical Society.)

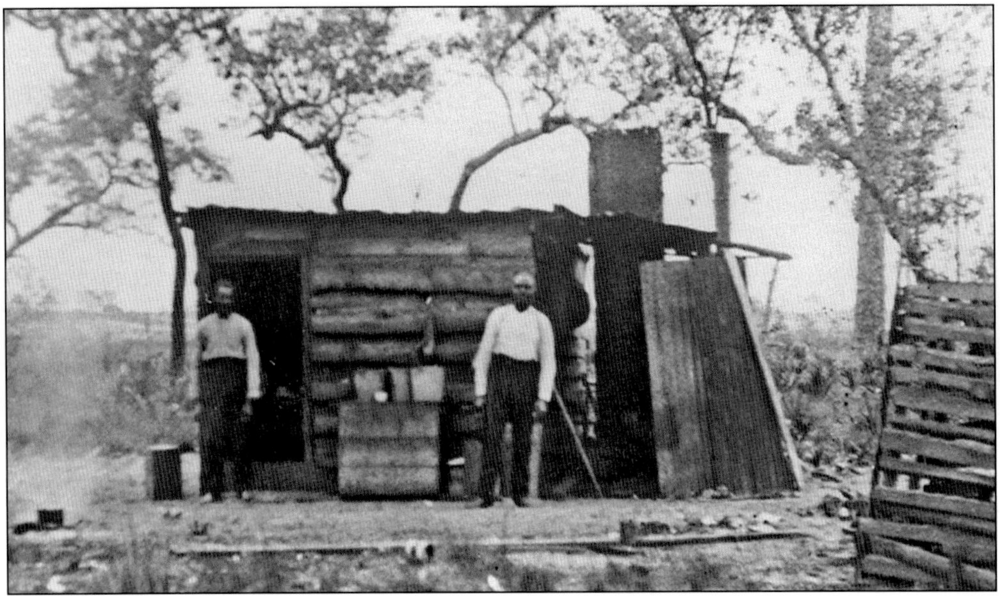

For new arrivals, a first Sebring home was rather simple. Most lived in tents, lean-to structures, or small temporary cabins built with wood from the sawmill. These living conditions typically improved over time, and it was not uncommon for the most advantaged families to move into a succession of larger homes within the first decade. (Courtesy Sebring Historical Society.)

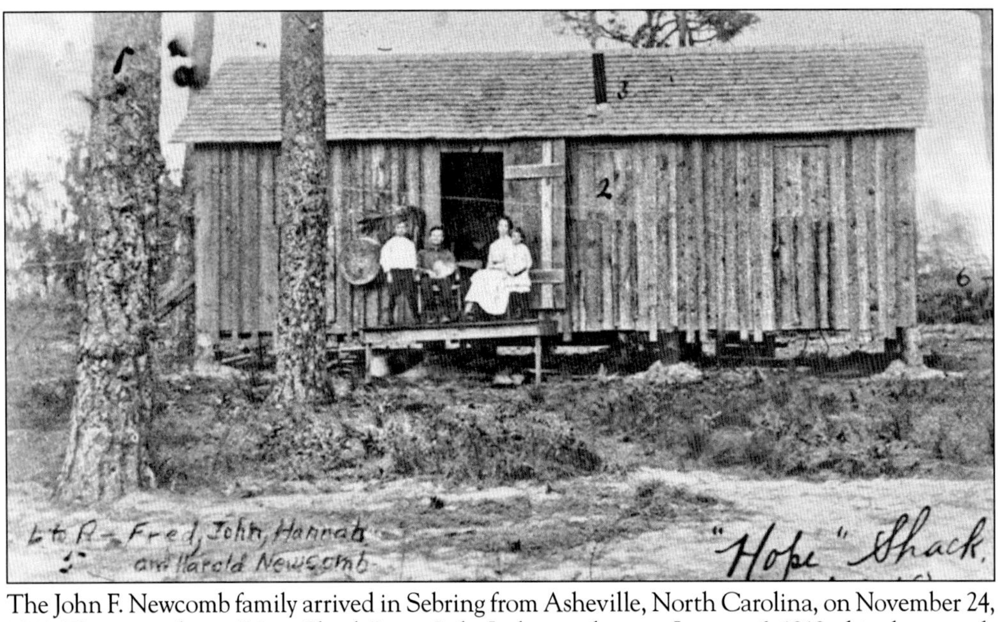

The John F. Newcomb family arrived in Sebring from Asheville, North Carolina, on November 24, 1911. They moved into "Hope Shack," near Lake Jackson, where on January 6, 1912, this photograph was taken of (front left to right) Fred, John F., Hannah Hayes Newcomb, and Harold. They moved to a home on North Pine Street purchased from William and Mary Trumble in April 1912. Daughter Maude joined the family later that summer. (Courtesy Sebring Historical Society.)

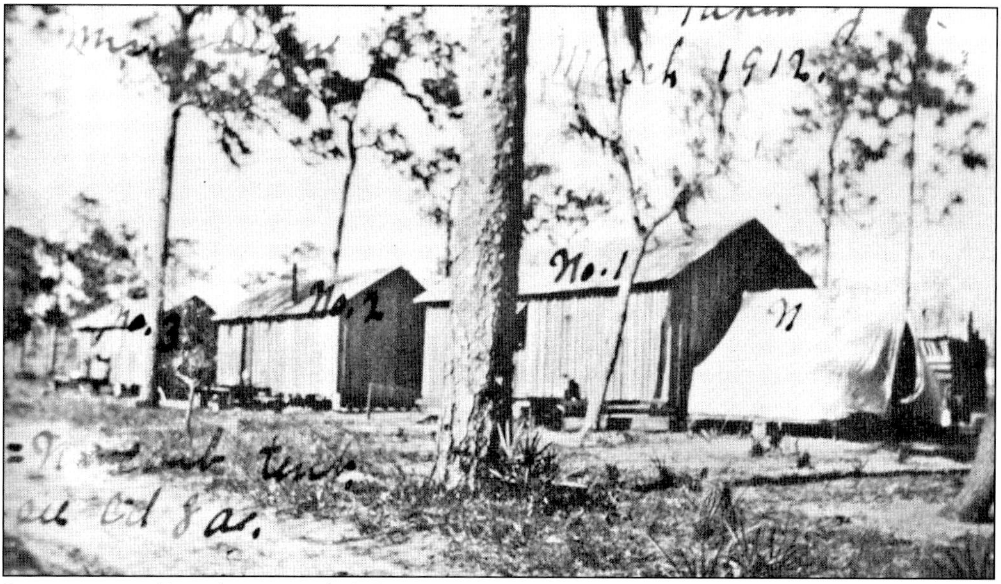

Pioneer sawmill workers provided the name Shackleton to this small group of residences that sprang up on what became North Lakeview Drive shortly after Sebring was founded. The Newcomb family lived in shack No. 2, which they called "Hope Shack." This March 1912 photograph also shows the Newcomb family tent. This lot was later occupied by the homes of the Evans and Albright families. (Courtesy Sebring Historical Society.)

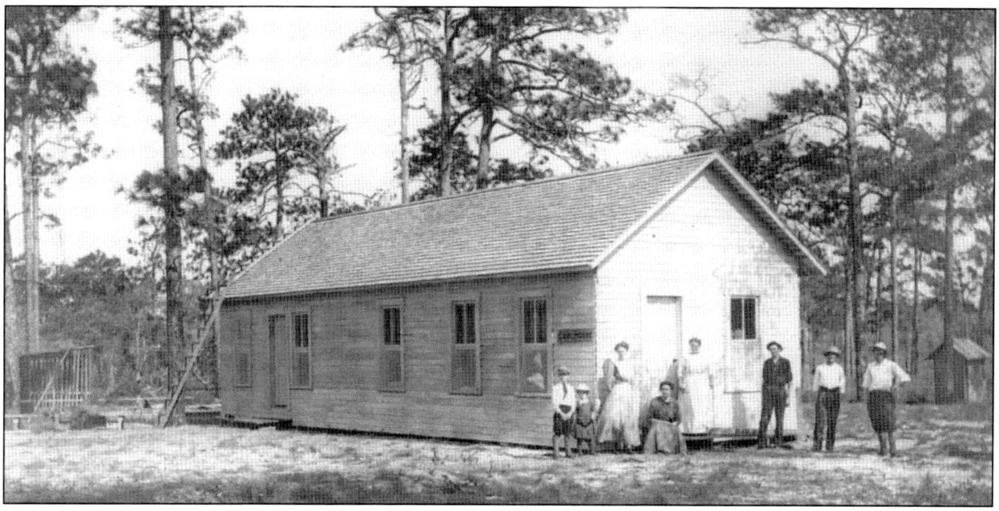

The Buckeye Clubhouse (1912) was one of the first structures erected in Sebring, serving as a dining and lodging hall for visitors. As an early social hub, it was featured in many early photographs and postcards. This frame building was located at the present site of the Buckeye Building (1922) on the northeast corner of Circle Drive and North Ridgewood Drive. (Courtesy Sebring Historical Society.)

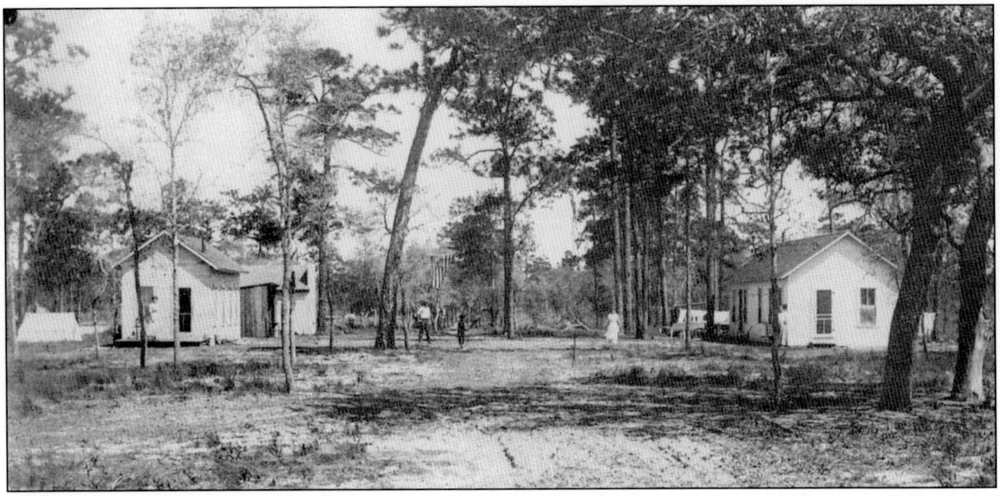

This was the view from the Circle in early 1912 looking north along what would become Ridgewood Drive. At the left (west) is the first Sebring Real Estate Company building (1911), which had doubled as the temporary home of the George E. Sebring family. The Buckeye Clubhouse is to the right, painted white with a green roof. (Courtesy Sebring Historical Society.)

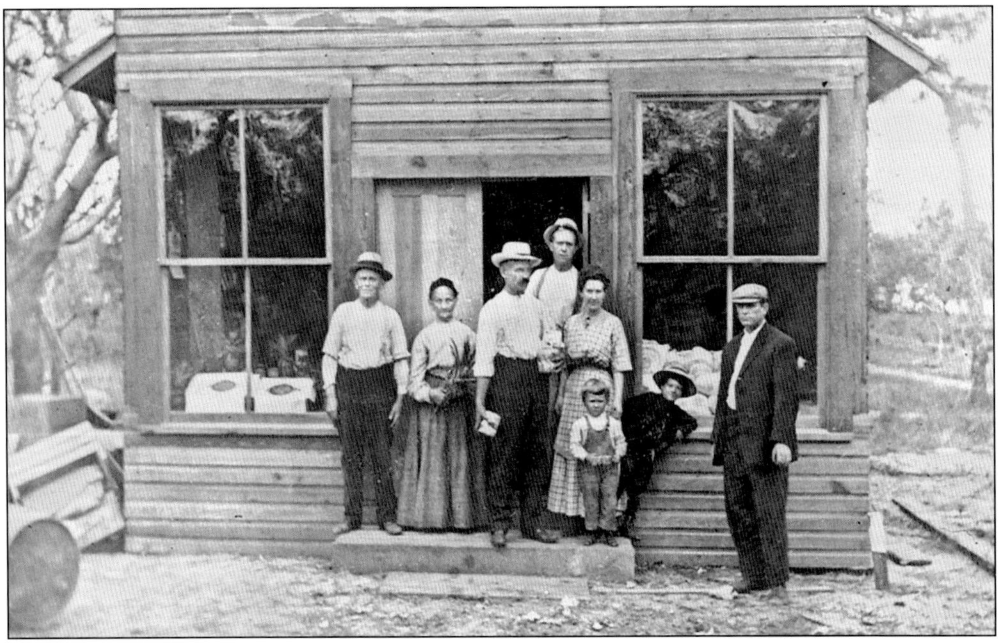

This photograph shows the Harrison Building on the south corner of Circle Drive and Center Avenue (occupied December 27, 1911) containing Milt Baker's grocery, which opened January 27, 1912. Baker's first customers included (from left to right) Postmaster John Harrison, the first man to live on the Circle; Mrs. George Harrison, John's mother; George E. Sebring, holding store goods; Milt Baker; Mrs. Milt Baker; Miles Baker; Harold Newcomb; and Aaron Withers. (Courtesy Sebring Historical Society.)

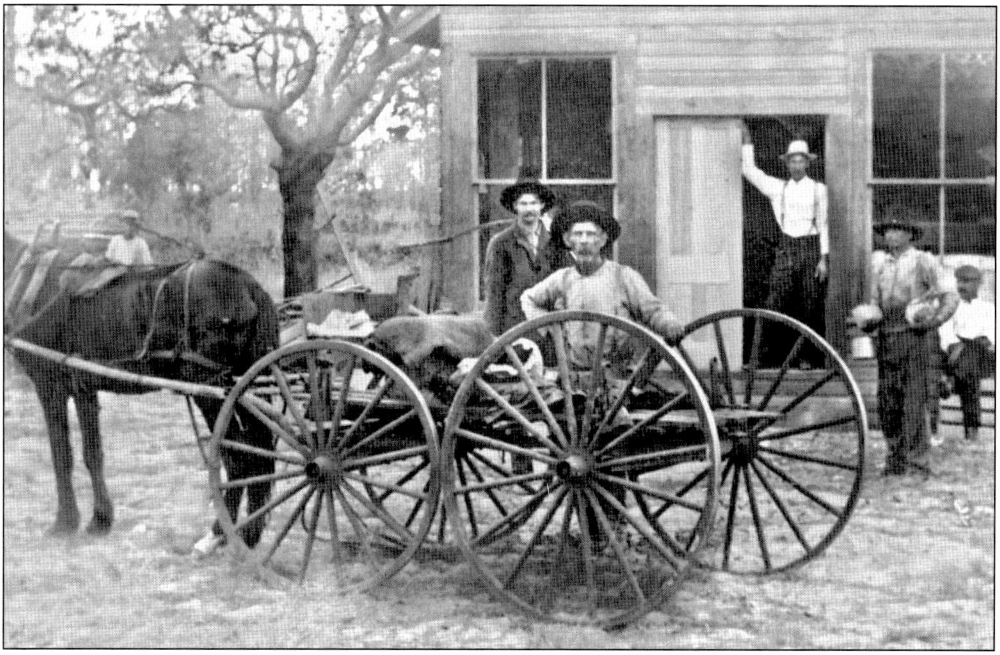

This January 1912 group in front of Milt Baker's store included, from left to right, Mr. Harrison, in the distance behind horse; "Orn" Howard; Mr. Pollard Sr.; Milt Baker(?); "Billy" Smith; and George E. Sebring, seated. Baker built and moved into a larger store later the same year. (Courtesy Sebring Historical Society.)

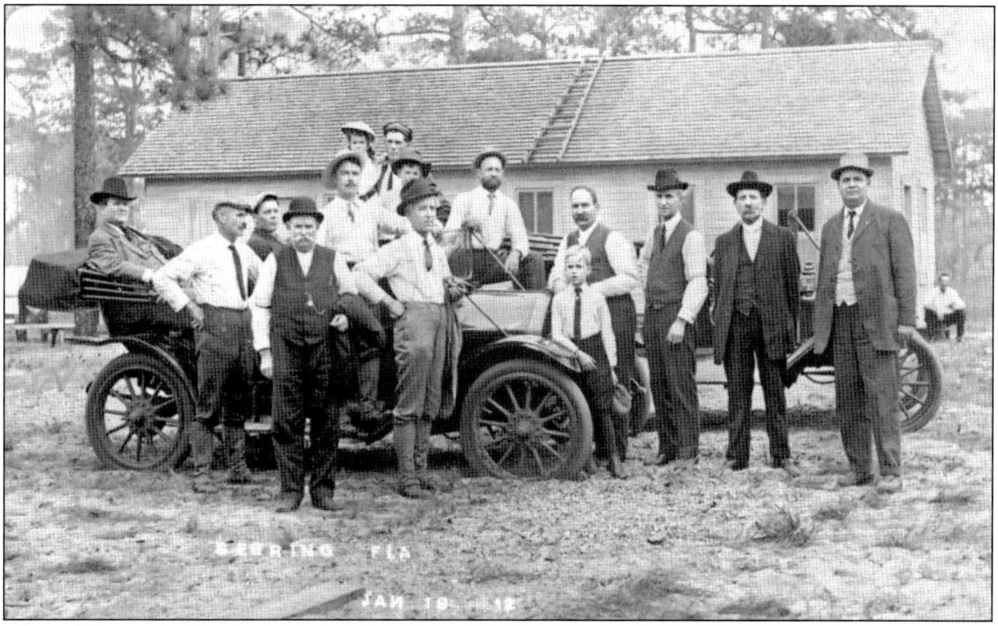

The Sebring Real Estate Company and the Sebring Development Company were founded by George E. Sebring and worked to promote Sebring to potential buyers. One such group was the Pittsburg Party from Pennsylvania, visiting in mid-January 1912 and pictured posing in front of the Buckeye Clubhouse. One of the leaders of this contingent was John Zeall, who later developed area citrus groves and served as Sebring's mayor. (Courtesy Sebring Historical Society.)

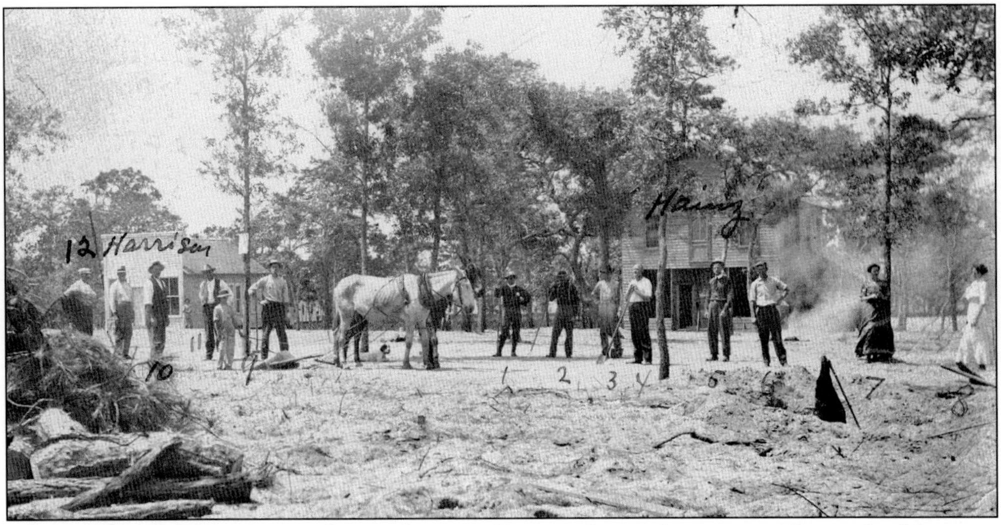

The Circle was cleared in early April 1912. This southwest-facing view shows the Harrison Building and Edward L. Hainz's new rooming house at the north corner of West Center Avenue. Among those identified by John F. Newcomb in 1933 are (1) himself, (7) Mrs. George E. Sebring, (8) Annie Riley, (10) Aaron Withers, and (12) George E. Sebring. Milt Baker's new grocery was started to the right of the Hainz building on April 18. (Courtesy Sebring Historical Society.)

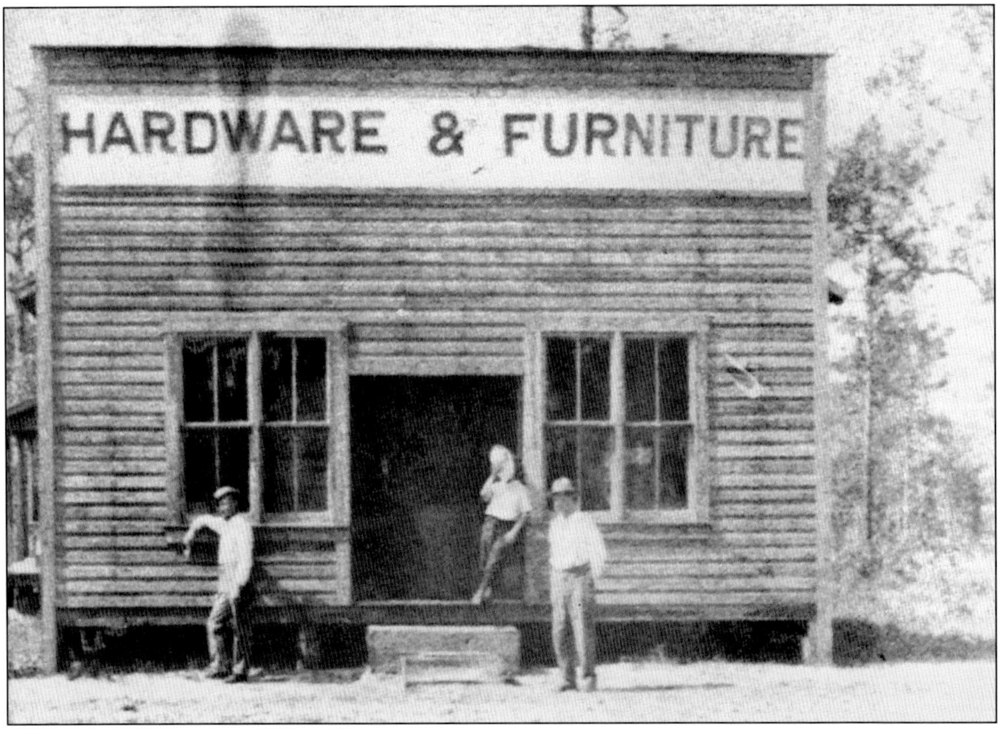

The Spencer Building was the fifth structure erected on the Circle, with work beginning on February 22, 1912. Operated as a hardware and furniture store by Mr. and Mrs. C. E. Spencer, an elderly couple from the west, it was located at the southeast corner of Circle Drive and South Ridgewood Drive. Since 1922, the J. B. Brown Building has occupied this building site. (Courtesy Sebring Historical Society.)

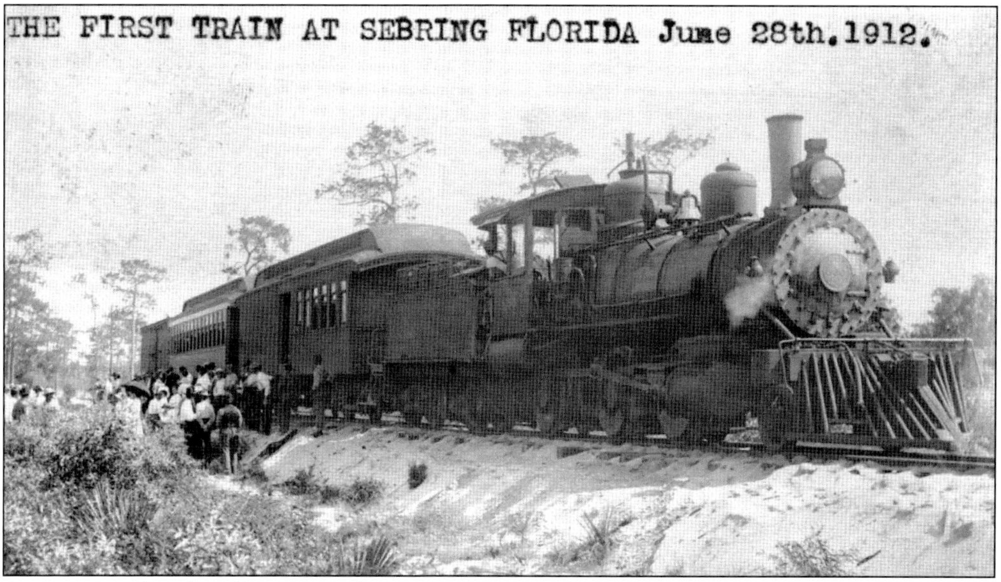

Access to railroad traffic was vital to attract potential land buyers and to bring tourists to this still-rural section of the state. The Atlantic Coast Line Railroad moved south from Jacksonville toward Avon Park by 1911; the first work train to enter Sebring laid tracks to the terminal at the north end of Commerce Avenue on June 12, 1912; and the first passenger train arrived on June 28. (Courtesy Sebring Historical Society.)

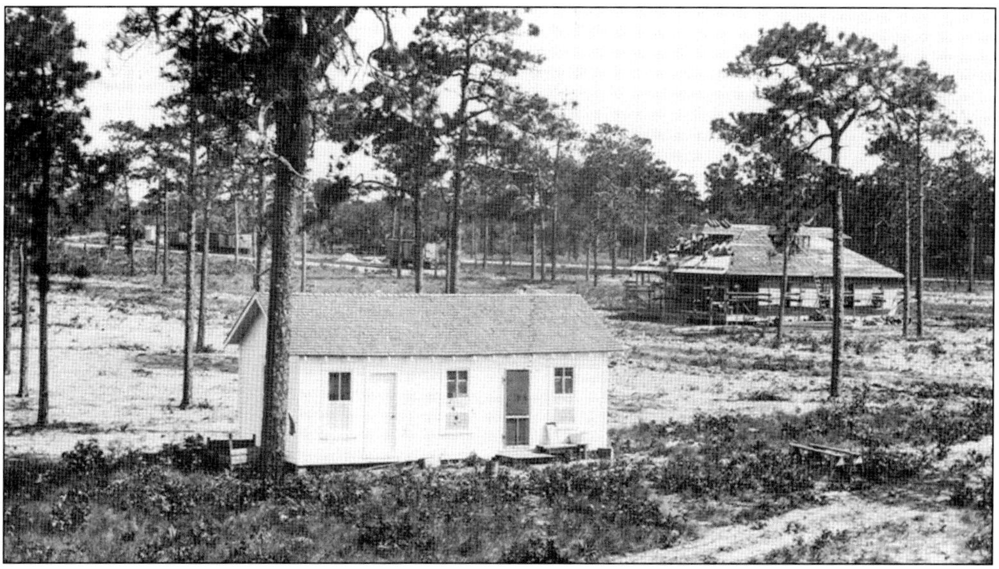

The Chamberlain cottage, immediately north of the Arrowhead Hotel, was occupied by Frank B. Chamberlain while the hotel was under construction. The unfinished Henry Henning home on Lakeview Drive is seen beyond the cottage in this August 1912 image. The original, in-town spur of the Atlantic Coast Line Railroad is evident near where the first railroad station was constructed. (Courtesy Sebring Historical Society.)

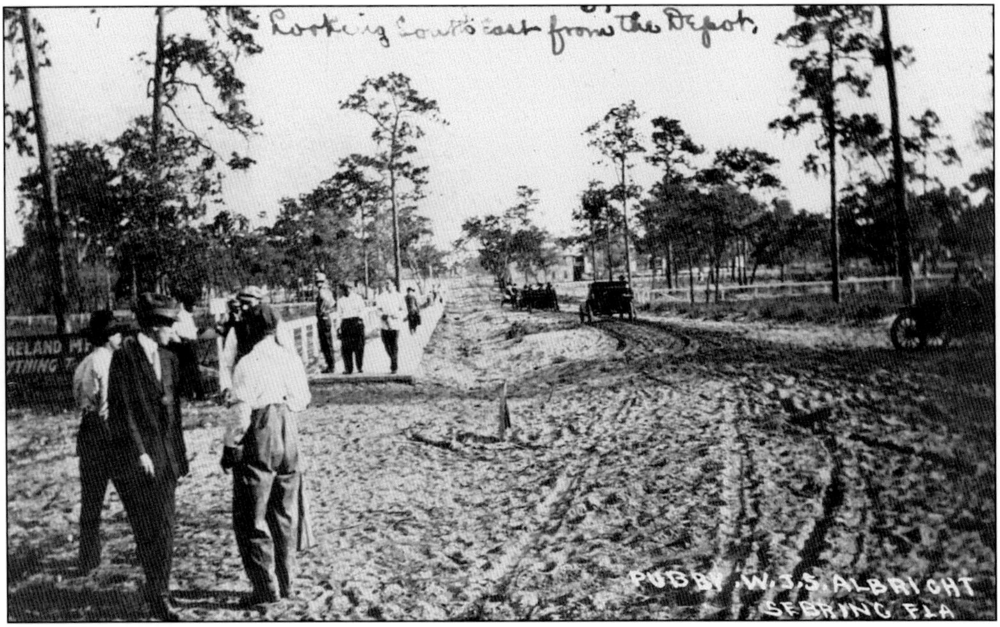

This c. 1913 view looks southeast along North Commerce Avenue toward the Circle from the Atlantic Coast Line Railroad passenger depot. Soft, sandy roads were an adventure, particularly for northern drivers. Northern automobiles were built with a narrower tread width than southern vehicles (54 inches versus 60 inches), which navigated unpaved sections more successfully. (Photograph by W. J. S. Albright, courtesy Sebring Historical Society.)

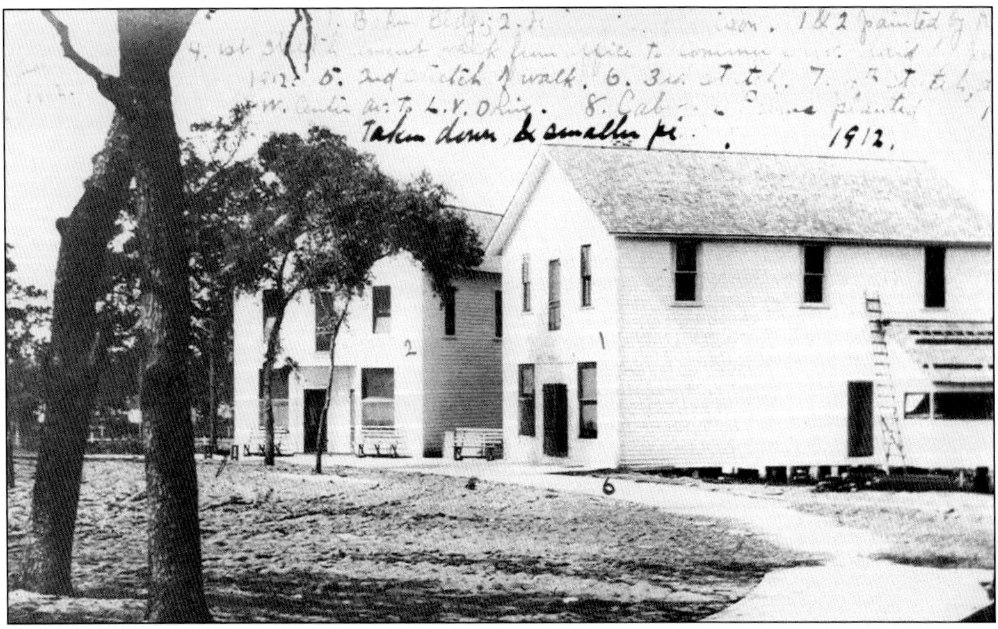

This August 1912 photograph from the Milt Baker collection was notated by John F. Newcomb. It depicts the Hainz and Baker buildings, both having been painted by a Mr. Ryal. By this date, a Mr. Jenkins had laid four sections of cement sidewalk counterclockwise from the Sebring Real Estate office to West Center Avenue, and southwest to Lakeview Drive. The area was landscaped with cabbage palm trees. (Courtesy Sebring Historical Society.)

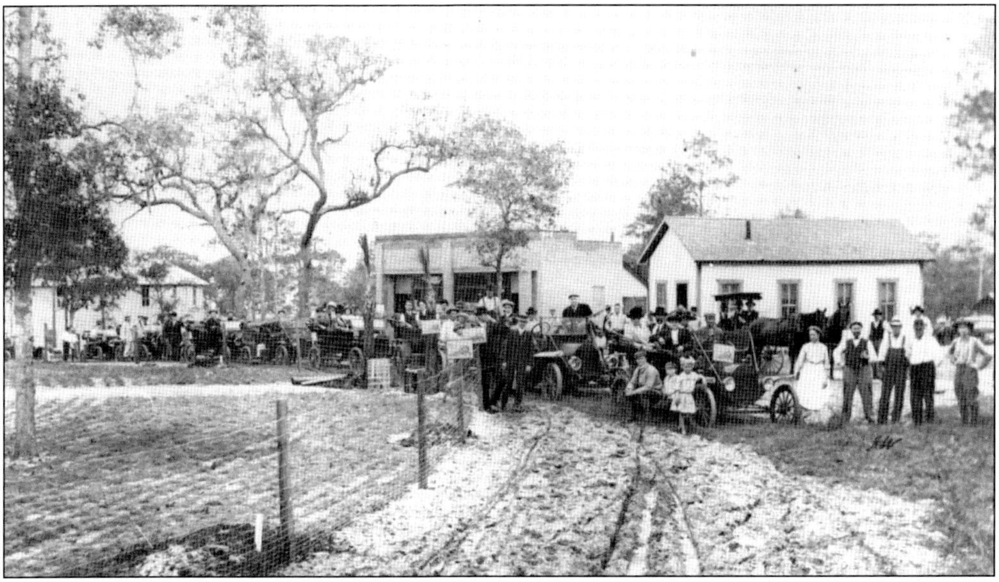

This view of citizens on the Circle likely dates from 1912. Many are holding signs showing a train locomotive, perhaps to promote the June arrival of the railroad. From left to right are what appears to be the I. G. Collier Building (1912) at the corner of North Commerce Avenue and Pomegranate Avenue, the brick Albright Building (1912), and the Sebring Real Estate Company building (1911). (Courtesy Sebring Historical Society.)

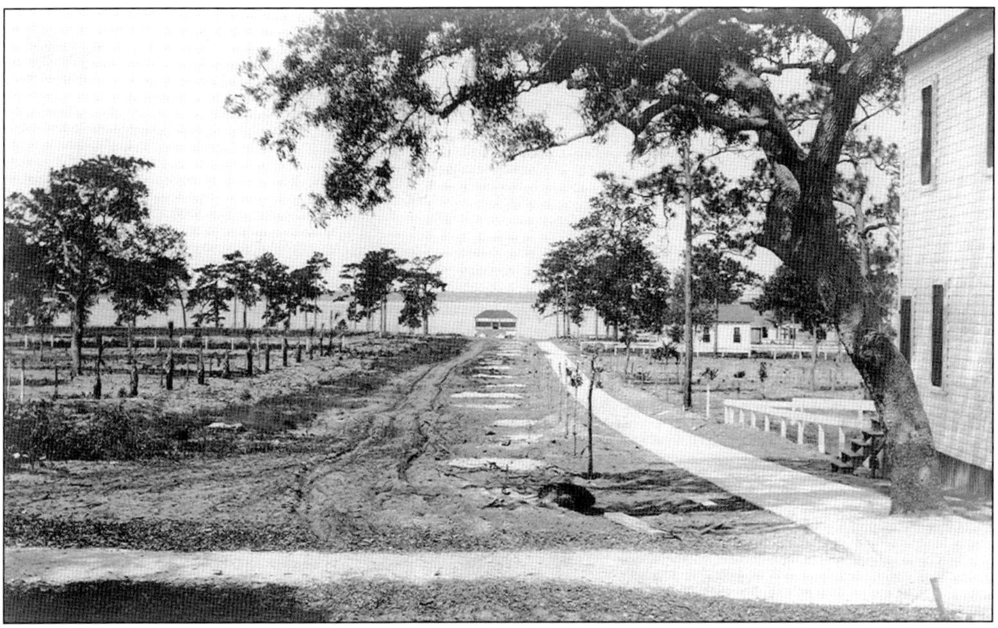

The 300-foot wooden Lake Jackson pier and two-level pavilion are visible in the distance southwest from the Circle along West Center Avenue; the street is unpaved, but a cement sidewalk had been laid. The Sebring Real Estate Company constructed the pier by mid-1912. The Hainz rooming house is seen at right. An early view of the pier from Lake Jackson is on page 99. (Courtesy Sebring Historical Society.)

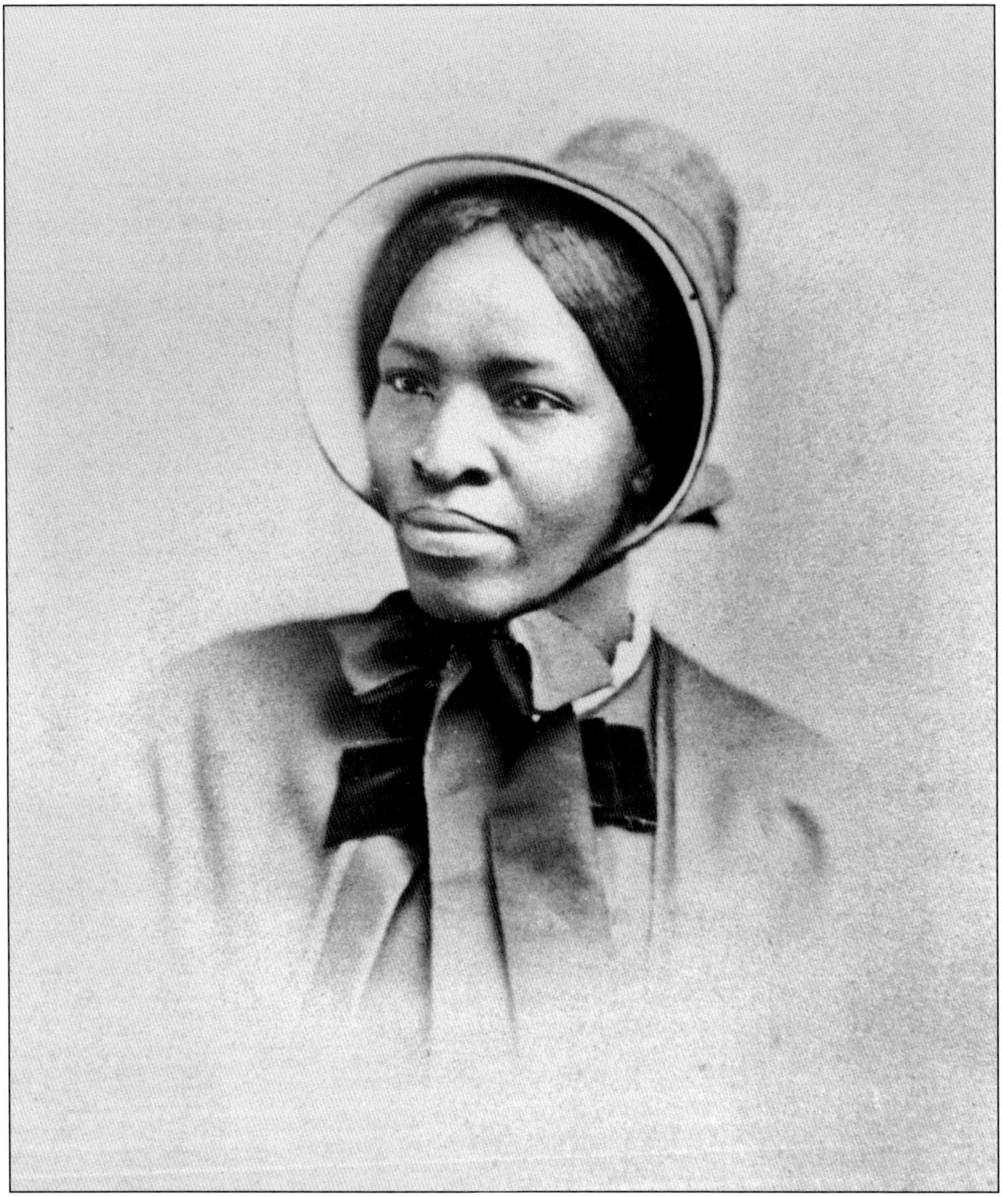

Amanda Berry Smith (1837–1915) was a former slave, evangelist, and renowned member of the Women's Christian Temperance Union during the second half of the 19th century. Her ministry began in 1869 and took her from African Methodist Episcopal churches across the Midwest and eastern United States to England, India, Liberia, and other countries. She returned to the United States in 1890, published her autobiography in 1893, and in 1899 founded an orphanage in Harvey, Illinois, near Chicago. George E. Sebring met Smith at a religious conference in Ohio, came to admire her ministry, and developed a friendship with her. He built her a home in Sebring directly across the street from his on Lake Jackson, and she moved there in 1912, remaining until her death in February 1915. She had not been universally welcomed in Sebring, but George E. Sebring was unstinting in his friendship, as recounted by Julia A. Savage in an April 1915 article in the *A.M.E. Church Review*: "If everyone else moves away, Amanda Smith and I [George] will remain." (Courtesy Sebring Historical Society.)

Two

The Circle and Downtown

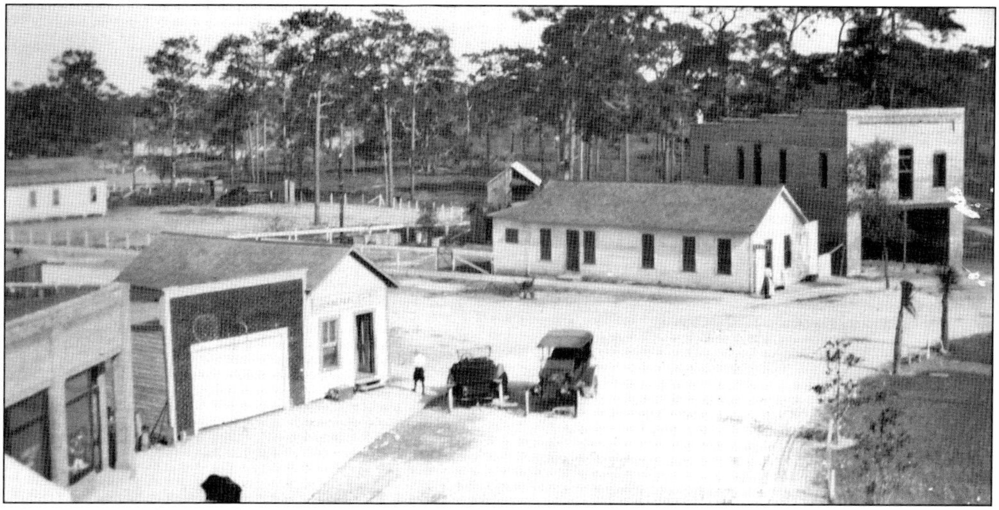

This view of the Circle dates from approximately 1914 and appears to have been taken from atop the Skipper Bank Building, looking northeast. From the lower left to right are the Albright Building (1912), the two-lane bowling alley, the first Sebring Real Estate Company building (1911), North Ridgewood Drive, the Buckeye Clubhouse (1912), and the Zachary Building (1914), under construction. (Courtesy Sebring Historical Society.)

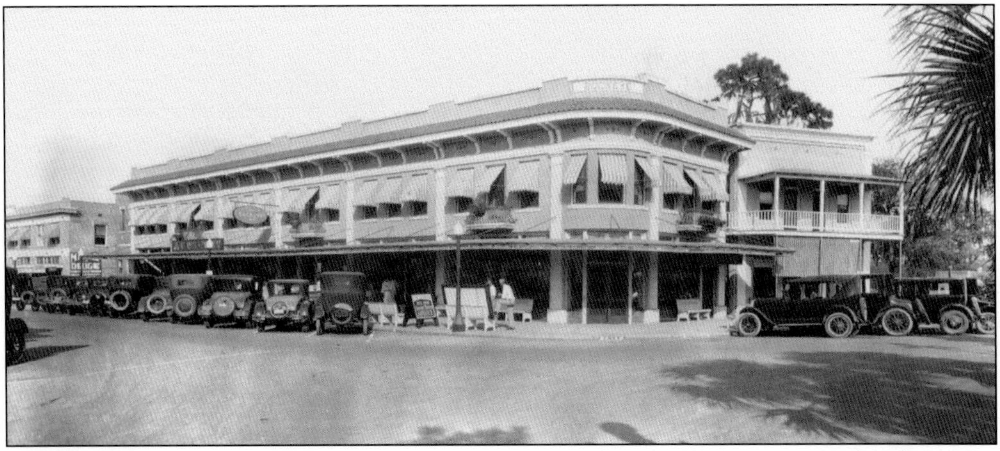

The attractive Buckeye Building, home of the 22-room Buckeye Inn, was constructed at the corner of Circle Drive and North Ridgewood Drive in 1922 south of the Salvation Army Building (1916). The Buckeye Building contained The Greater Atlantic and Pacific Tea Company, better known as A&P grocery. The corner storefront advertised Lake Sebring home sites, and the Zachary Building stands to the right. (Photograph by Woodward, courtesy Sebring Historical Society.)

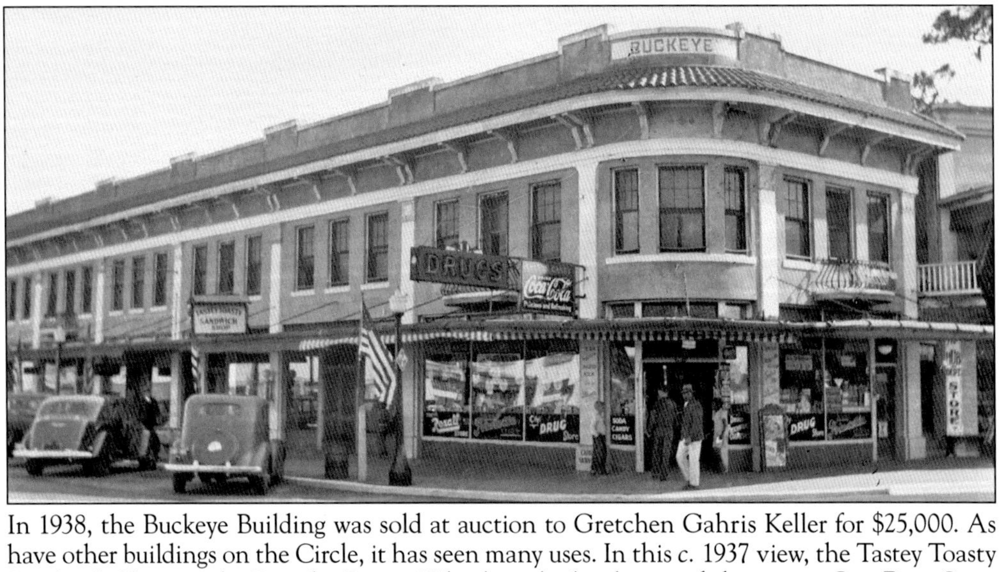

In 1938, the Buckeye Building was sold at auction to Gretchen Gahris Keller for $25,000. As have other buildings on the Circle, it has seen many uses. In this c. 1937 view, the Tastey Toasty Sandwich Shop run by Dorothy Doane Wheeler, a barbershop, and the corner City Drug Store are most prominent. A sign for the Hub Department Store is at the edge of the Zachary Building. (Courtesy Sebring Historical Society.)

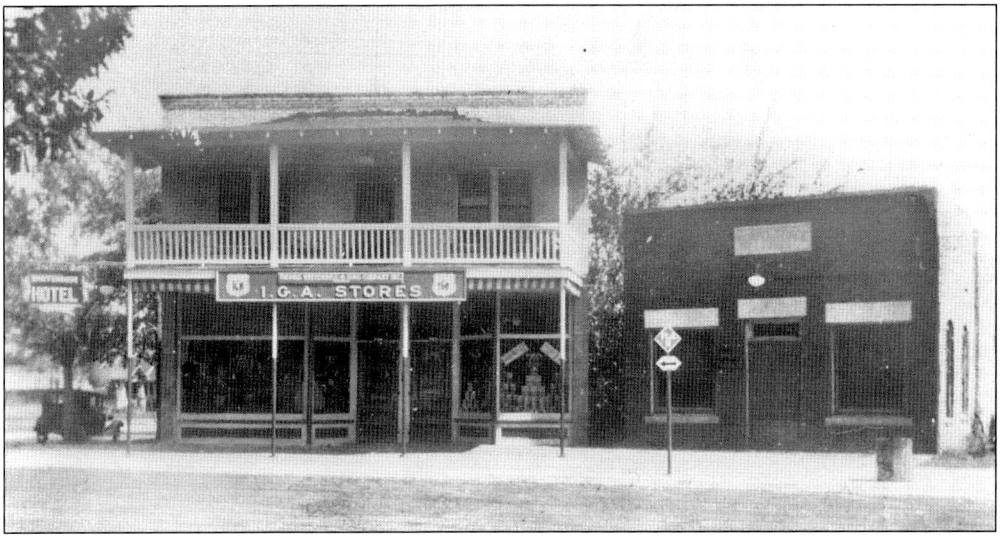

Englishman Thomas Whitehouse operated a dry goods and grocery store, with hotel rooms upstairs, out of his Whitehouse Building (c. 1915) on the east block of the Circle. This undated image shows his IGA grocery adjacent to the 1916 Board of Trade Building. The Board of Trade, organized in 1914 by H. Orvel Sebring, promoted Sebring as the county seat of newly formed Highlands County, and later merged with the chamber of commerce. (Courtesy Sebring Historical Society.)

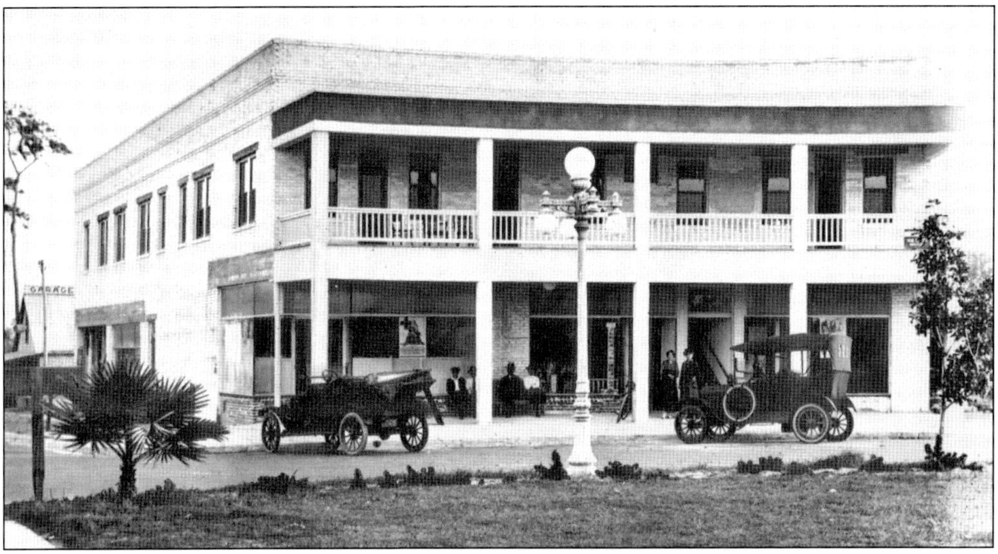

The Roanoke Hotel, with a concave facade, was constructed on the southeast block of the Circle in 1917 by the Sebring Development Company. Hotel rooms were on the second floor, with the first level divided into business storerooms. The Roanoke hosted dances during the 1920s, developing as a social center for Sebring. In recent years, the landmark Cat House Restaurant occupied the South Commerce Avenue side of the building. (Courtesy Sebring Historical Society.)

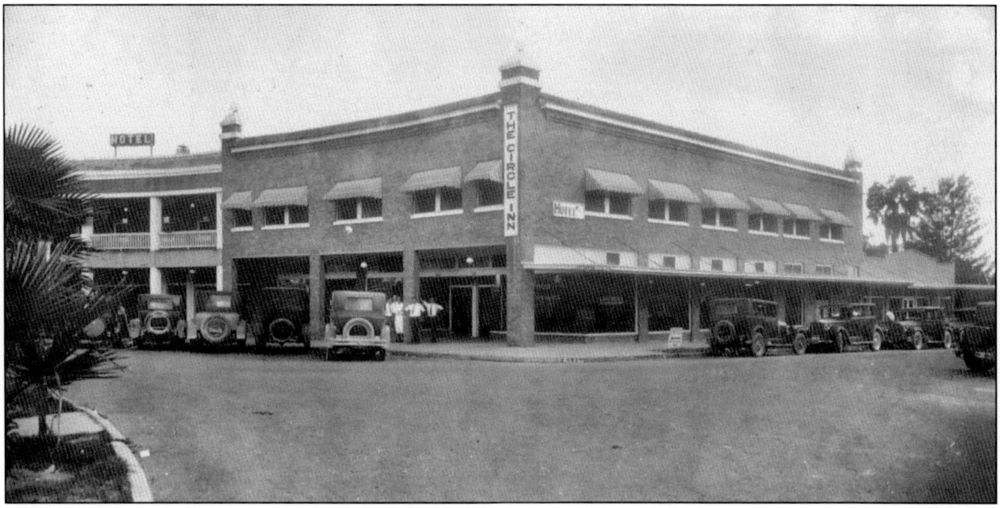

The J. B. Brown Building (1922) was constructed west of the Roanoke Hotel at the east corner of South Ridgewood Drive. The building was home to Jesse B. Brown's hardware store, the S. R. Hart Furniture Company, and Milt Baker's grocery. The 22-room Circle Inn was on the second floor. The city of Sebring purchased the building in 1929 and used a first-floor portion as the city hall until 1933. (Courtesy Sebring Historical Society.)

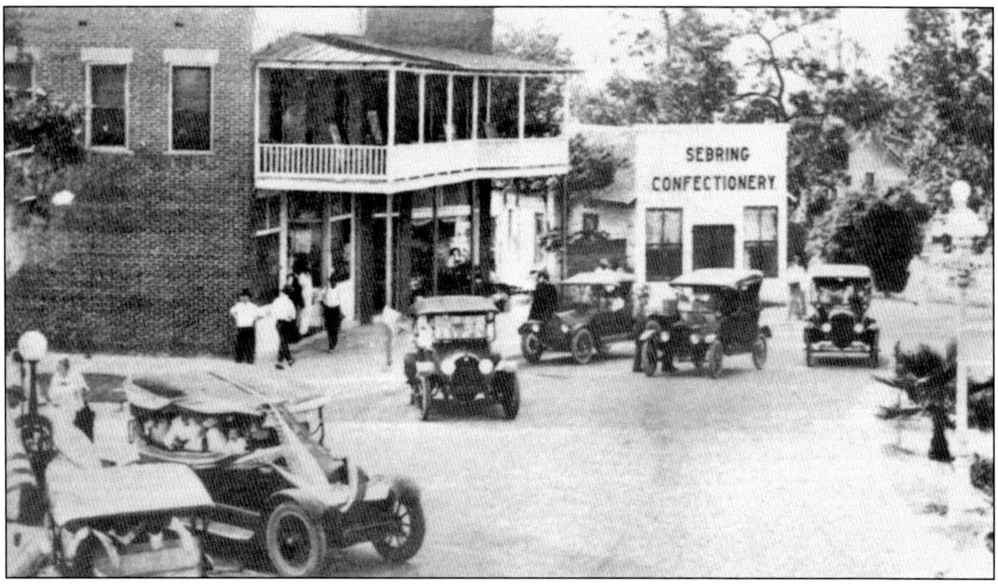

The A. E. Withers Building (1913) at the corner of Circle Drive and South Ridgewood Drive stands adjacent to the J. B. Zeall Building (*c.* 1915). The Withers Building was the second brick building erected on the Circle. The Sebring Confectionary was in the Harrison Building, which in 1926 was replaced by the Tobin Building. This picture is believed to date from before 1921. (Courtesy Sebring Historical Society.)

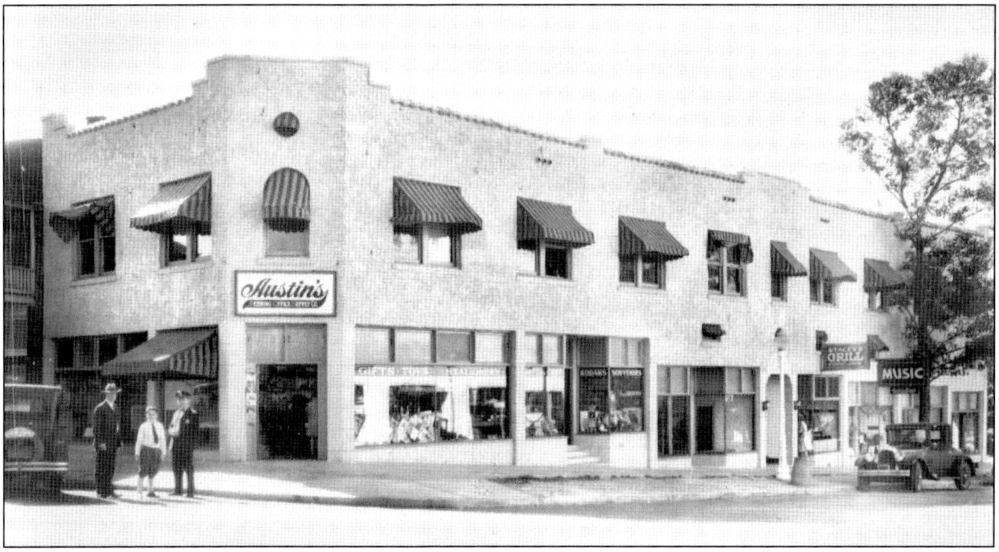

The Tobin Building (1926) is seen in this image from the late 1920s or early 1930s. Located at the corner of West Center Avenue, it was home to Austin's Sebring Office Supply Company, Harry Stacey's Grill (which advertised "Good Java"), and a music store. The Tobin Building is included in the Sebring Downtown Historic District. The lower facade is now covered with decorative stone. (Courtesy Sebring Historical Society.)

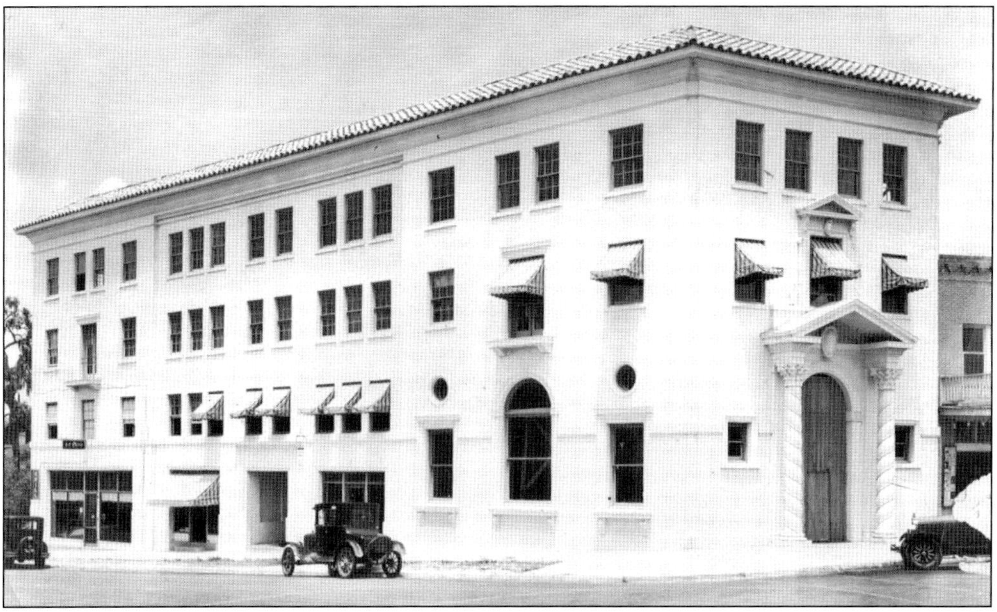

The Harder Hall Building stood at the north corner of Circle Drive and West Center Avenue. Constructed in 1926, it housed the offices of the Harder Hall real estate development and the Sebring *Daily American* newspaper. Among the professional offices in the Harder Hall Building was Dr. Herman Martin's second floor dental practice. The Elks Lodge met here, and a ground-level restaurant faced West Center Avenue. (Courtesy Sebring Historical Society.)

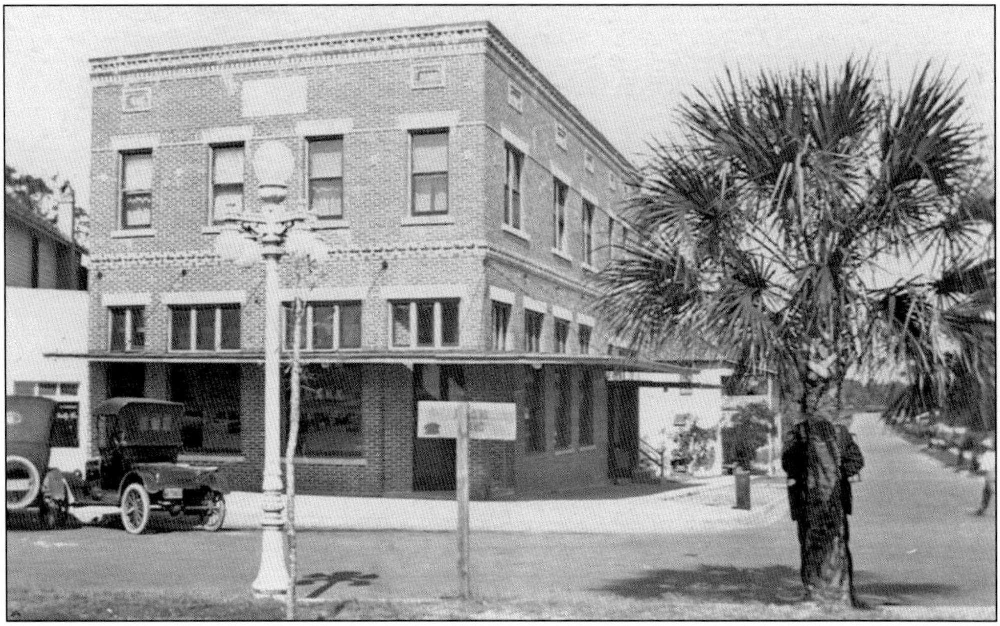

The First National Bank shared the E. E. Skipper Bank Building (1913) with the post office and the Sebring Real Estate Company. The building stands on the Circle at the corner of North Commerce Avenue and had apartments and offices upstairs. At far left is Milt Baker's grocery, and beyond the Skipper Bank Building is a structure that in 1917 was replaced by the new Sebring Post Office. (Courtesy Sebring Historical Society.)

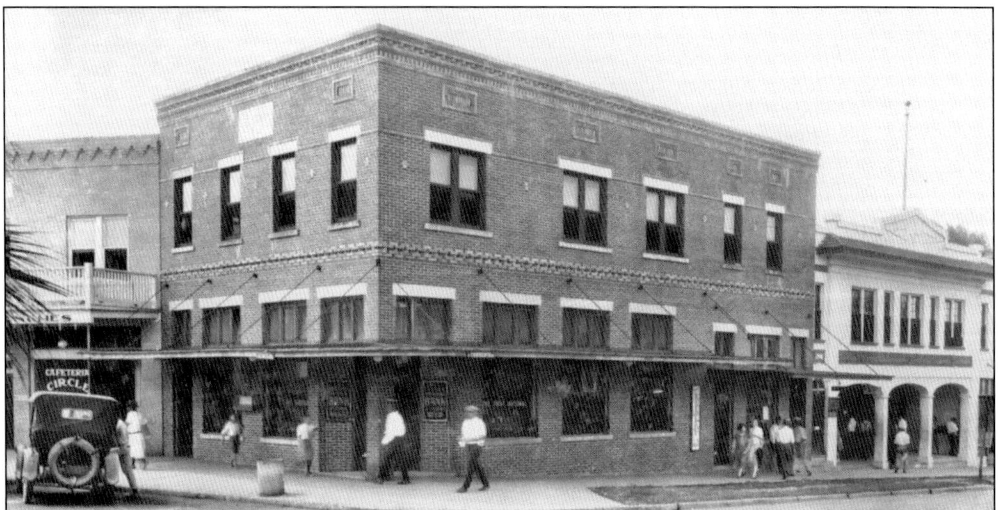

This view of the E. E. Skipper Bank building was taken between 1920 and 1924. The adjacent Dingus Building (1920) was first home to a cafeteria and then to a hardware store after 1924. The Sebring Post Office on North Commerce Avenue is visible at right. The E. E. Skipper Bank building was the site of city hall from 1933 until 1969. (Courtesy Sebring Historical Society.)

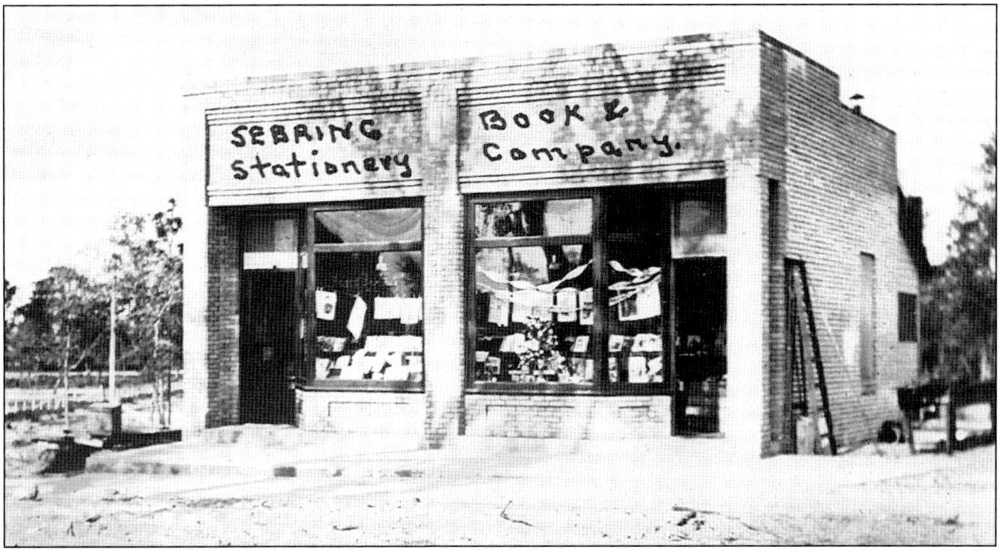

The Albright Building, the city's first masonry structure, was constructed at the north corner of Circle Drive and North Commerce Avenue during the summer of 1912 from bricks manufactured in Sebring. The building served as a book and stationery store, a drug store and doctor's office, and a gift shop before Fisher Sauls purchased the property and established Fisher's Restaurant. The building was destroyed by a fire in May 1977. (Courtesy Sebring Historical Society.)

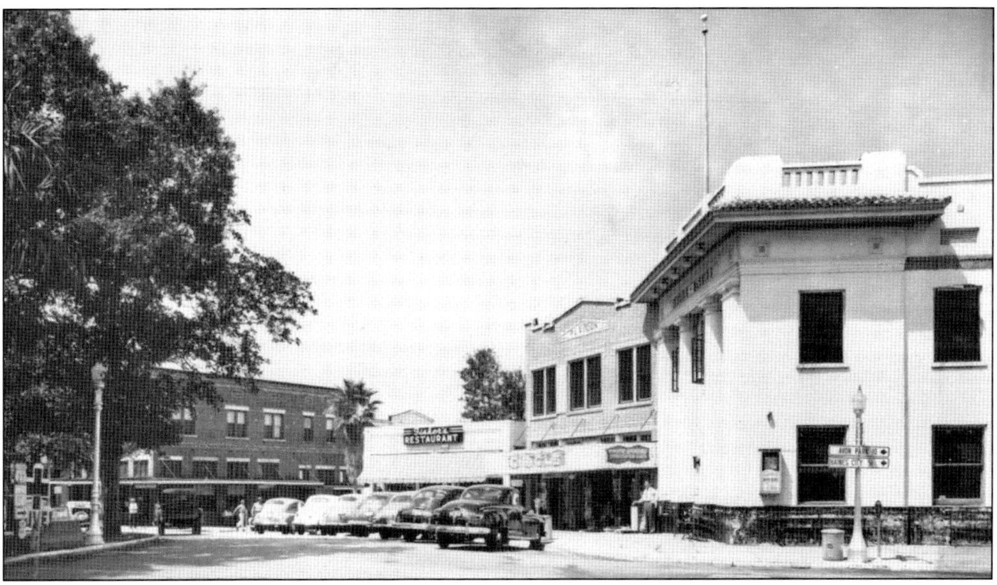

This c. 1950 photograph shows the E. E. Skipper Bank building at left adorned with a "City Office" sign. The next block includes Fisher's Restaurant in the Albright Building, the Circle Theater in the (Paul) P. L. Vinson Building (1923), and the old Highlands Bank and Trust Building at the corner of North Ridgewood Drive, at that time adorned with the lettering "Sebring—Haskins." (Courtesy Sebring Historical Society.)

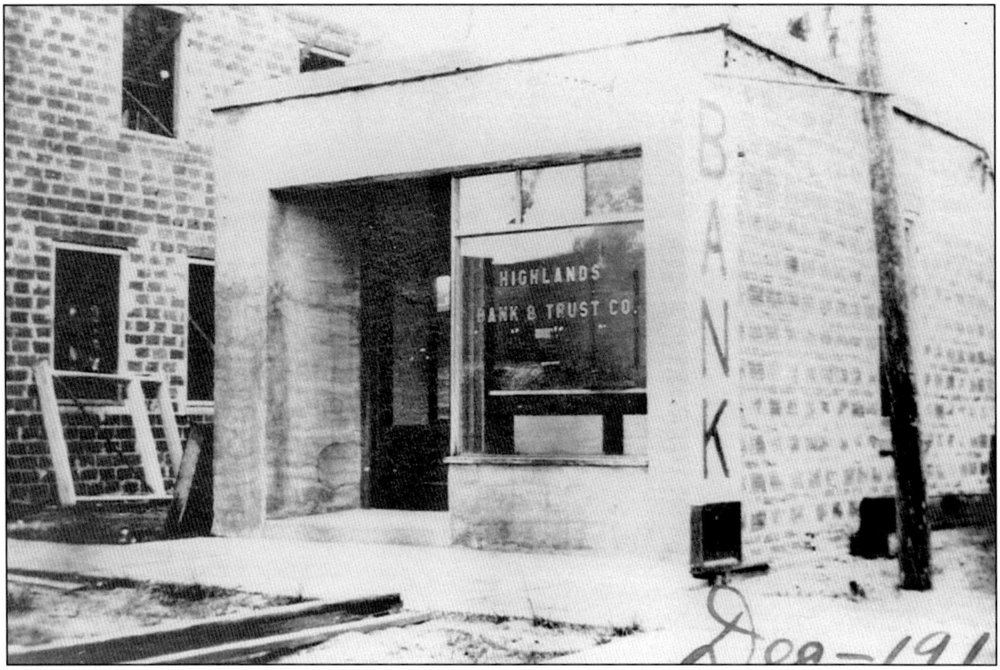

This Highlands Bank and Trust Company building is believed to have been located on North Ridgewood Drive at the present site of the Sebring Real Estate Company Building (1920). The new Highlands Bank and Trust Company Building was constructed in 1919, eliminating the need for this structure. (Courtesy Sebring Historical Society.)

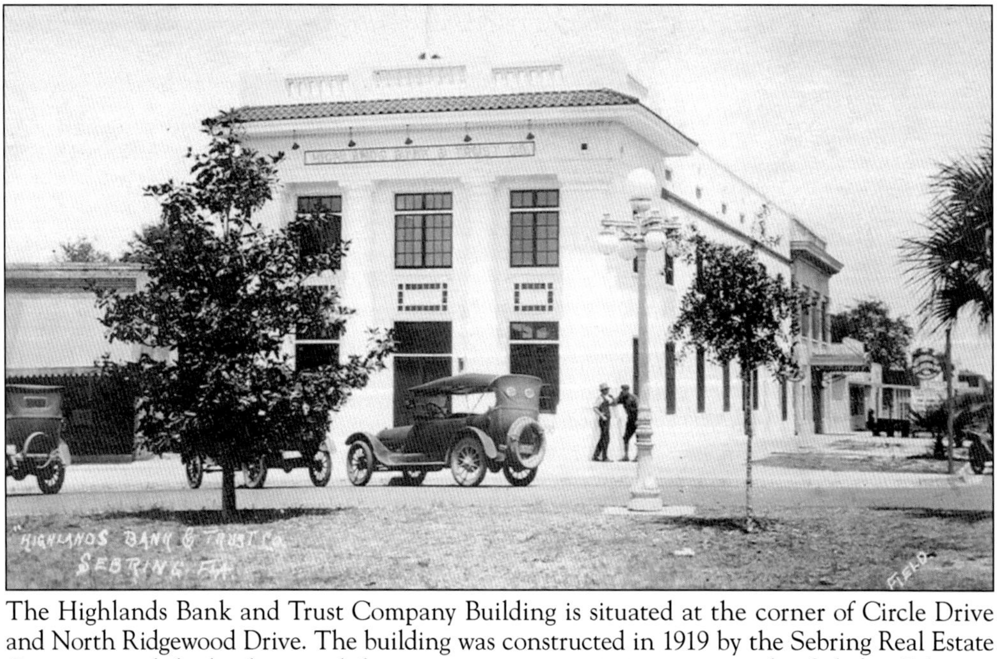

The Highlands Bank and Trust Company Building is situated at the corner of Circle Drive and North Ridgewood Drive. The building was constructed in 1919 by the Sebring Real Estate Company, and the bank opened the next summer, remaining open until it failed in February 1929. The building at left preceded the 1923 P. L. Vinson Building, which became home to the Circle Theater. (Photograph by Field, courtesy Sebring Historical Society.)

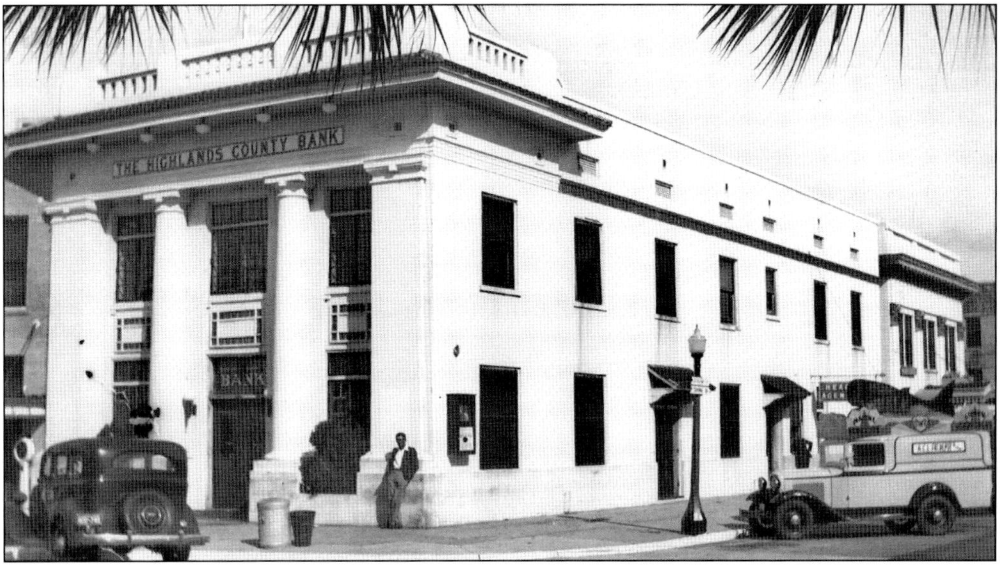

Re-branded as the Highlands County Bank following the Depression, by the mid-1930s, the bank building also housed the Heacock Agency, with first-floor offices accessible through an entrance on the side of the building. By the time of this photograph, the frontage on North Ridgewood Drive had been narrowed, closer to the present width. The truck is advertising a "London Flea Circus" and "Marine Wonders." (Courtesy Sebring Historical Society.)

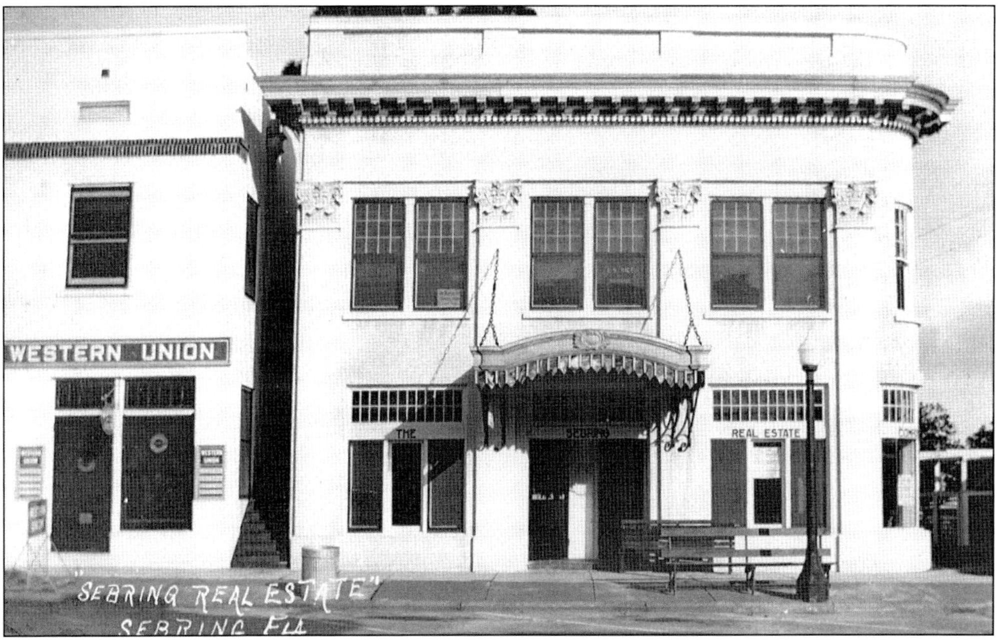

The Sebring Real Estate Company Building is a magnificent structure tucked behind the Highlands County Bank building on North Ridgewood Drive. Constructed in 1920, it is included in the Sebring Downtown Historic District. The building was sold to the Highlands Security Abstract and Title Company owned by Fairfax T. Haskins and Chelsea A. Skipper later that decade. (Courtesy Sebring Historical Society.)

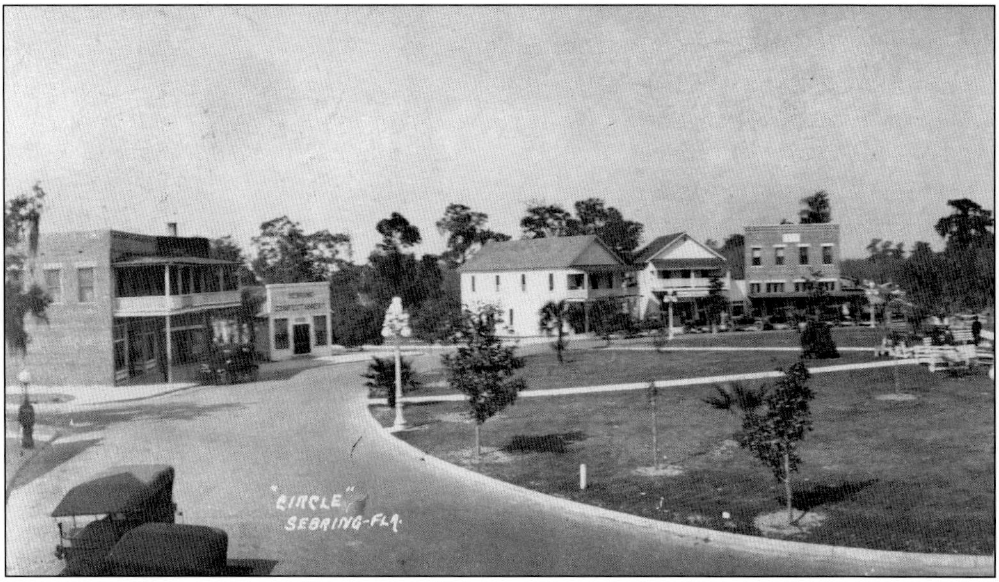

This photograph, facing northwest toward Circle Park, was taken between 1915 and 1919, and is half of a panoramic view continued on the next page. Likely taken from the top of the Roanoke Hotel, these landmarks are visible from left to right: the Withers Building (1913), the Zeall Building (1915), the Harrison Building (1911), the Hainz rooming house (1912), Baker's grocery (1912), and the E. E. Skipper Bank Building (1913). (Photograph by Field, courtesy Sebring Historical Society.)

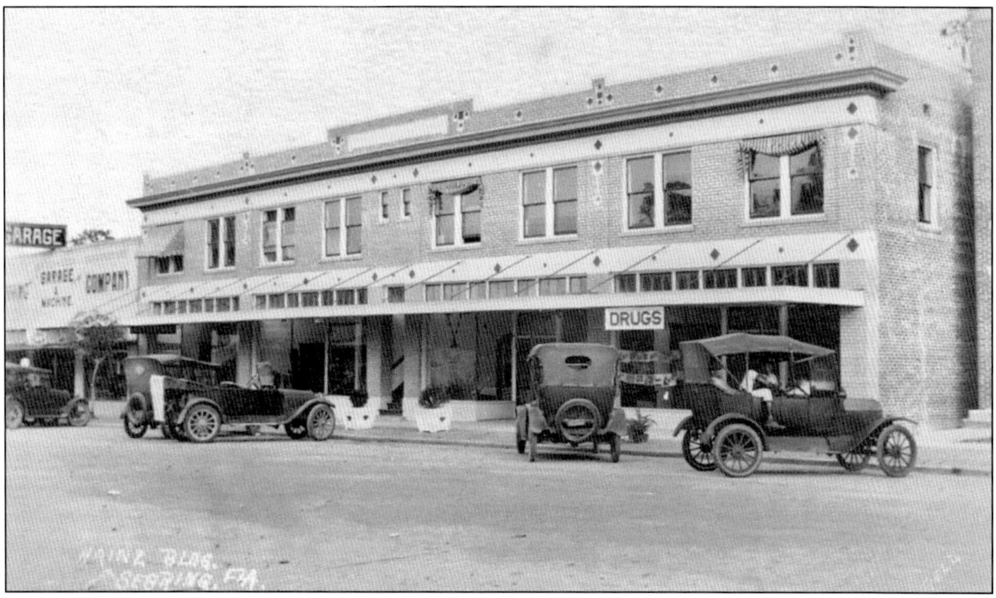

The E. L. Hainz Building (1923) was constructed by businessman Edward L. Hainz and the Sebring Real Estate Company south of the Sebring Garage and Machine Company with four stores on the ground level and with offices on the second floor. The Hainz Building housed the Highlands County Courthouse offices from 1923 to 1927, and still stands at 130–138 North Ridgewood Drive across from the former Nan-Ces-O-Wee Hotel. (Photograph by Field, courtesy Sebring Historical Society.)

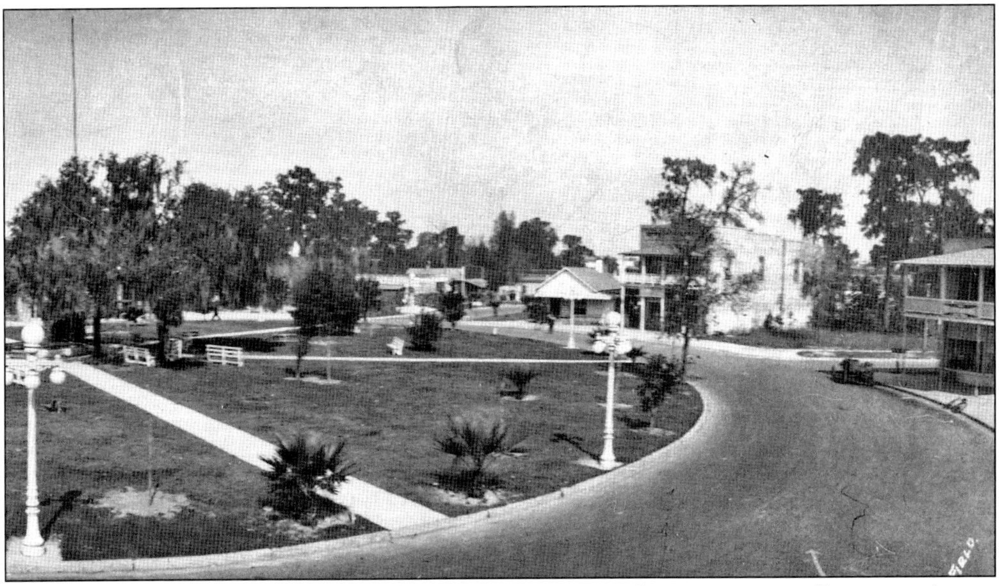

This photograph is the second half of the panoramic view on the previous page. Facing northwest, it is possible to identify the following: the pre-1919 Highlands Bank and Trust Company (?) and an unidentified storefront on North Ridgewood Drive, the Buckeye Clubhouse (1911), the Zackary Building (1914), and the Whitehouse Building (c. 1915). (Photograph by Field, courtesy Sebring Historical Society.)

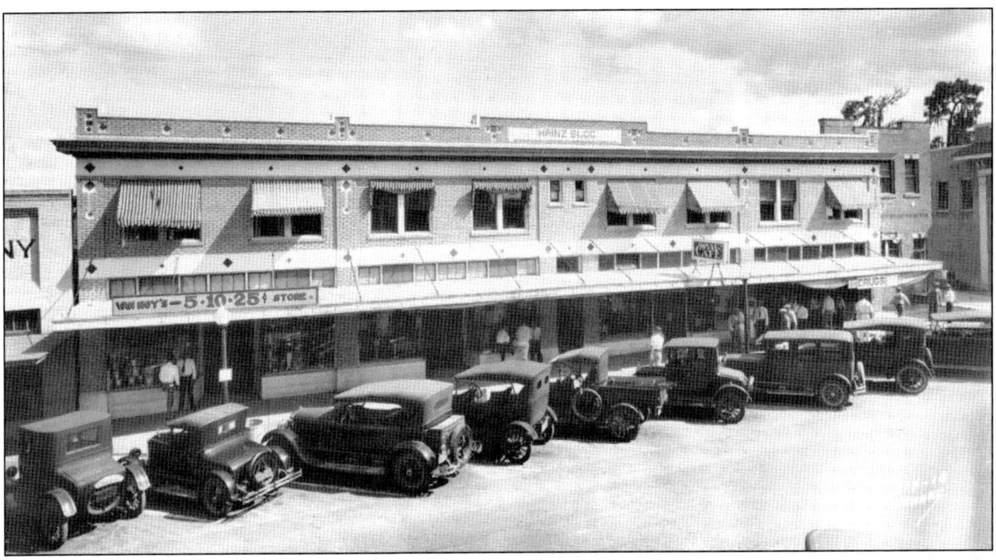

Around 1927, the E. L. Hainz Building was home to Van Noy's 5-10-25¢ Store, the Royal Café, and the Manley Drug Company. The Salvation Army and Buckeye Buildings can be seen at the right in this photograph. The building was renovated by Sam Corson beginning in 2002, and as the Hainz Professional Center, the stately building is once again an important business address. (Photograph by Woodward, courtesy Sebring Historical Society.)

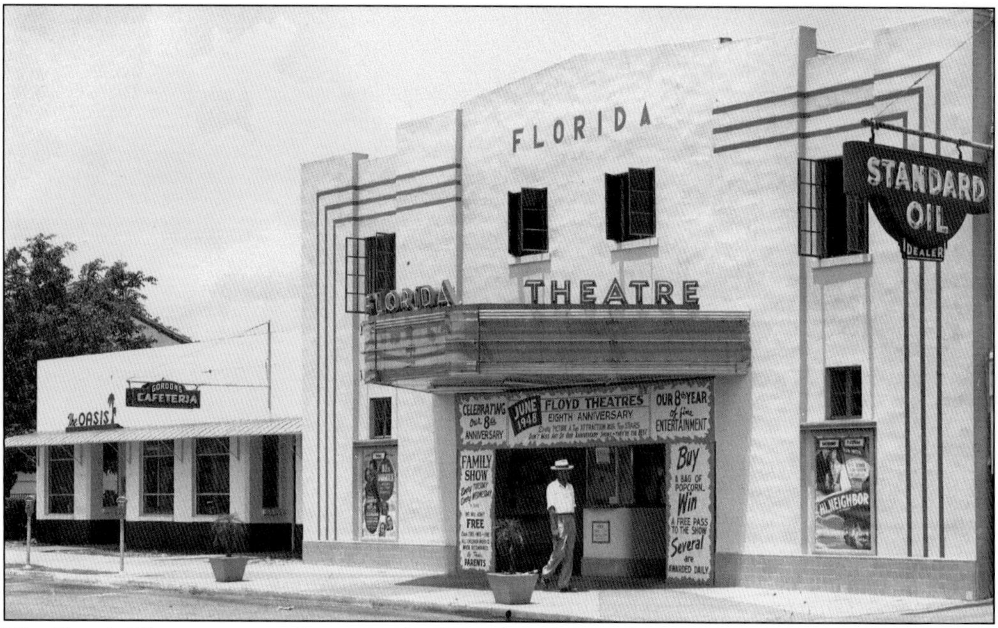

The Florida Theater was on the west side of North Ridgewood Drive near Lime Street. When the theater opened in 1940, Eugene "Gene" Sauls purchased the first ticket and won free admission for a year. This image is from June 1948; the theater was demolished after 1962. The Oasis and Gordon's Cafeteria were next door in a building that later was home to Annette's Shop. (Photograph by Ted Shoemaker, courtesy Sebring Historical Society.)

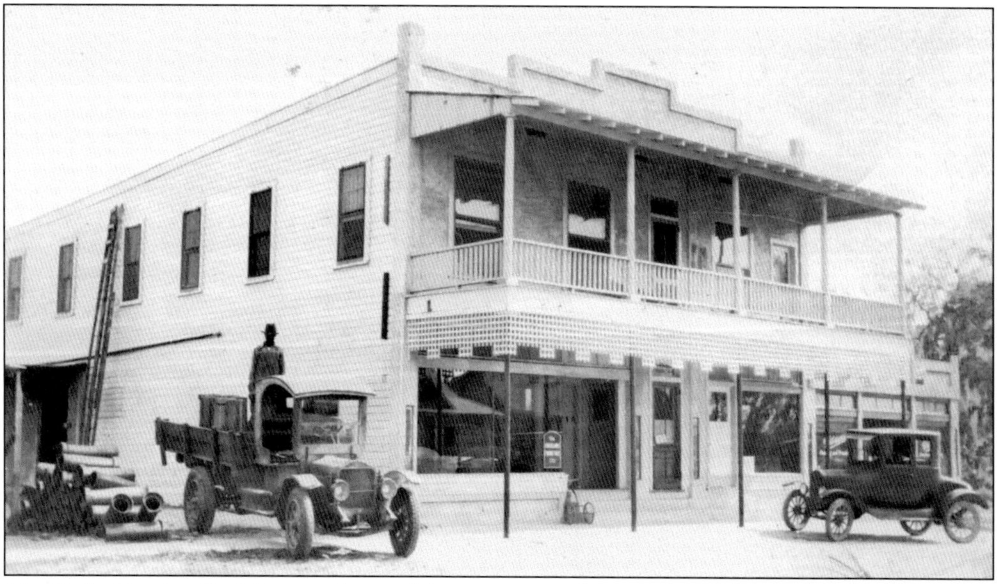

The P. G. Gearing Building was located downtown, perhaps on North Ridgewood Drive; a sign out front advertises "The Highlands Furniture Co." The adjacent building has window lettering reading "Wilson's." Gearing also owned a furniture warehouse at 33 South Commerce Avenue in the 1920s. He served as coach and manager of the Sebring fire department baseball team and was known as "Mr. Baseball" throughout central Florida. (Courtesy Sebring Historical Society.)

Three

Homes and Neighborhoods

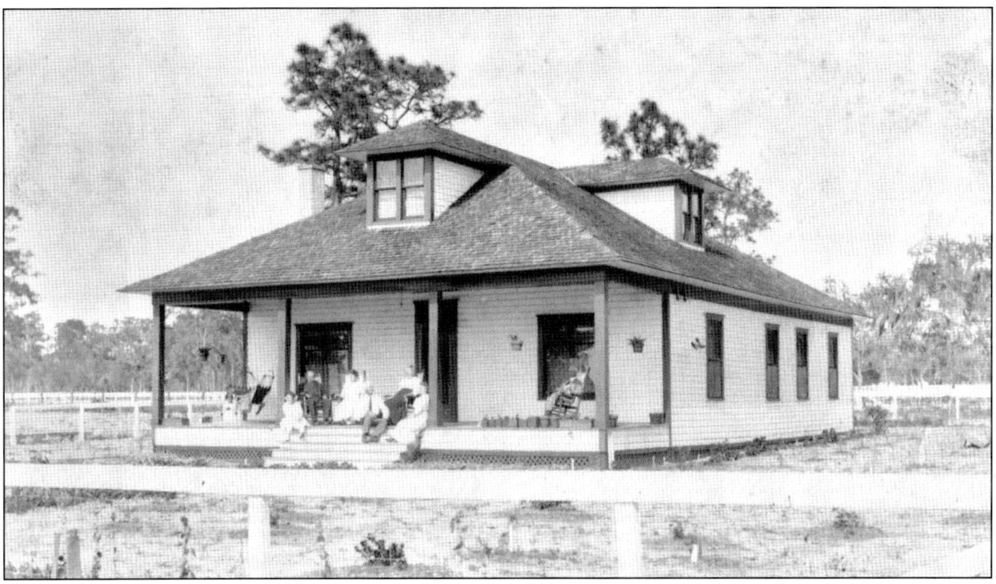

The Henning House on Lakeview Drive NE is Sebring's oldest surviving residence, having been constructed during the summer of 1912 for Henry Henning and his family. Henning first visited Sebring as a member of the Pittsburg Party in January 1912. He was one of the first local citrus grove owners, with an extensive grove southeast of the Circle along South Commerce Avenue. (Courtesy Sebring Historical Society.)

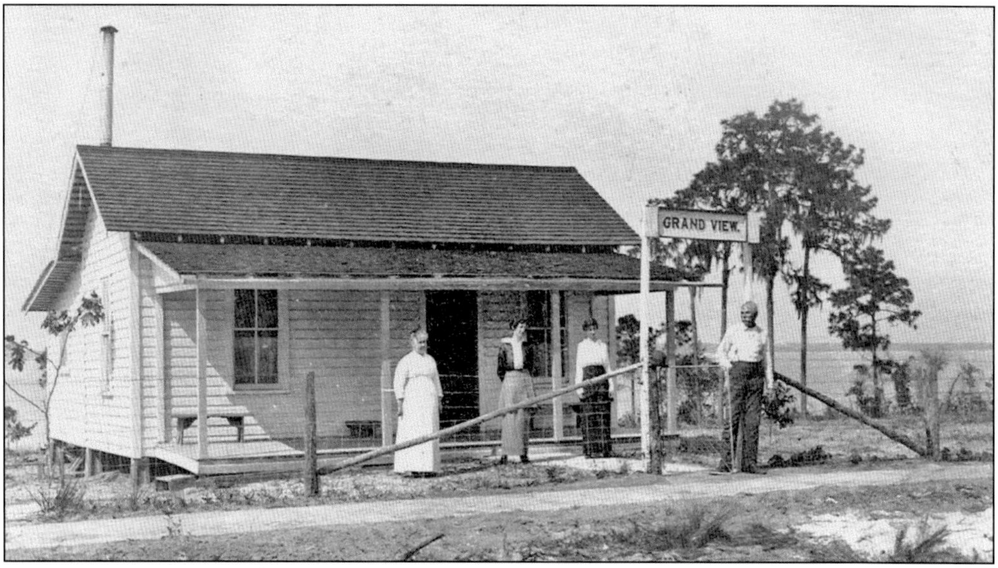

This small home on the shore of Lake Jackson had what the owner advertised as a grand view. Early yards were required to be fenced to keep roving hogs and herds of cattle out, and to help the town marshal control the movement of chickens. In 1918, the city commission voted to surround the entire town with a fence with gated roadways to protect residences and city property. (Courtesy Sebring Historical Society.)

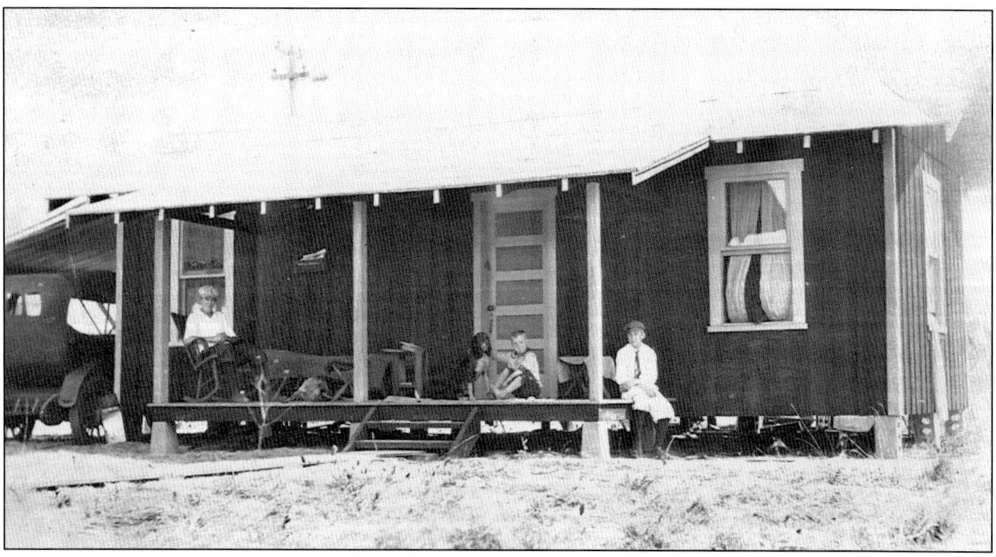

John Engle and Lila Woodward Graham moved their six children, nieces, and nephews to Sebring from Roanoke, Virginia, in 1916 and made their home in "Too Little." John Graham, an inventor, served several terms on the town council, including as president in 1921. The family later moved to the Vinson-Graham House on Lakeview Drive NE. (Courtesy Sebring Historical Society.)

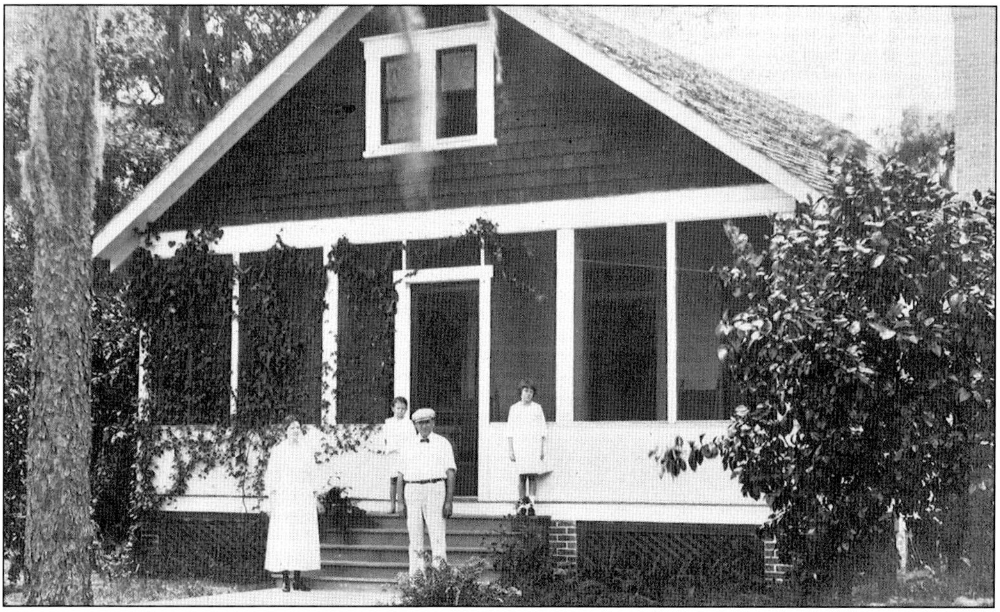

The P. G. Miller family is shown in front of their home at 133 North Commerce Avenue, one of Sebring's three original "permanent" houses. It was purchased in 1921 by Herman Dresto. North Commerce Avenue was first known as Railroad Avenue, and shrewd investors realized that proximity to the railroad depot was good business. Lots were bought and sold along this road by speculators capitalizing on the location. (Courtesy Sebring Historical Society.)

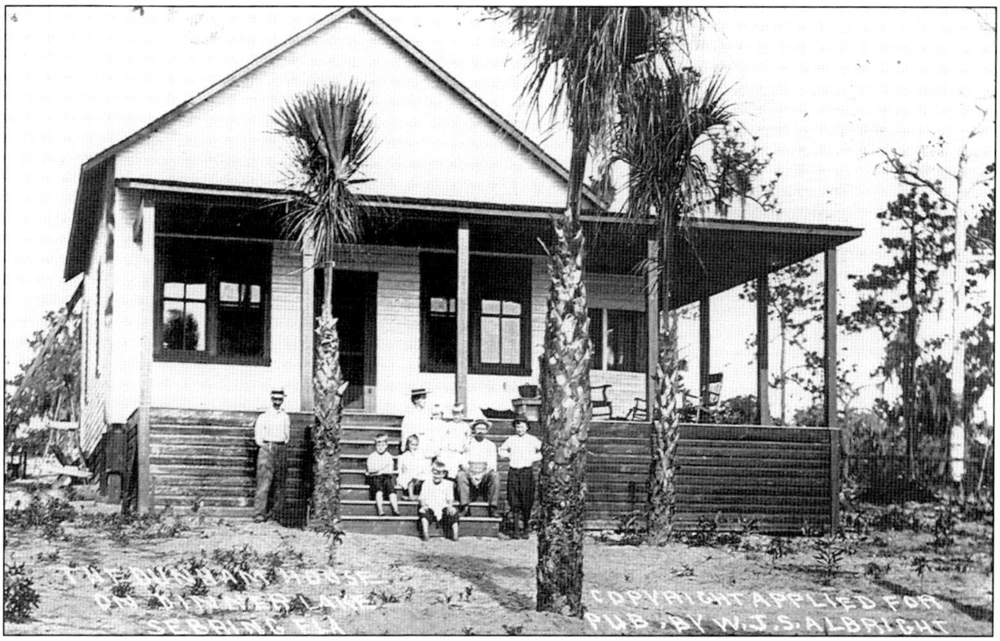

Salvation Army brigadier David Dunham, who led many of the pioneer religious services, built his family's home facing Dinner Lake in 1912. Major Irvings is shown at far left in this photograph. Photographer Sewell Albright was the circulation manager for the first local newspaper, which was published by H. Orvel Sebring. (Photograph by W. J. S. Albright, courtesy Sebring Historical Society.)

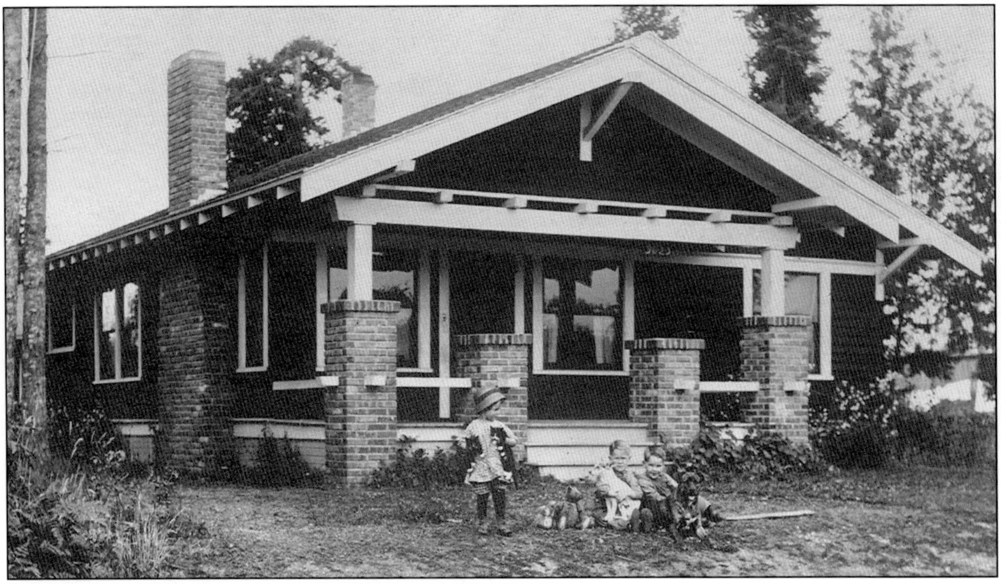

Teddy bears, cats, and dogs—these young children had it all. The *Sebring White Way*—named for the streetlights that illuminated the city—reported on the latest building craze on June 2, 1916, as builders Chauncey Heagle and William F. Ashley formed a partnership to build bungalows on spec. Their five-room homes ranged in price from $1,500 to $2,300, included a bath and a porch, and were located within several blocks of the Circle. (Courtesy Sebring Historical Society.)

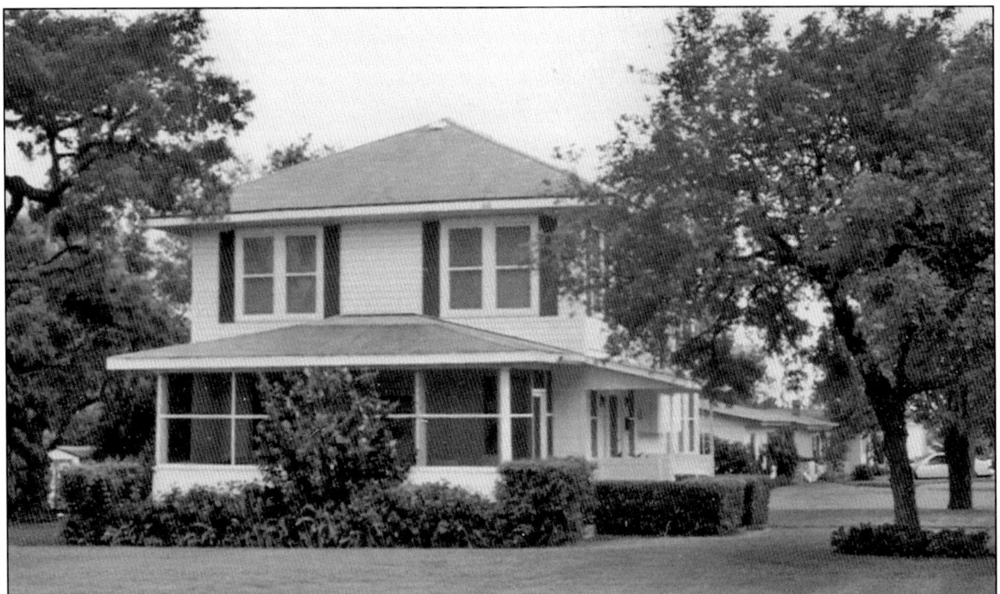

The Haskins House was built in 1913–1914 by the Sebring Realty Company for horticulturist Ryland G. Haskins, who had arrived in November 1911 to work for George E. Sebring in developing the new community. The home was located on the northeast corner of North Ridgewood Drive and North Pine Street, and was moved in 1954 by Ray T. Graddy to its present location on Nancesowee Avenue. (Courtesy Sebring Historical Society.)

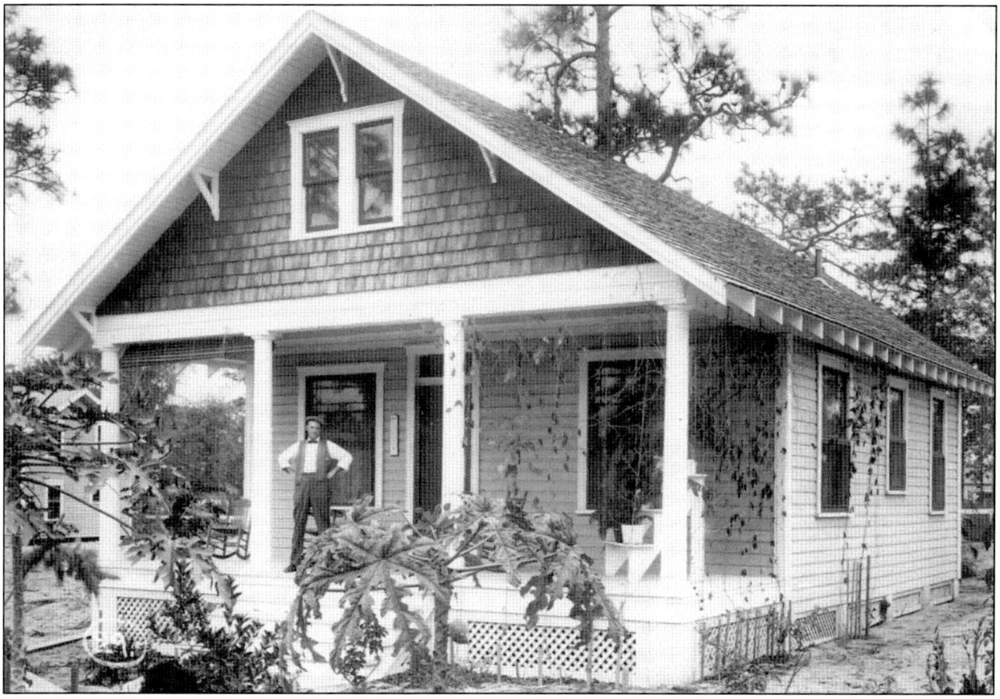

The owner of this attractive home, believed to have been located on North Commerce Avenue, took full advantage of Sebring's temperate climate with papayas in the yard, potted ferns on the porch, and trained vines against the house. A Cola-Cola thermometer hung next to the door. Willis Kugler produced photographs and real-photo postcards in the 1910s, and commercially-printed postcards as late as the 1930s. (Photograph by Kugler Photo, courtesy Sebring Historical Society.)

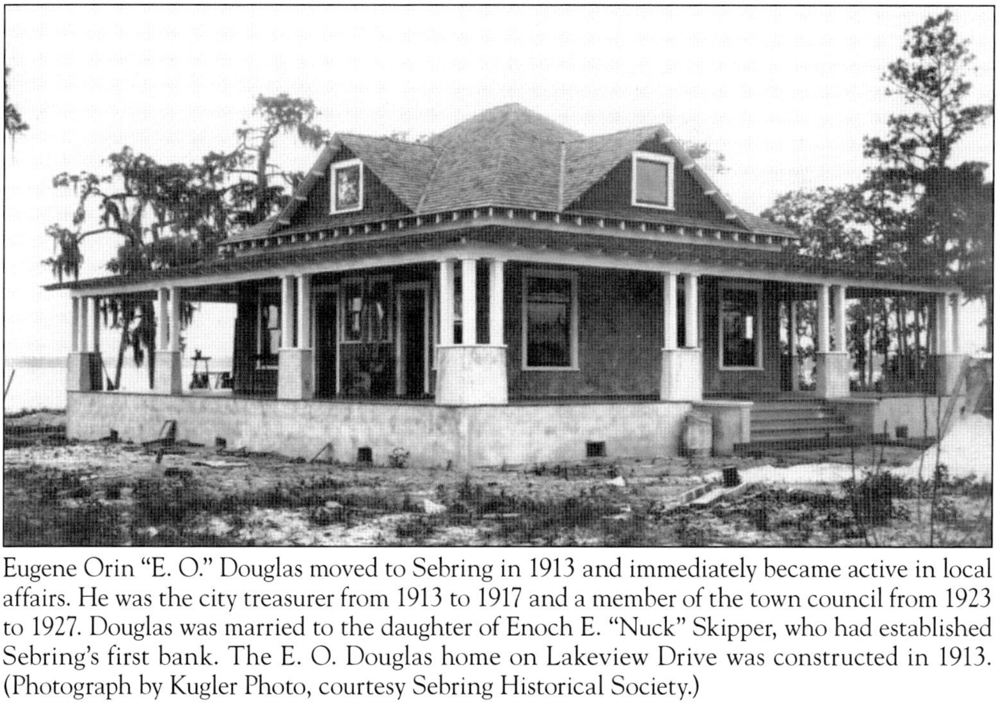

Eugene Orin "E. O." Douglas moved to Sebring in 1913 and immediately became active in local affairs. He was the city treasurer from 1913 to 1917 and a member of the town council from 1923 to 1927. Douglas was married to the daughter of Enoch E. "Nuck" Skipper, who had established Sebring's first bank. The E. O. Douglas home on Lakeview Drive was constructed in 1913. (Photograph by Kugler Photo, courtesy Sebring Historical Society.)

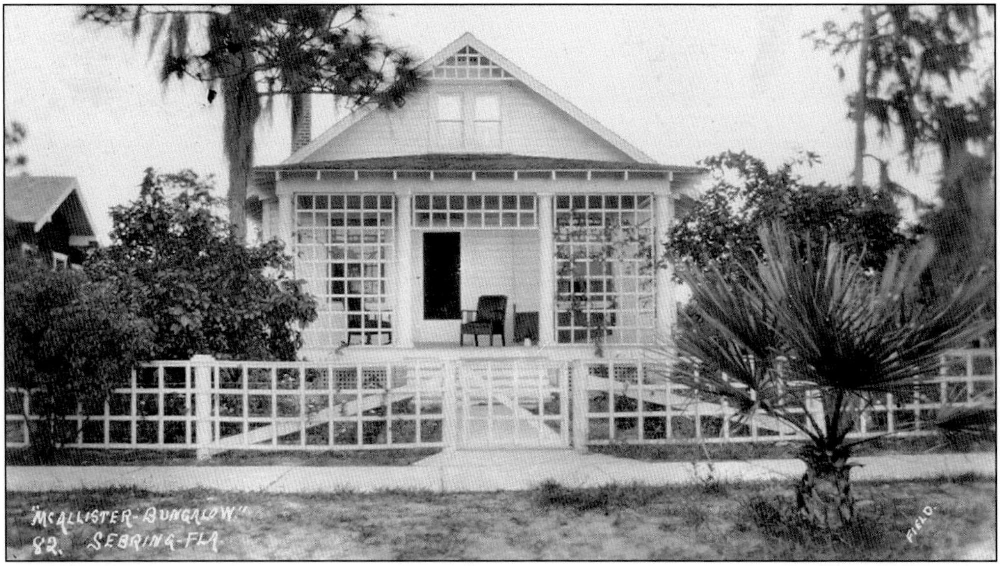

The McAllister bungalow was one of more than 100 bungalows in early Sebring. These homes were characterized by a low profile and a prominent porch, and most included all living space on one level. In June 1916, Sebring was referred to as "Bungalow Town" in the local press. (Photograph by Field, courtesy Sebring Historical Society.)

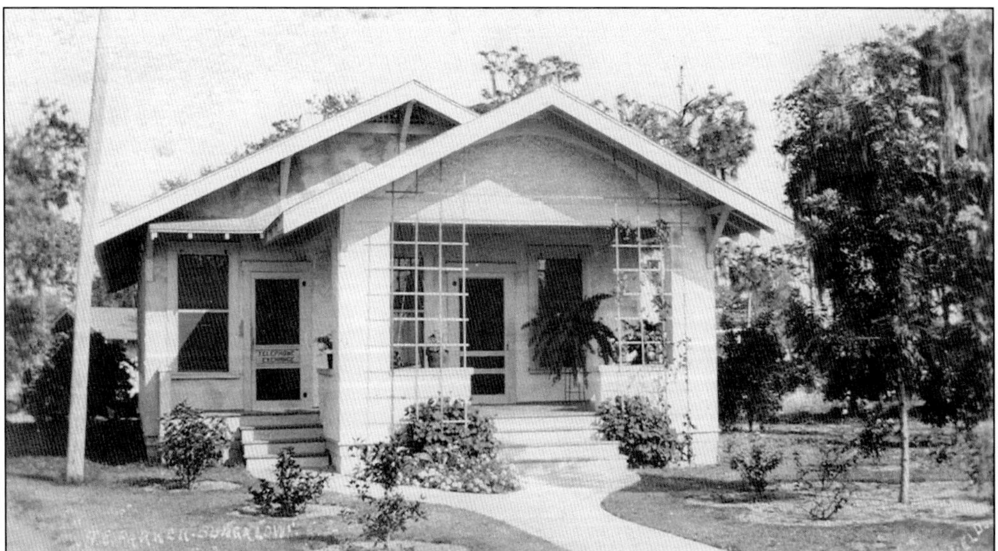

The Jerome E. Parker Bungalow was home to the Sebring telephone exchange in the 1920s. Discussed since 1914, the earliest telephone service reached Sebring in November 1916. Service was $1.50 per month with several telephones hung on trees in the Circle. When Parker purchased the franchise in July 1917, residential rates were increased to no more than $27 per year, and businesses rates were capped at $36. (Photograph by Field, courtesy Sebring Historical Society.)

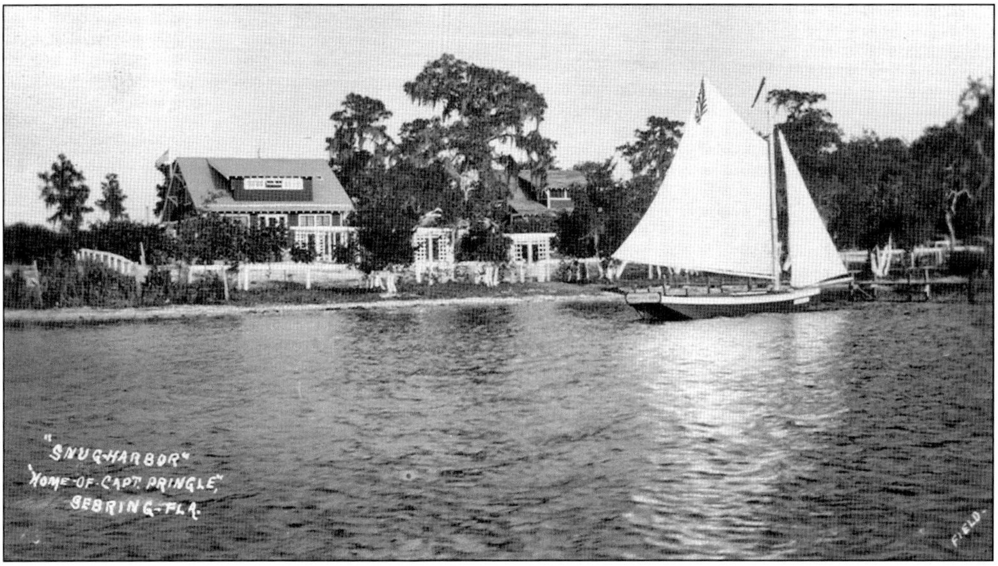

Captain Pringle of Sebring built a home nicknamed "Snug Harbor" on the east shore of Lake Jackson. With long, sweeping roofs on the front and rear, and open and screened porches facing Lakeview Drive, this distinctive, two-story frame building was the backdrop for this 1920s view from the lake. The home was moved to the east side of Lakeview Drive on January 18, 2006. (Photograph by Field, courtesy Sebring Historical Society.)

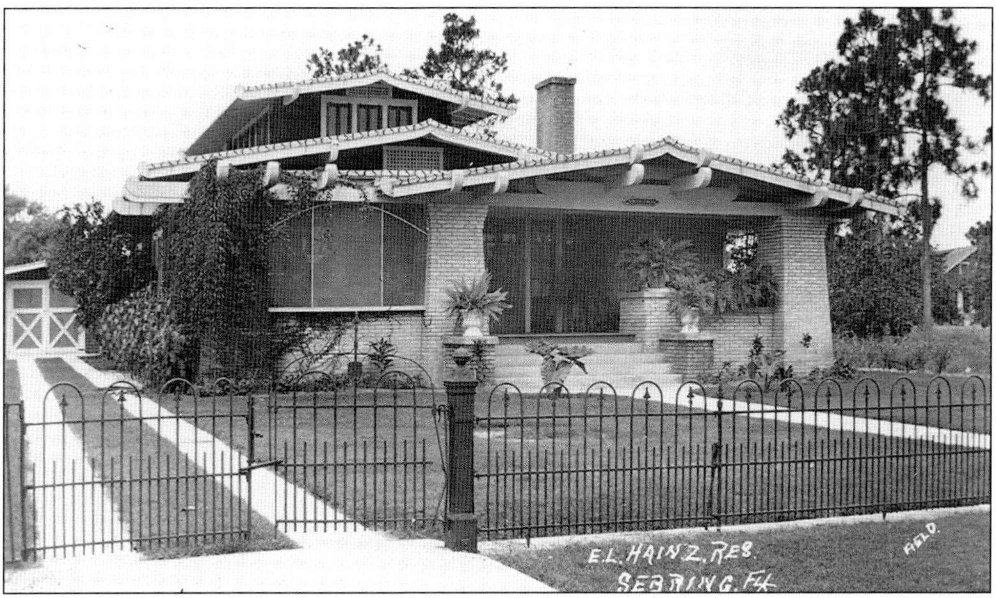

The Edward L. Hainz residence (1917), also shown on the bottom of page 98, stands on West Center Avenue. The sign above the porch entrance reads "Linger Longer." This striking airplane-style bungalow was added to the National Register of Historic Places in 1989. Hainz was a charter member of both the Board of Trade and the Rotary Club. (Photograph by Field, courtesy Sebring Historical Society.)

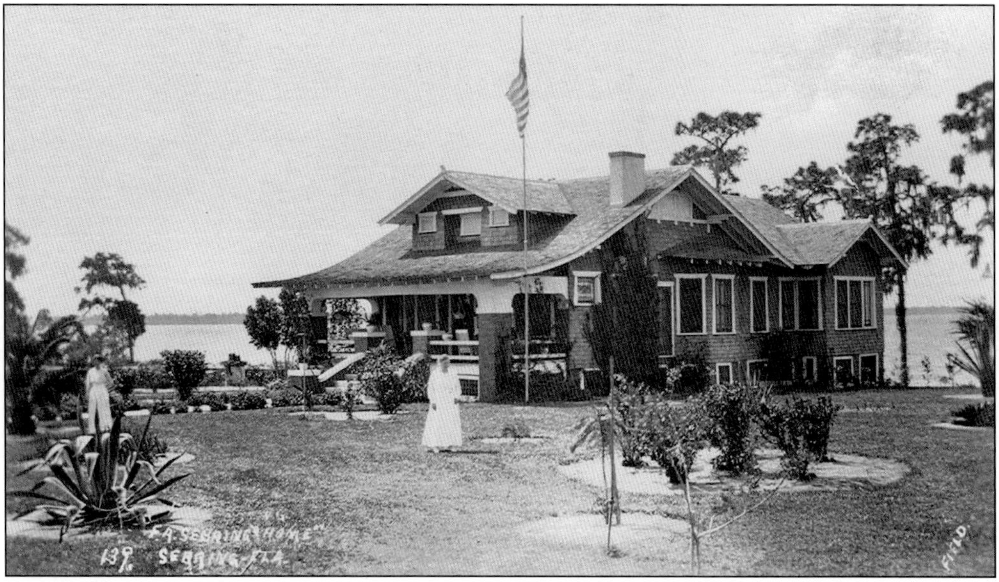

Frank Albert Sebring (1865–1936) was a younger brother of George E. Sebring. This photograph depicts the home of F. A. and Emma Sebring in the 1920s. As the 1921 president of the Board of Trade, Sebring was instrumental in the development of Tuscawilla Park and other beautification initiatives. He was a partner in a corporation that purchased Kenilworth Lodge in 1923. (Photograph by Field, courtesy Sebring Historical Society.)

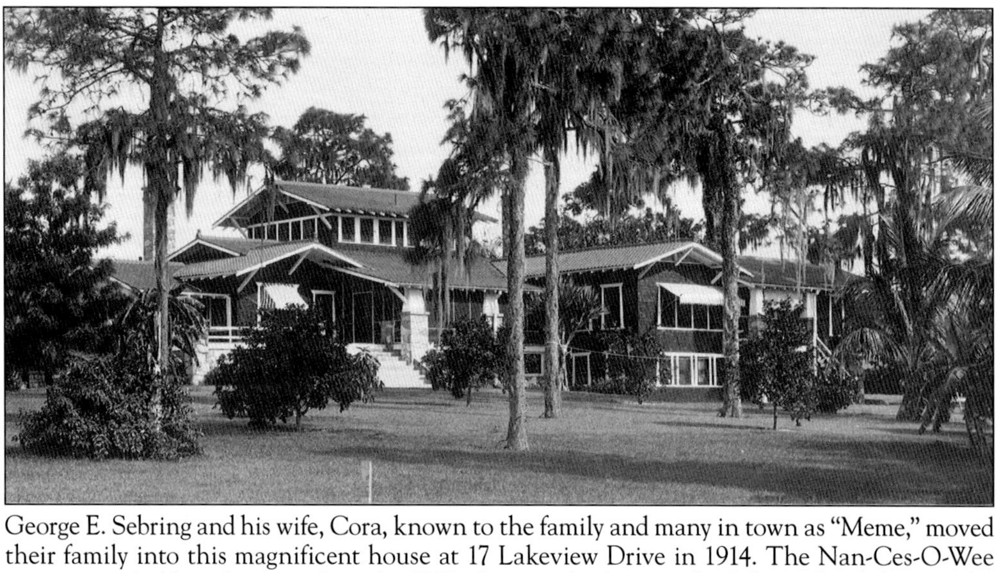

George E. Sebring and his wife, Cora, known to the family and many in town as "Meme," moved their family into this magnificent house at 17 Lakeview Drive in 1914. The Nan-Ces-O-Wee pageant was held on the grounds in the 1930s, but mostly, this was the Sebring family home. The house was demolished to make way for the Sebring Public Library by the late 1960s. (Photograph by Woodward, courtesy Sebring Historical Society.)

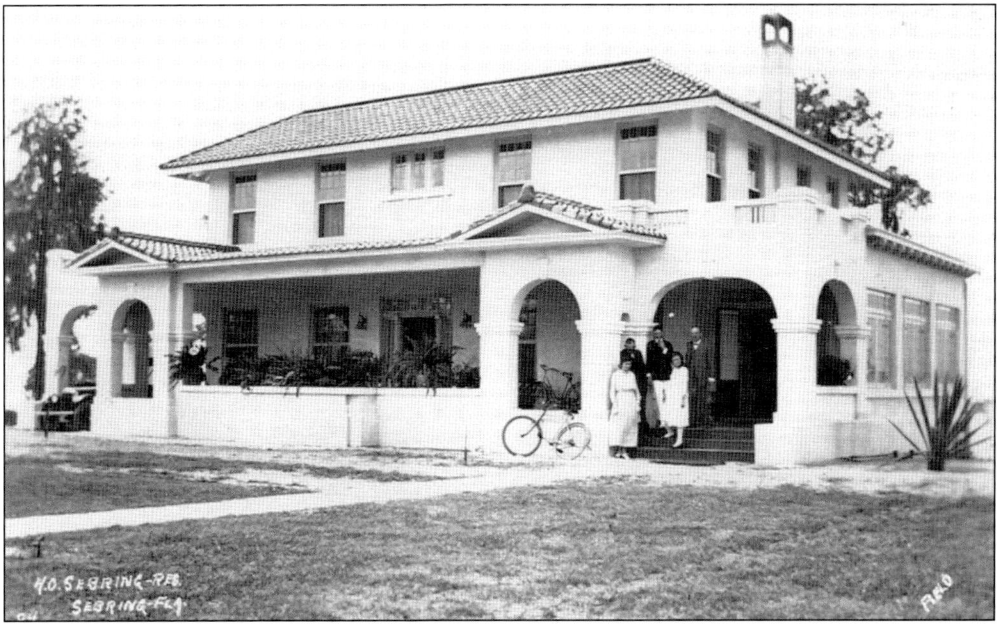

One of the city's best-recognized residences is the H. Orvel Sebring home, constructed in 1919 on Lakeview Drive SE. Designed by acclaimed Tampa architect M. Leo Elliott, the home was added to the National Register of Historic Places in 1989. Sebring was his father's enthusiastic partner in the development of the city, and he played an active role in local affairs until his death in 1950. (Photograph by Field, courtesy Sebring Historical Society.)

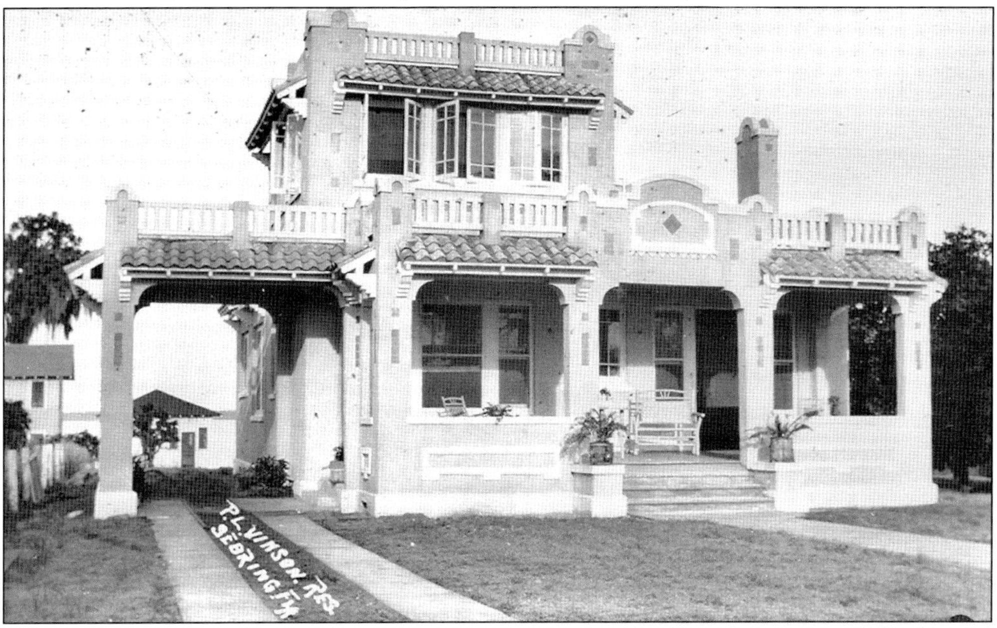

In 1923, Paul L. Vinson constructed the downtown building that bears his name and that housed the Circle Theater. His attractive Mission-style residence on Lakeview Drive SE dates from the same period and is now known as the Vinson-Graham House, also named after John E. Graham. The house was added to the National Register of Historic Places in 1989. (Photograph by Field, courtesy Sebring Historical Society.)

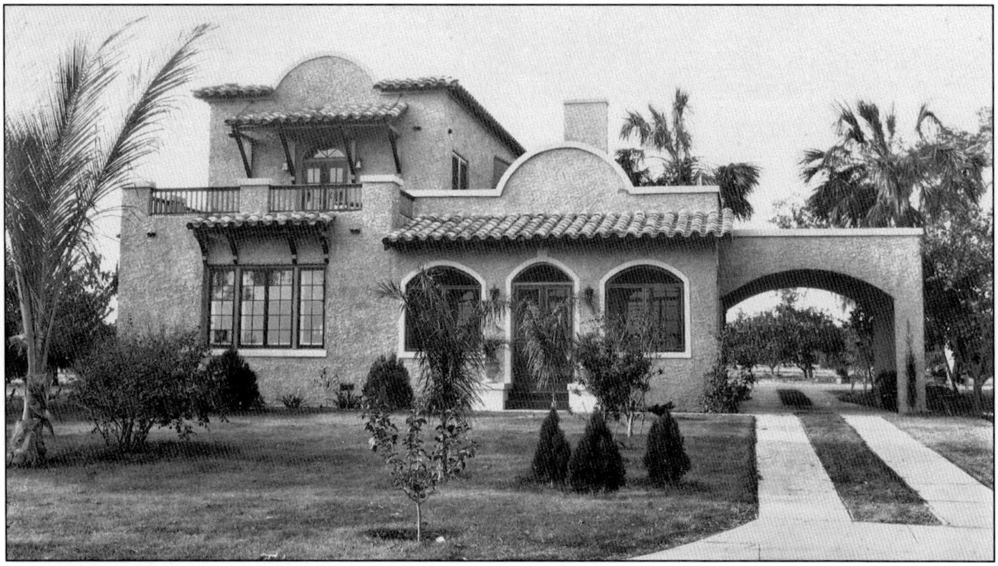

Sebring pioneers Aaron Withers and Edward W. Harshman were citrus business partners, and their families also both lived at different times in the Withers-Harshman residence. Harshman was an engineer at the first electric plant, served four years on the city council, and was mayor from 1918 to 1920 and in 1922. (Courtesy Sebring Historical Society.)

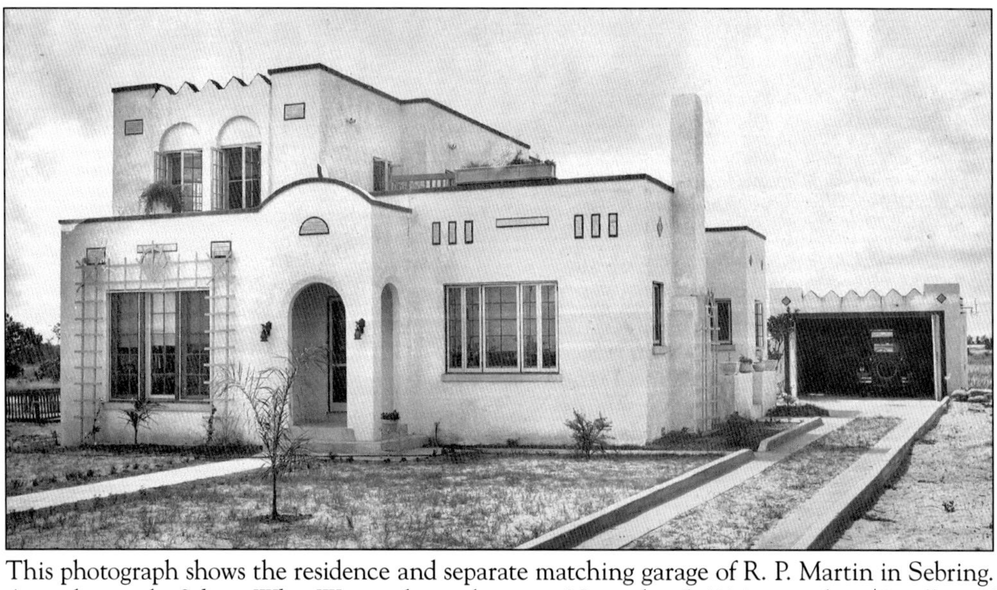

This photograph shows the residence and separate matching garage of R. P. Martin in Sebring. According to the *Sebring White Way*, in the week prior to November 5, 1924, more than $2 million of local property exchanged hands in six days. One local man purchased a lot for $2,800 on a Monday, selling it the next week for $5,000. Henry Pierson of Brooklyn, New York, invested $100,000 in three days. (Courtesy Sebring Historical Society.)

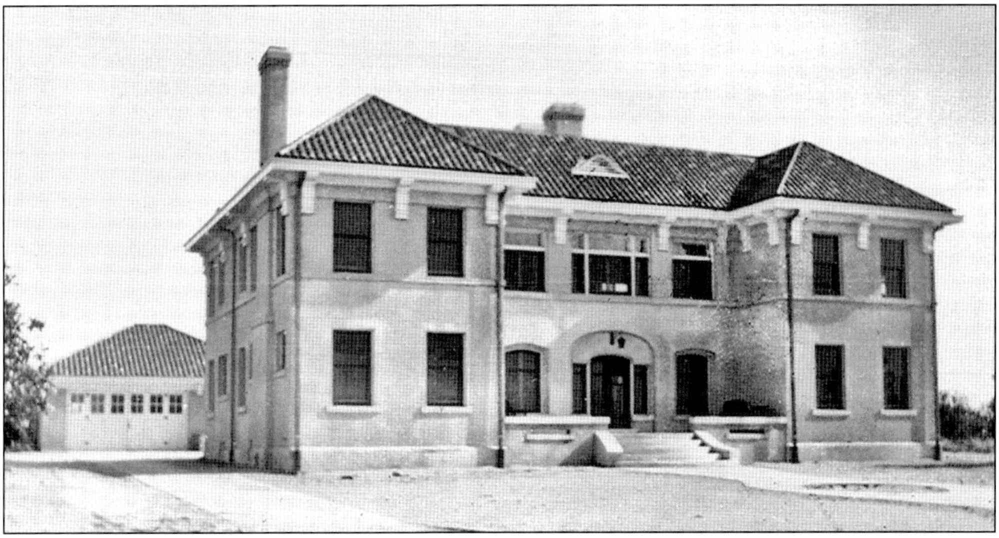

The Italian Renaissance–style Elizabeth Haines House was constructed on Summit Drive in the Sebring Heights subdivision in 1927. Subsequent owners included Charles Sebring in 1950, George E. Sebring III in 1967, and Jerry McCustion in 1973. The home was added to the National Register of Historic Places in 1993, and by 2003, it had been carefully renovated. (Courtesy Sebring Historical Society.)

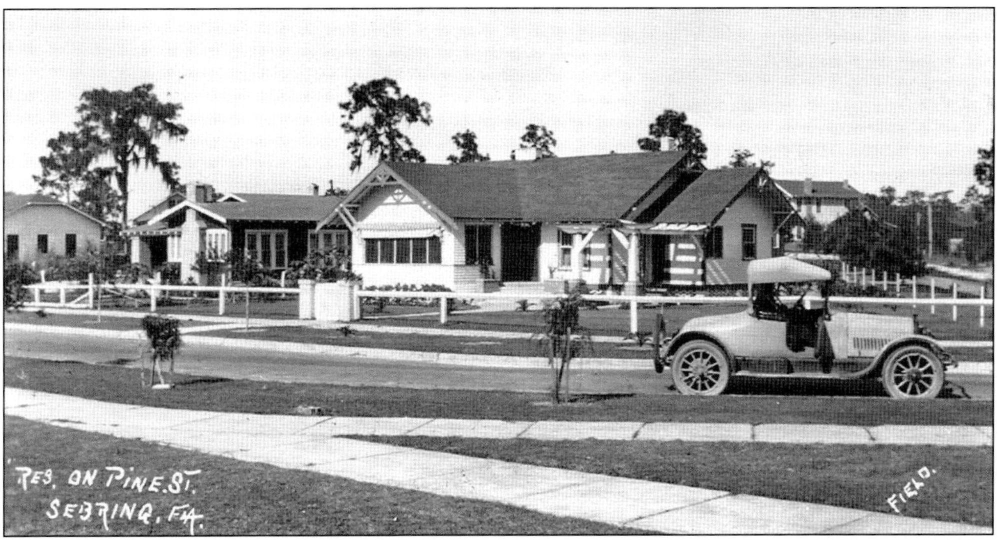

These Pine Street residences were among many in new subdivisions in the 1920s. In 2004, Alice Ruth Gettel Gingrich recalled in *The Historian* when she lived in a three-story house on Pine Street near the Church of the Brethren in the 1940s. The home was known as Gettel's Apartments, and tenants included servicemen and, after World War II, Pennsylvania Dutch residents. (Photograph by Field, courtesy Sebring Historical Society.)

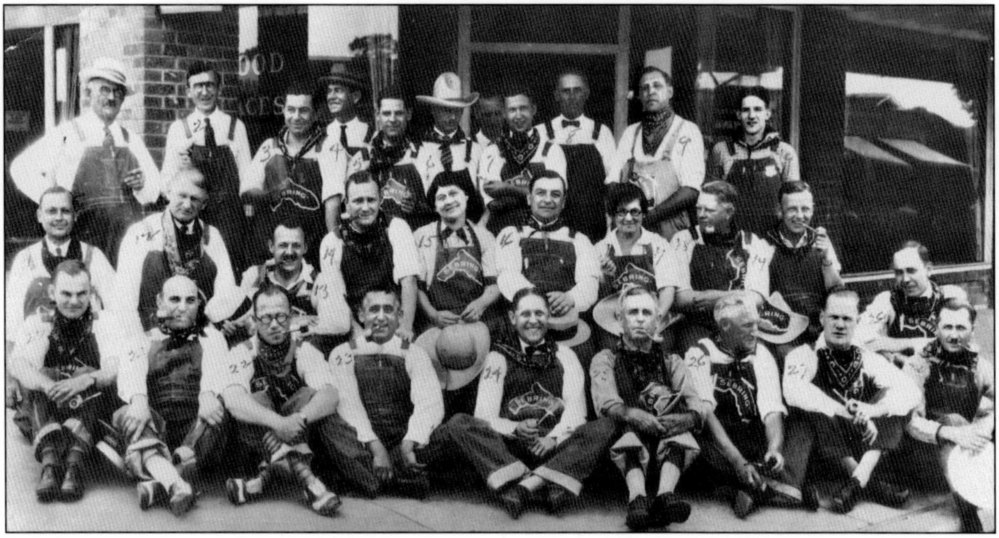

The area surrounding the Harder Hall resort included the Lakewood Terraces development. The 1925 sales force included these identified individuals: (1) George E. Sebring, (2) Harry McCorkle, (14) Dorland Cook, (15) Maude Manley, (16) William Parrish, (19) Paul Cheney, (20) Skeet Naylor, (24) ? Norris, and (26) C. D. Hout. The Lakewood Development Corporation was the first major local victim of the Florida land bust. (Courtesy Sebring Historical Society.)

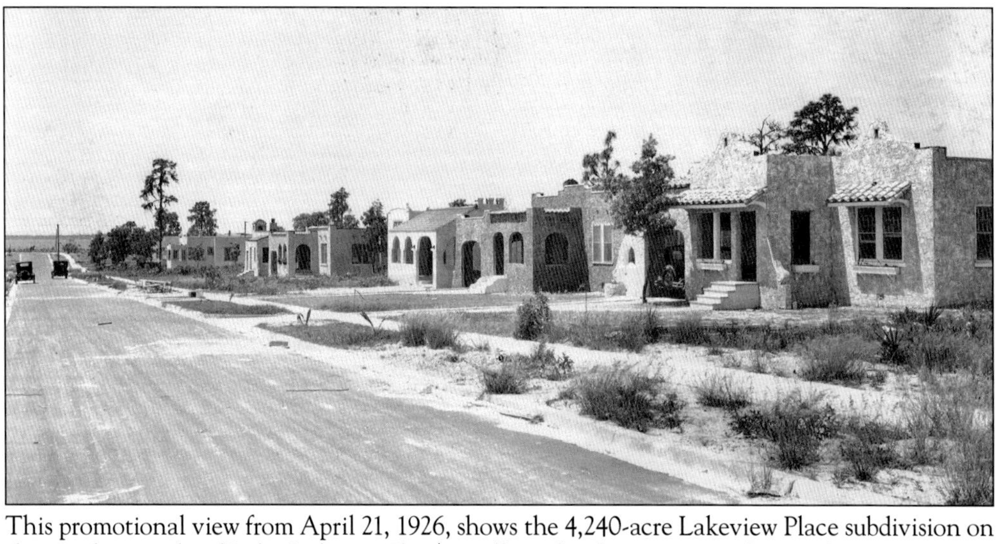

This promotional view from April 21, 1926, shows the 4,240-acre Lakeview Place subdivision on the northeast side of Lake Jackson. The $1 million development was designed as an exclusive neighborhood with Spanish Mission–style homes, Seminole Indian–inspired street names, and included several small parks extending to the lake. The most expensive homes cost more than $5,000. (Photograph by Burgert Brothers Tampa, courtesy Sebring Historical Society.)

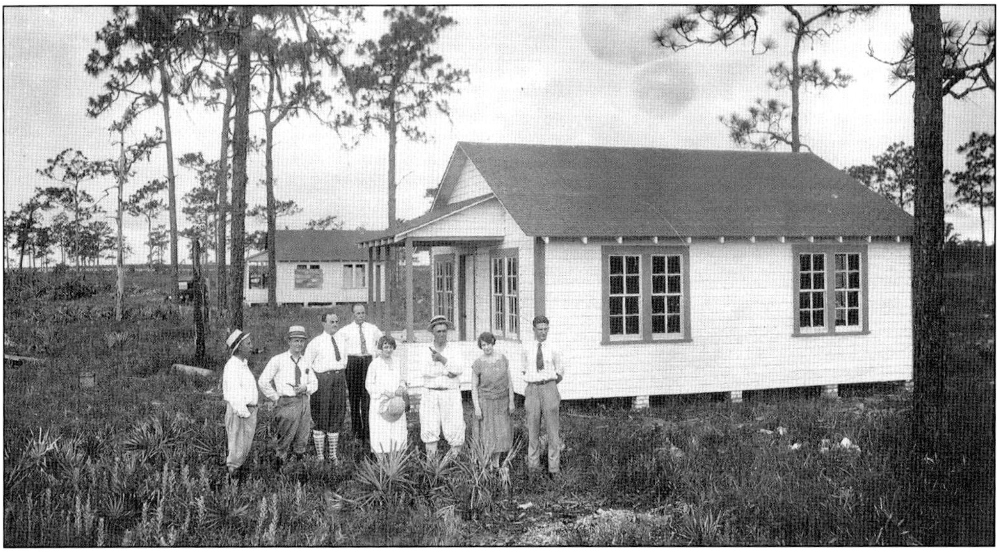

Pictured near rural farm cottages in this c. 1930 image is one of Sebring's most famous citizens, accomplished novelist Rex Beach (1877–1949), third from right. Beach and his wife, Edith, purchased some 7,000 acres of land used for farming, supported the development of Highlands Hammock State Park, and anonymously assisted needy families during the Depression. Among those shown are Fred Stone, Warren Atlerson, and Lottie and Louis Alsmeyer. (Courtesy Sebring Historical Society.)

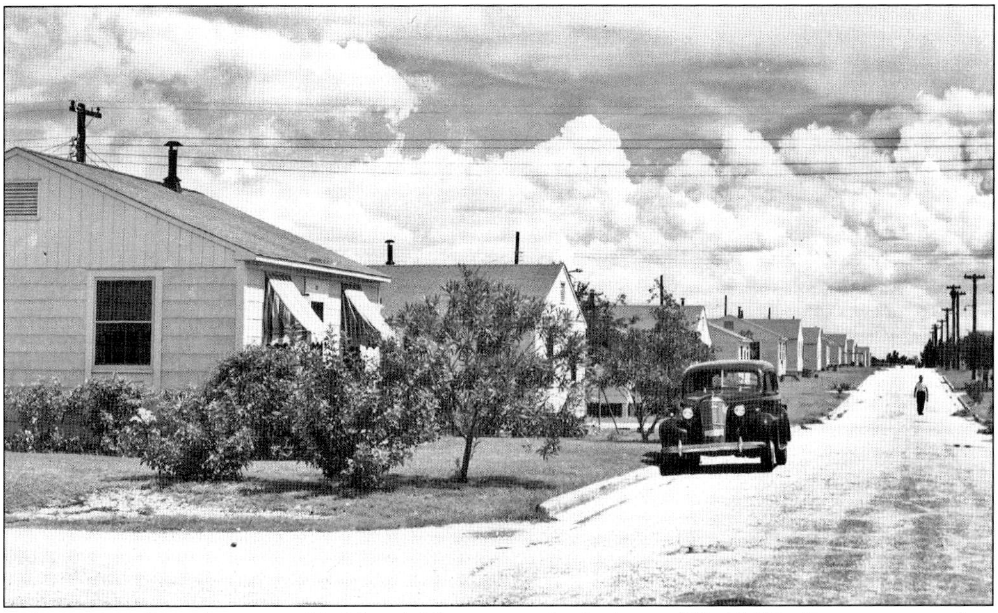

Splinter City, later known as Highlands Homes, was built during World War II to accommodate non-commissioned officers and civilians affiliated with Hendricks Field. Married officers lived along Lakeview Drive SE in 50 new homes; the area was nicknamed "Snob Hollow." Many wives and girlfriends of servicemen followed them to Sebring. A rent control board was established to maintain reasonable local lodging rates. (Courtesy Sebring Historical Society.)

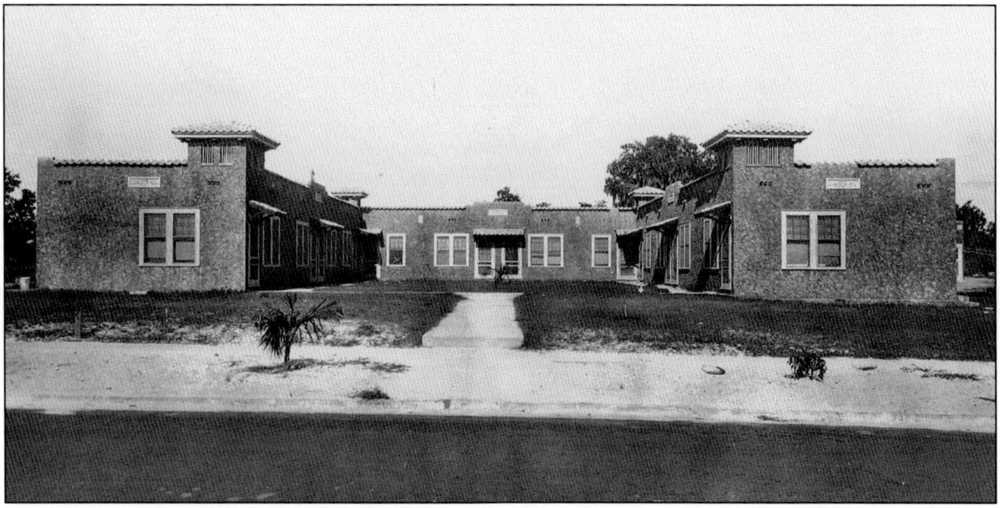

The *Sebring White Way* on October 31, 1924, includes an advertisement for Lake View Court, better known as Lakeview Terrace Apartments. Still located on Lakeview Drive NE, the apartments featured "one large room, clothes press, Murphy bed, bath room and kitchenette" leased at $300 for the season. Need a garage? One was available for only $25 more. (Photograph by Woodward, courtesy Sebring Historical Society.)

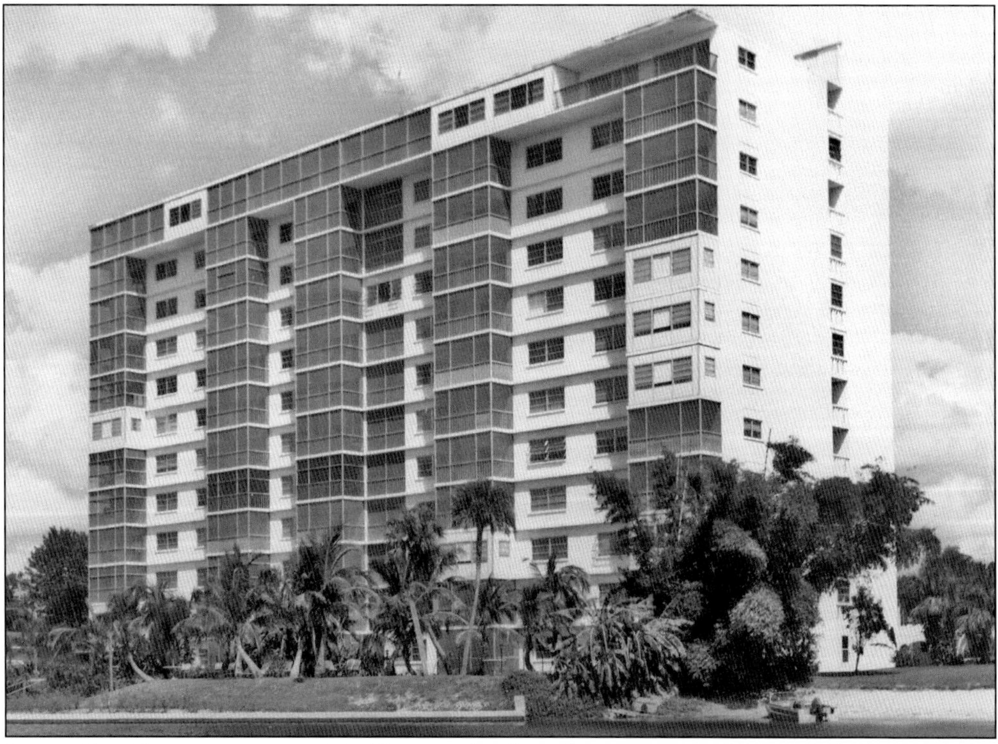

Inevitably, old gives way to new. The Fountainhead condominiums overlooking Lake Jackson were constructed in 1966 north of Edgewater Arms. A sign outside the new tower advertised "This is the Private World of Fountainhead: Condominium, Apartment, Residences . . . 2 bedroom, 1 1/2 bath—2 bedroom, 2 bath . . . Priced from $10,450. You can own your own for as little as 57¢ per day." (Courtesy Sebring Historical Society.)

Four

HOUSES OF WORSHIP

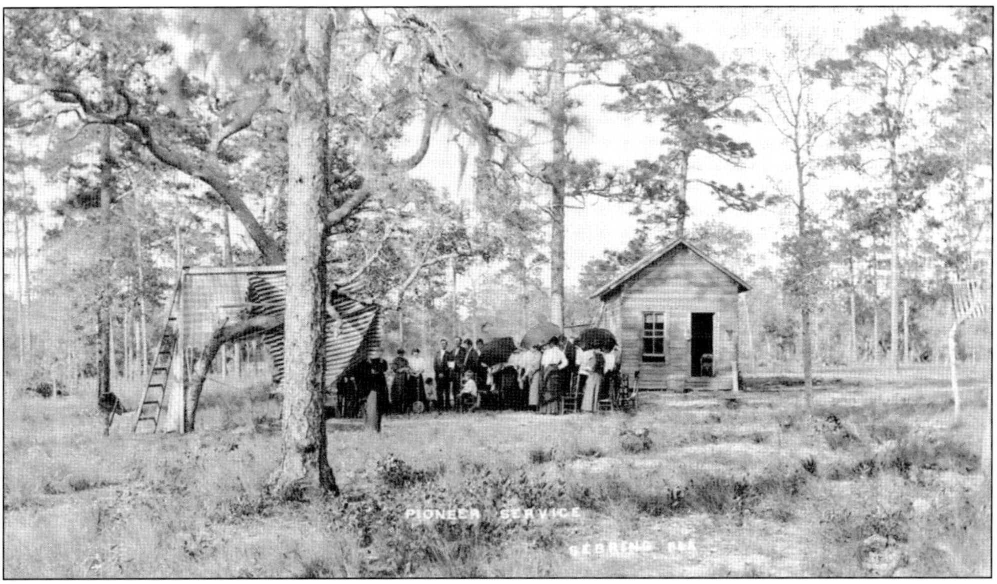

The "Church of the Trees" was the site of this religious service on January 28, 1912, held at the northern edge of the Circle. Records of the earliest services were preserved by retired Salvation Army officer John F. Newcomb. Both the local Methodist and Salvation Army congregations grew from these non-denominational outdoor services. George E. Sebring encouraged the establishment of local congregations and provided land for church sites. (Courtesy Sebring Historical Society.)

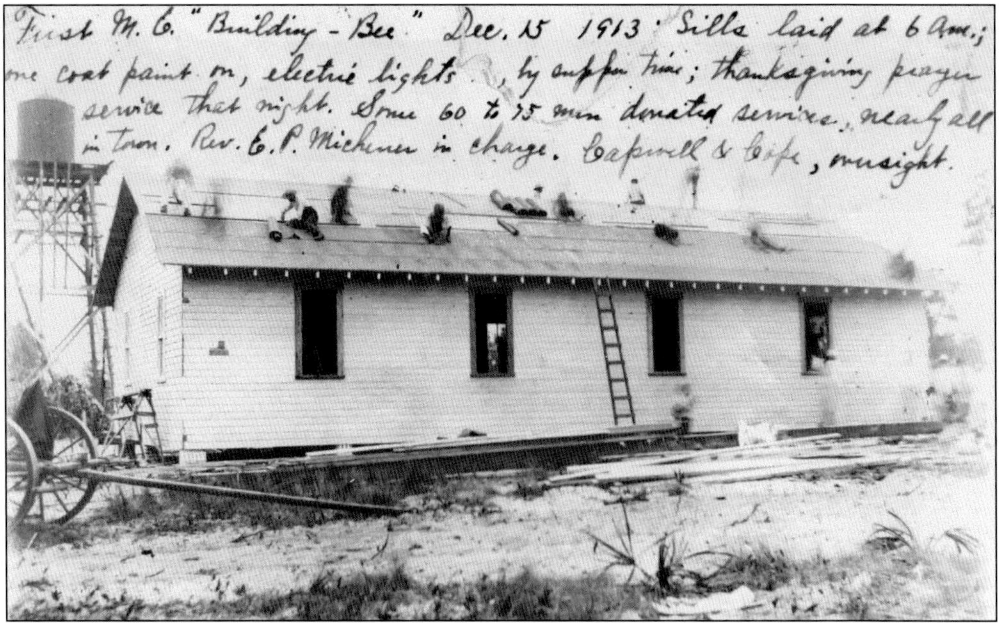

The First Methodist Church building was erected by 60 volunteers on December 15, 1913, at the corner of Pine Street and North Ridgewood Drive. Work commenced at 6:00 a.m., and by the end of the day, it had been painted, had electric lights, and was furnished, all in time for evening services. Rev. E. P. Michener was in charge, with oversight from Mr. Capwell and B. A. Cope. (Courtesy Sebring Historical Society.)

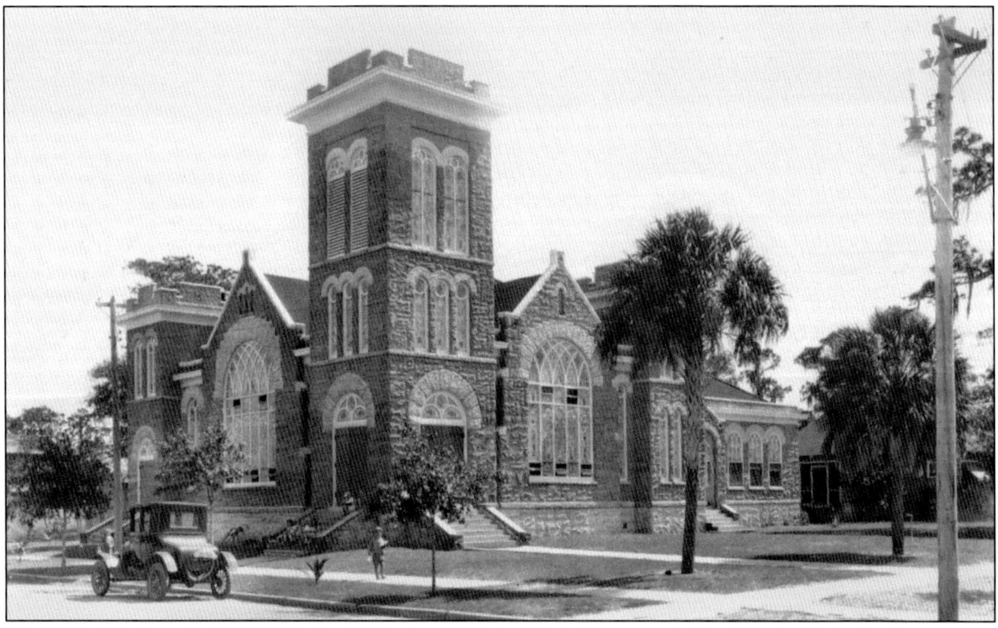

The *Sebring White Way* reported on June 2, 1916, on the construction of the second sanctuary for the First Methodist Church at the east corner of South Pine Street and East Center Avenue. The concrete, stone, and brick building, modeled after the First Methodist Church of Eustis, was forecast to cost approximately $20,000 and was to be built by Sebring residents. (Photograph by Woodward, courtesy Sebring Historical Society.)

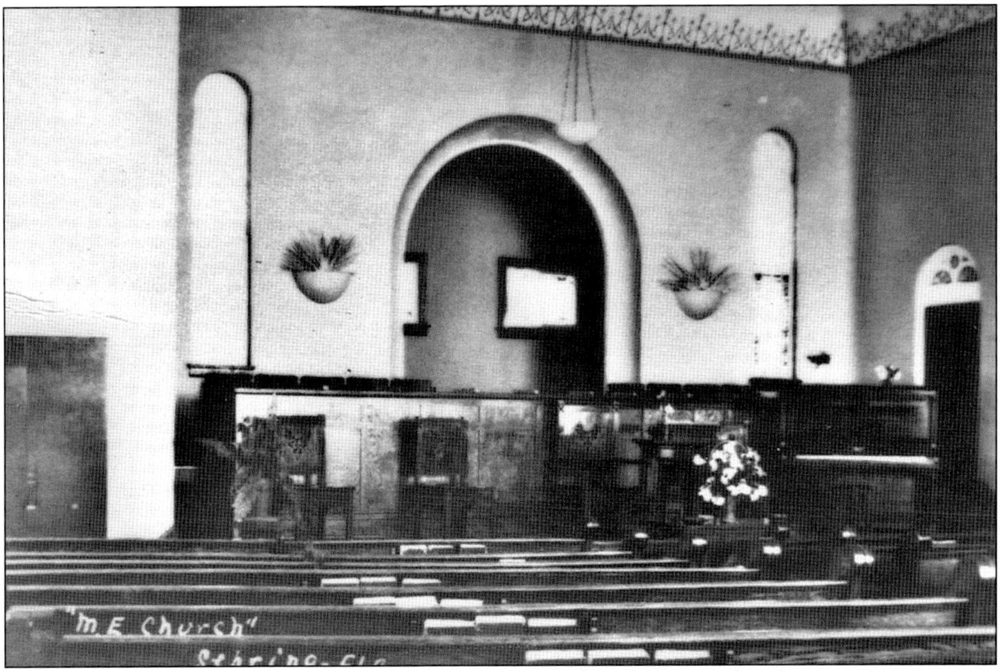

The interior of the 1916 First Methodist Church included native Florida pine decor, a pipe organ, carpet, decorative stained-glass windows, a heating system, lavatories, and other modern conveniences. The *Sebring White Way* reported that "money will not be spared to make the building a thing of beauty and a joy forever." A 1928 hurricane severely damaged the church, but the church building was successfully repaired. (Courtesy Sebring Historical Society.)

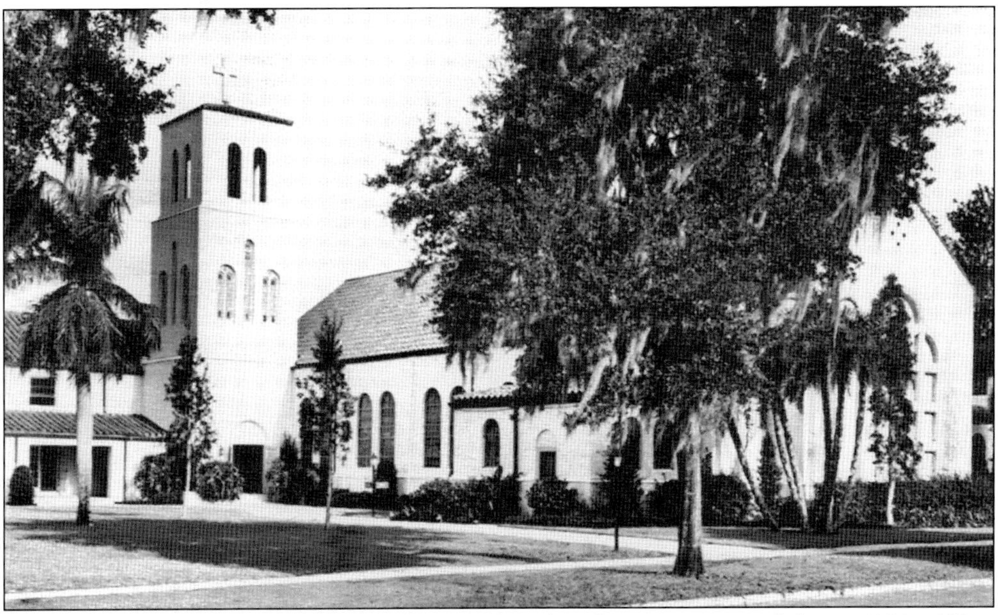

The third sanctuary of the First United Methodist Church was constructed during 1952–1953 at 126 South Pine Street during the pastorate of Dr. E. F. Carwithen and was opened on May 31, 1953. This photograph dates from about 1962. The families of many of the early congregants are represented in today's First United Methodist Church. (Courtesy Sebring Historical Society.)

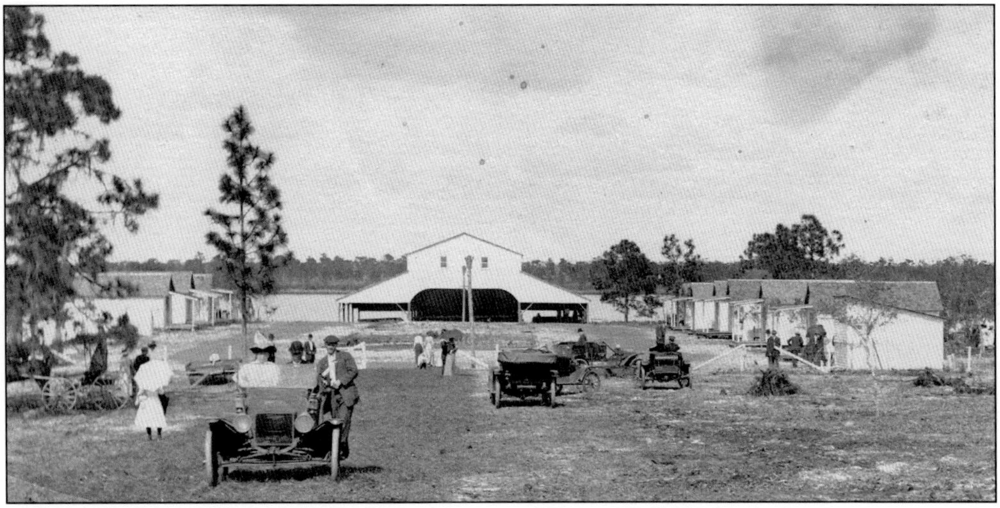

A 1912 Sebring Real Estate Company advertising brochure entitled "The Consummation of a Great Idea" promoted Salvation Point, "a large assembly grounds on the shore of one of the most beautiful lakes in this picturesque community . . . in the midst of fruit and flowers in the land of perpetual June." The grounds included cottages and an open-air pavilion on the southwest shore of Dinner Lake. (Courtesy Sebring Historical Society.)

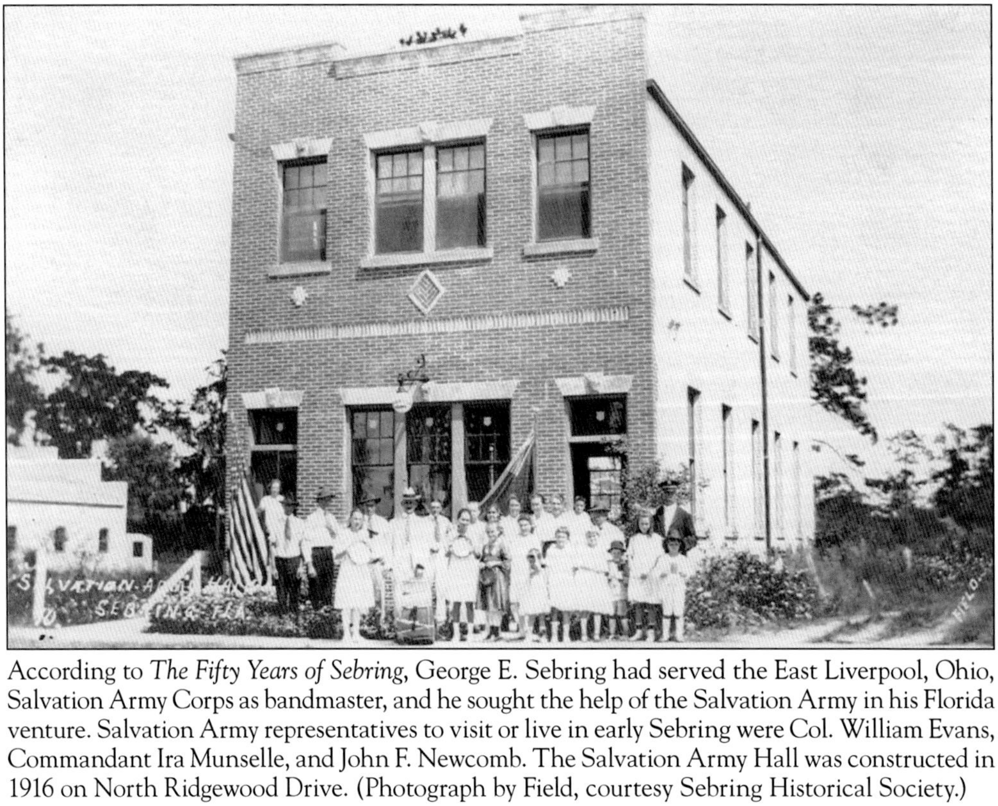

According to *The Fifty Years of Sebring*, George E. Sebring had served the East Liverpool, Ohio, Salvation Army Corps as bandmaster, and he sought the help of the Salvation Army in his Florida venture. Salvation Army representatives to visit or live in early Sebring were Col. William Evans, Commandant Ira Munselle, and John F. Newcomb. The Salvation Army Hall was constructed in 1916 on North Ridgewood Drive. (Photograph by Field, courtesy Sebring Historical Society.)

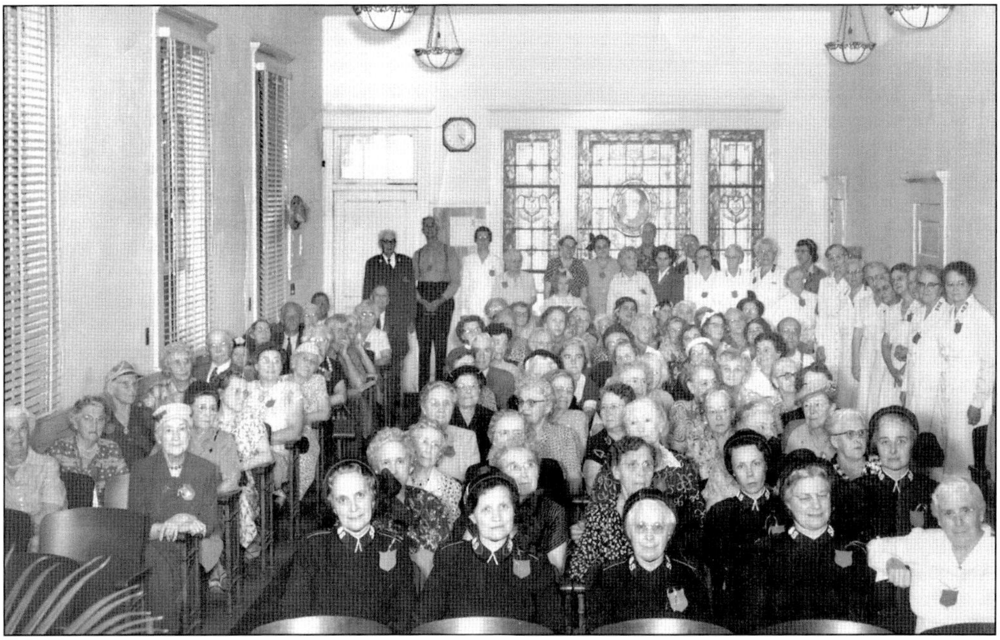

Among attendees at an early 1950s Salvation Army Home League annual meeting were Carrie Weigle, Mrs. Ray Gearing, Mrs. Clifford, Mrs. Young, Mrs. Gordon MacGilvary, Col. Elizabeth Anderson, Cecile Bair, Mrs. McAdams, Alice Dunn, Mrs. O. D. Garrett, Ruth Wolfe, Mildred Talmash, Maj. Pearl Tanner, Mrs. Sowers William, Susie Munselle, Martha Kimmell, Gertrude Vanderville, and Mr. and Mrs. Herbert K. Anderson. (Courtesy Sebring Historical Society.)

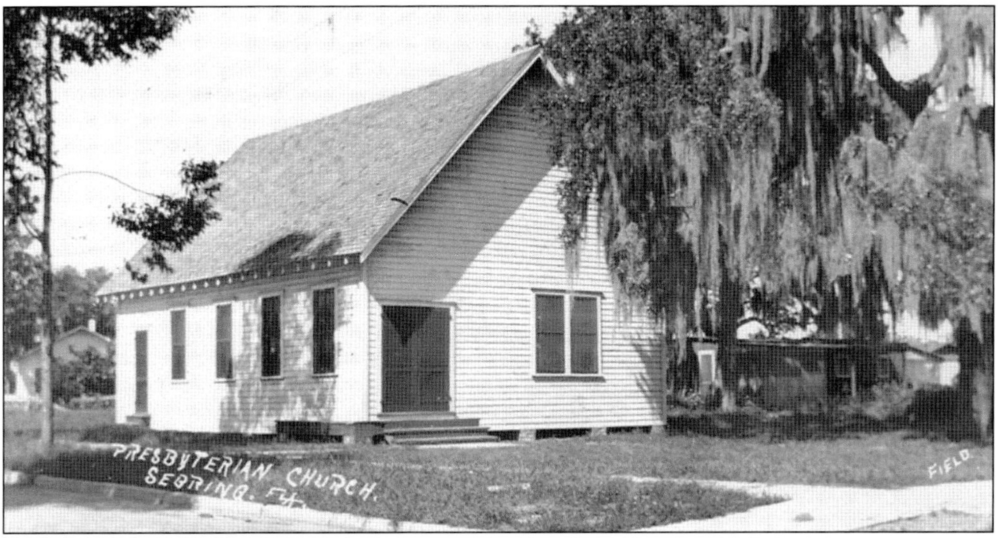

The First Presbyterian Church was organized on May 3, 1914, and met in this frame structure on North Pine Street. This photograph dates from the early 1920s when the congregation experienced sustained growth. Howard Crawford, in *The Seventy-Five Years of Sebring*, recounts that ushers borrowed chairs from neighbors to accommodate the large crowds, returning the chairs during the last hymn so that congregants could exit. (Photograph by Field, courtesy Sebring Historical Society.)

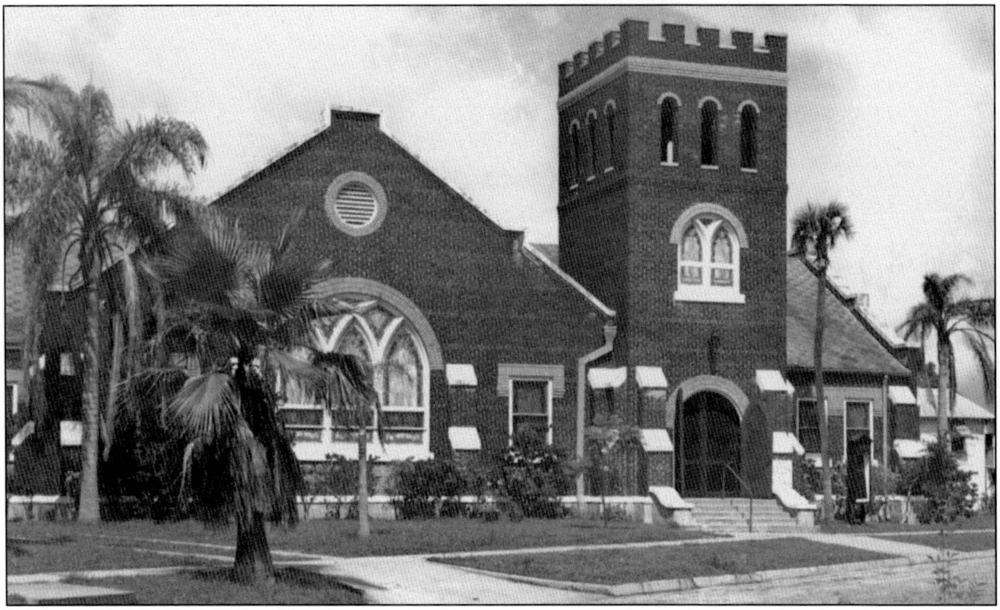

The cornerstone for the present-day First Presbyterian Church building was placed on November 13, 1925, with representatives of local denominations participating in the dedication ceremony. Constructed at the corner of Poinsettia Avenue and South Pine Street, First Presbyterian meets in one of Sebring's oldest sanctuaries in continuous use. An educational building was constructed in 1954. (Courtesy Sebring Historical Society.)

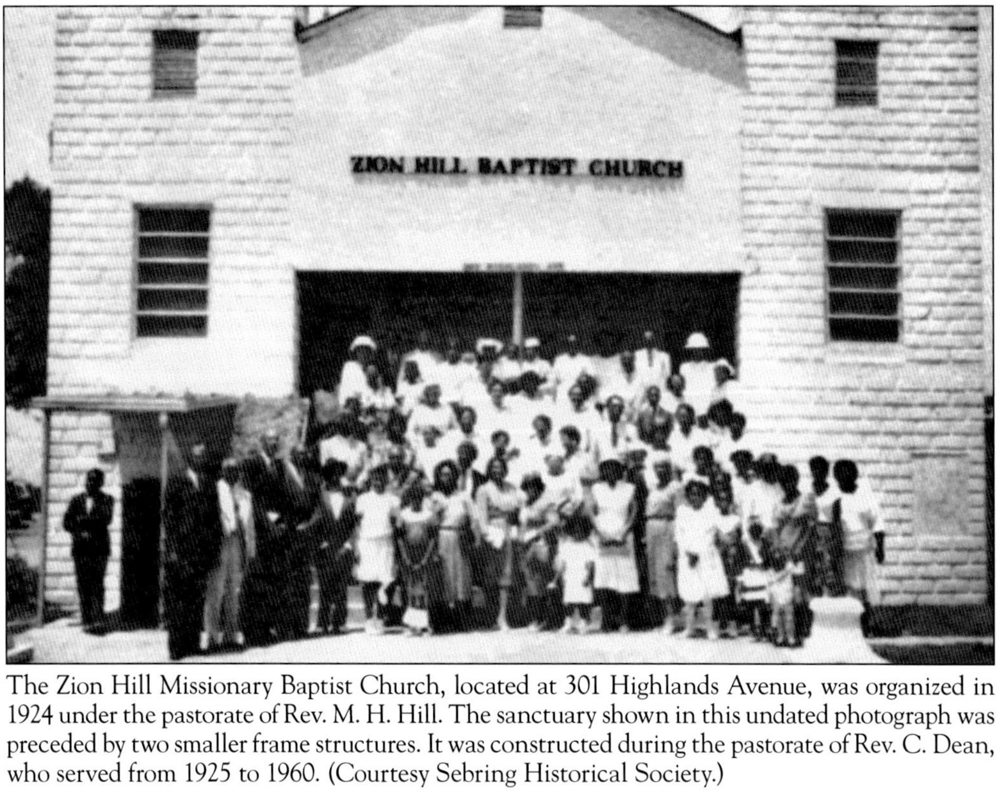

The Zion Hill Missionary Baptist Church, located at 301 Highlands Avenue, was organized in 1924 under the pastorate of Rev. M. H. Hill. The sanctuary shown in this undated photograph was preceded by two smaller frame structures. It was constructed during the pastorate of Rev. C. Dean, who served from 1925 to 1960. (Courtesy Sebring Historical Society.)

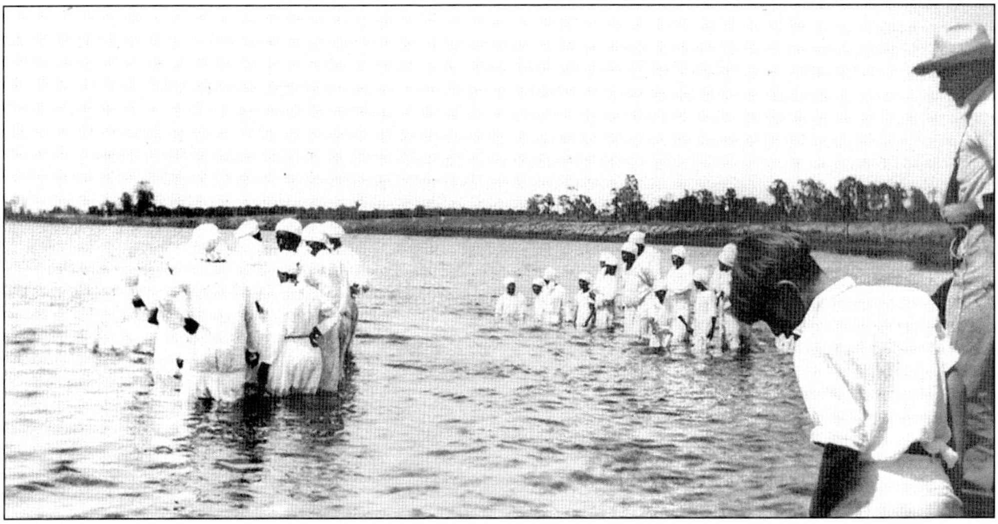

This photograph shows baptisms in Dinner Lake in the 1930s. Sebring's original First Baptist Church, which became First Calvary Baptist Church and subsequently First Missionary Baptist Church on Lemon Avenue, was organized in October 1913. For a time, their services were held in the sanctuary of the Greater Mount Zion A.M.E. Church, which was organized in 1915. By 2007, there were over 60 houses of worship in Sebring and the environs. (Courtesy Sebring Historical Society.)

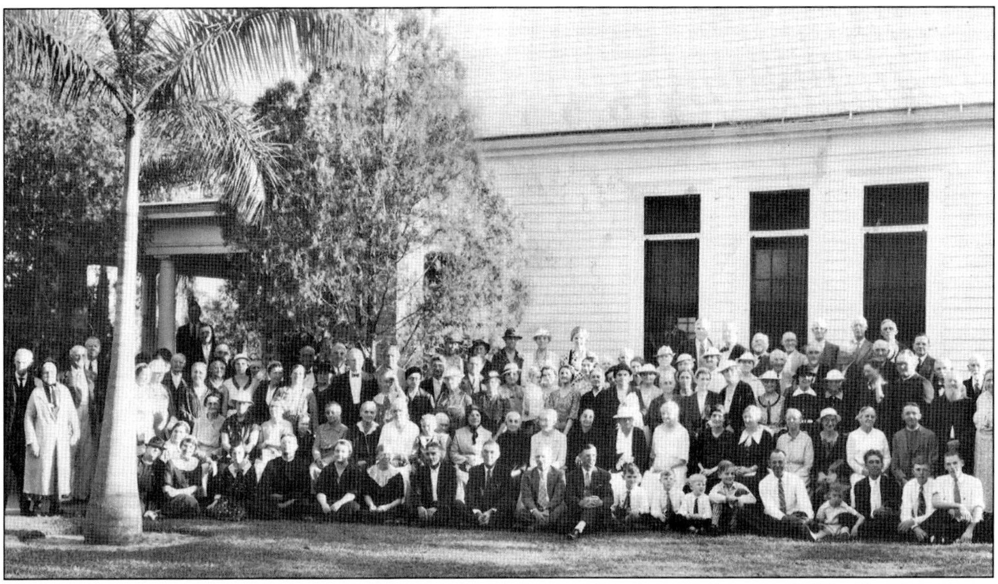

The Church of the Brethren was organized in 1916 under the guidance of Elder J. H. Moore, who wrote enthusiastically about the young community. When more Brethren arrived, George E. Sebring donated a parcel on Poinsettia Avenue for a bungalow-style sanctuary constructed by B. A. Cope. This *c.* 1933 photograph shows the second church after the congregation relocated in 1920 to the corner of Oak Avenue and South Pine Street. (Courtesy Sebring Historical Society.)

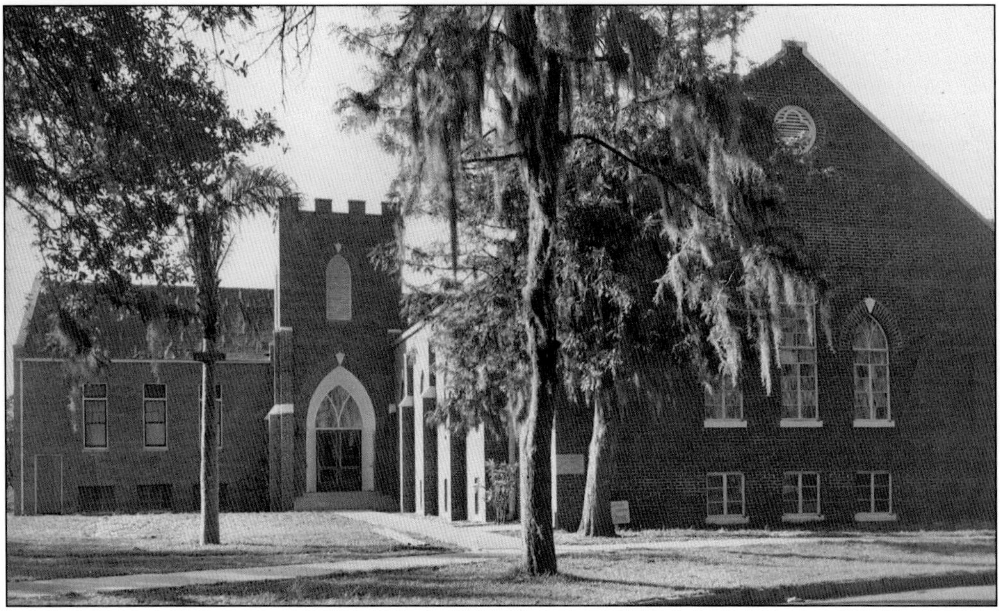

The Church of the Brethren Aid Society was established with Mrs. Moore as the first president in 1916, and the Sunday school first met in January 1917. After the church moved in 1920, a new sanctuary was constructed (now Garst Chapel), along with kindergarten and classroom buildings to accommodate church programs and ladies' sewing and quilting. The present sanctuary was constructed in 1950 and subsequently remodeled. (Courtesy Sebring Historical Society.)

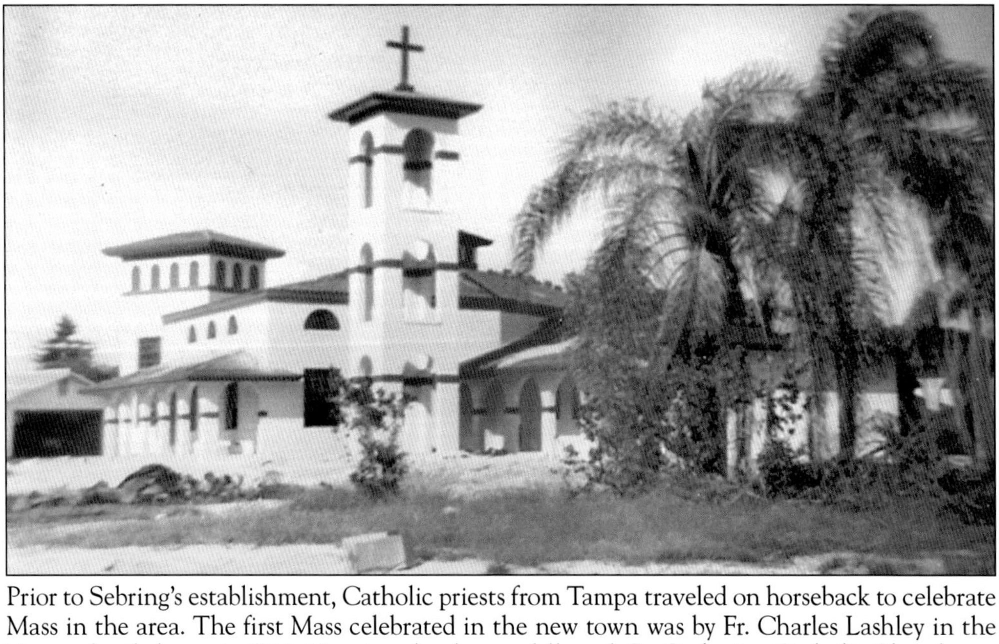

Prior to Sebring's establishment, Catholic priests from Tampa traveled on horseback to celebrate Mass in the area. The first Mass celebrated in the new town was by Fr. Charles Lashley in the Varena family home in 1918; Mass in other homes followed. St. Catherine Catholic Church was constructed in 1924 and was named for St. Catherine of Siena. This image depicts the current church building nearing completion in 1978. (Courtesy Sebring Historical Society.)

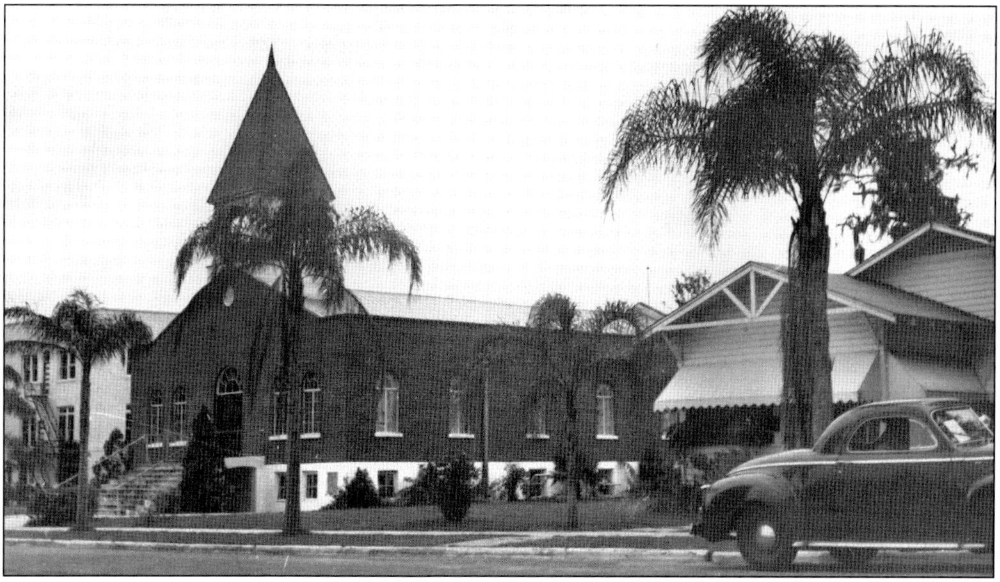

This 1935 brick building on Lemon Avenue near Pine Street was the second home of the First Baptist Church established in 1922; the second local congregation to bear that name. The church met first in the Tuscawilla Park pavilion, and in 1923 moved to a white frame sanctuary. From 35 to 40 servicemen attended Sunday services at First Baptist Church during World War II. (Courtesy Sebring Historical Society.)

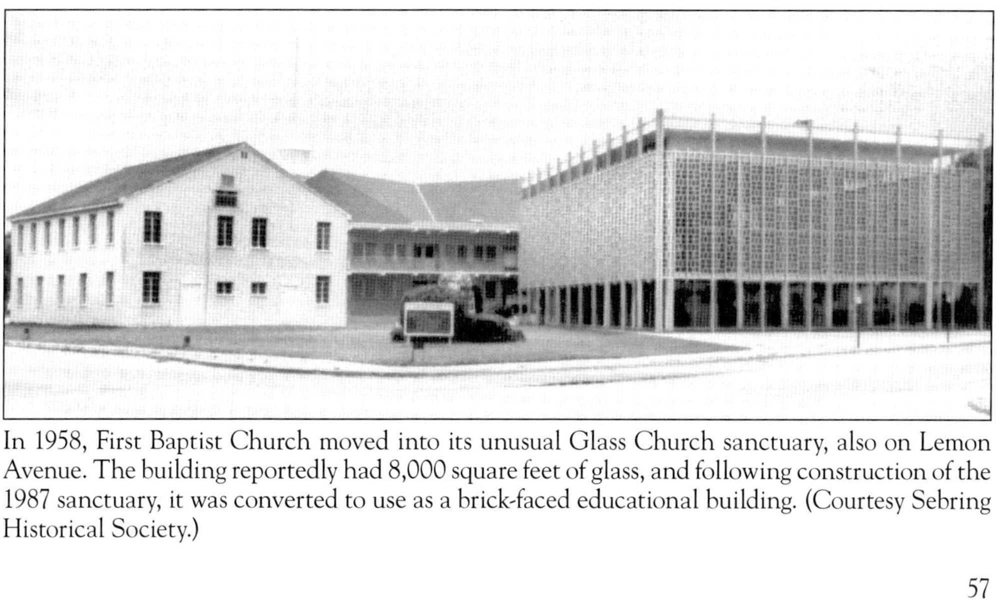

In 1958, First Baptist Church moved into its unusual Glass Church sanctuary, also on Lemon Avenue. The building reportedly had 8,000 square feet of glass, and following construction of the 1987 sanctuary, it was converted to use as a brick-faced educational building. (Courtesy Sebring Historical Society.)

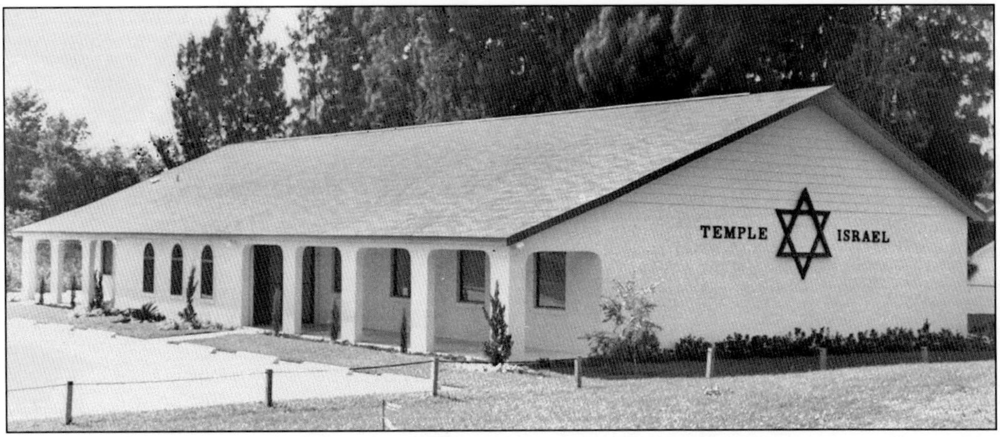

The Temple Beth Israel synagogue was built on Orange Street at Fernleaf Avenue in about 1927 on land donated by George E. Sebring. The temple was razed in the 1950s, and many of the members attended Temple Emanuel in Lakeland. The local temple was reorganized in the 1960s, Rabbi Morton M. Applebaum arrived in 1979, and the present-day Temple Israel, shown here, was dedicated in 1986. (Courtesy Sebring Historical Society.)

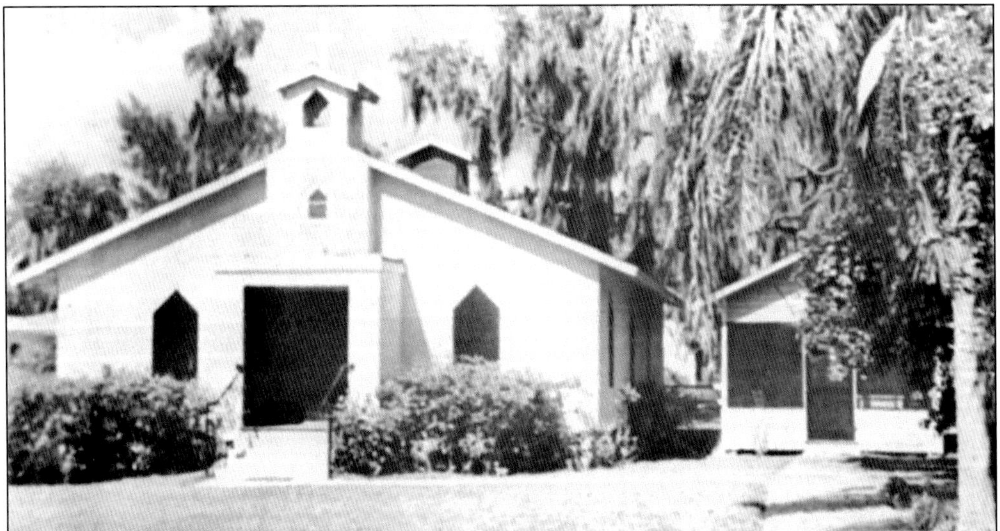

St. Agnes Episcopal Church was first known as the Mission Church of the Good Shephard when it was organized in the mid-1920s. Fr. John M. Luke was the vicar in 1929 when the congregation moved to a renovated house on Hickory Street, and the church was renamed St. Agnes Mission. Hilan Rogers served as clerk and treasurer from 1928 to 1958. (Courtesy Sebring Historical Society.)

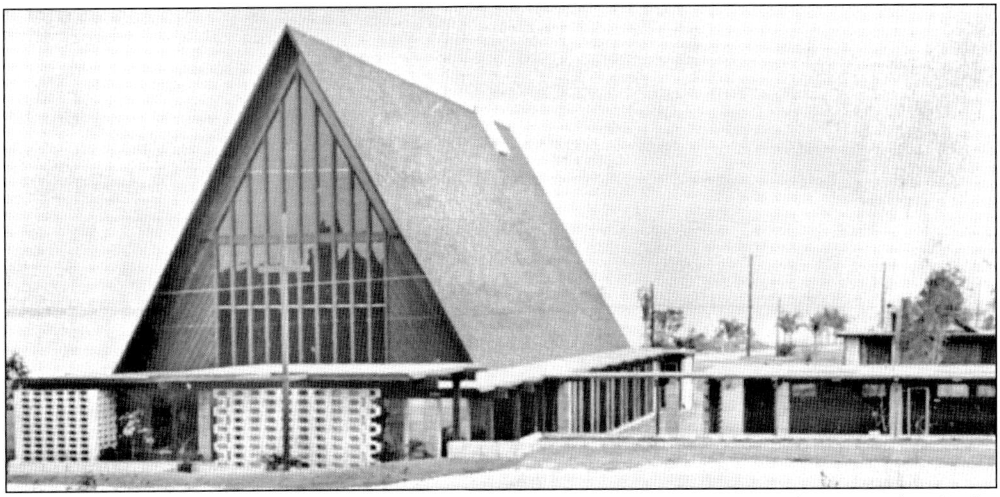

The present home of St. Agnes Episcopal Church is on Lakeview Drive on the west side of Lake Jackson. The church complex was dedicated on January 24, 1960, under the direction of Fr. Stuart M. Stewart, and the former property was sold to St. Catherine Catholic Church. (Courtesy Sebring Historical Society.)

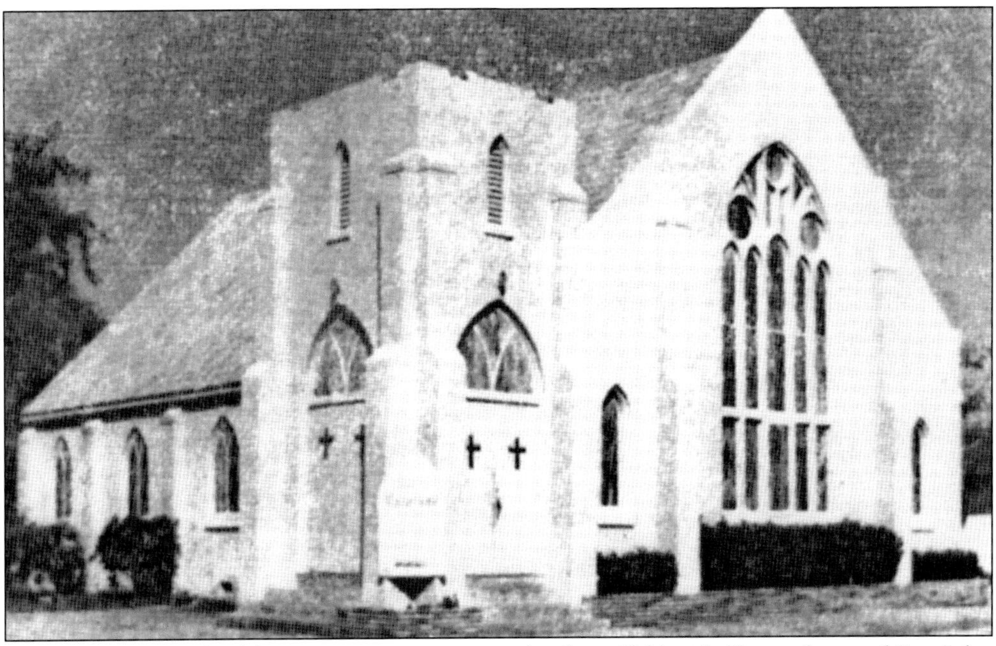

The Sebring Church of the Nazarene was organized in June 1944 with 13 members and Rev. John D. Rhame as the first pastor. The first church, shown here, was constructed as funds allowed at the corner of South Commerce Avenue and South Pine Street on land previously occupied by Joe Stiles's Standard Oil station. When completed in 1945, the building was debt free. The current church was dedicated in 1972. (Courtesy Sebring Historical Society.)

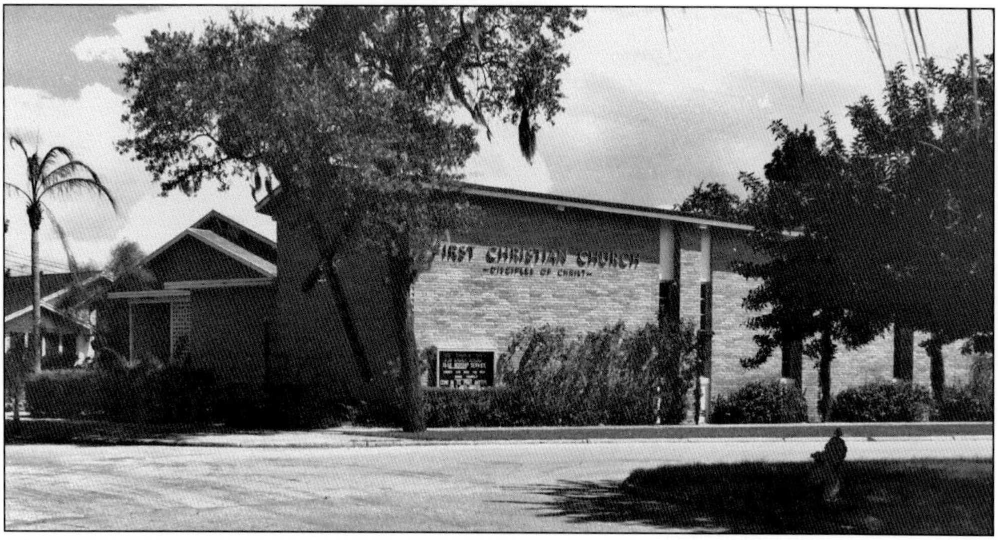

The First Christian Church (Disciples of Christ) was organized in the spring of 1926. The congregation held services at Tuscawilla Park and began construction of the church using wood first utilized as scaffolding for the new Highlands County Courthouse. This sanctuary was followed by a 1965 structure at Poinsettia Avenue and South Eucalyptus Street that is still in use. (Photograph by C. W. Burn, courtesy Sebring Historical Society.)

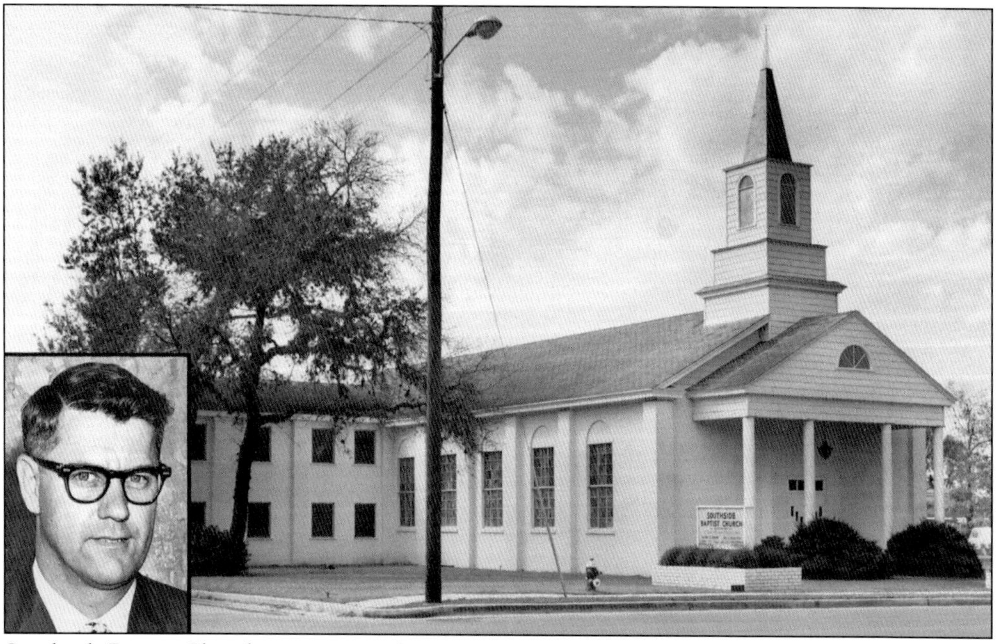

Southside Baptist Church was organized in 1947, and the first service in the new sanctuary at South Commerce and Orange Avenues was on Easter Sunday 1948. The inset on this *c.* 1960 photograph shows Rev. Leland E. Brooker, who served as pastor from 1954 until 1983. The church experienced marked growth and service during his tenure. (Courtesy Sebring Historical Society.)

Five

Schools and Government

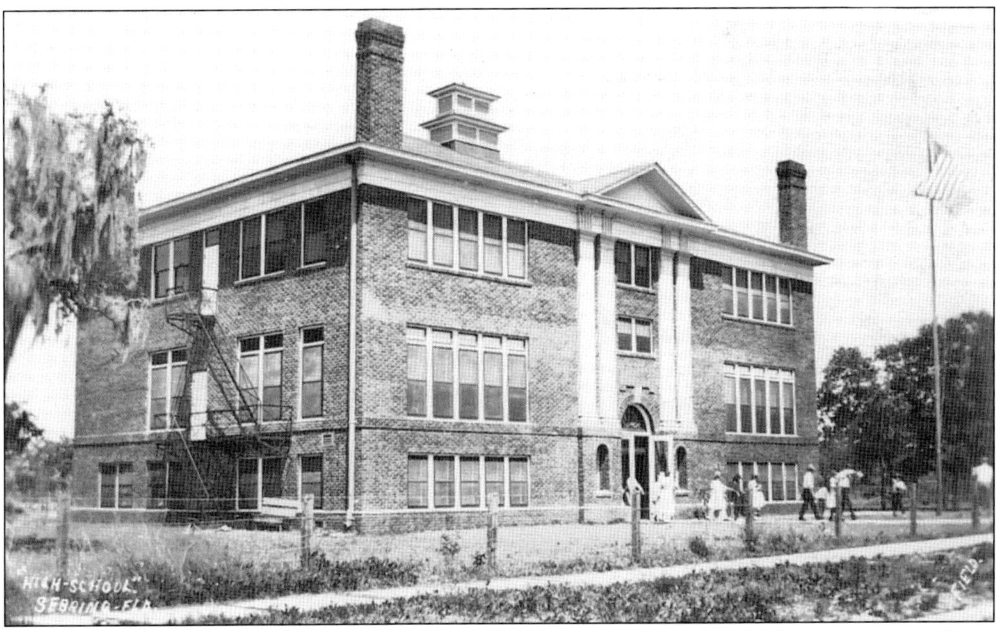

The Sebring School was a three-story, red brick building constructed in 1916 at the corner of Pine Street and Lemon Avenue for students in 1st through 12th grades. The school contained eight recitation rooms on the first and second floors, an auditorium, and four basement rooms used for domestic science, manual training, and science laboratory classes. The first class graduated in 1919. (Courtesy Sebring Historical Society.)

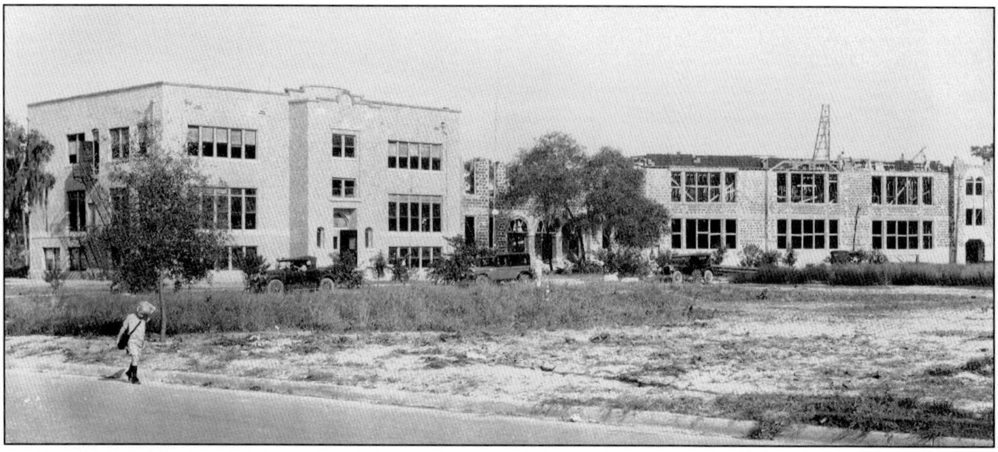

As the local school-age population grew, the need for a larger facility became evident, and the Sebring School was significantly expanded in 1925. The remodeled school became part of a superior Mediterranean and Mission-style structure, which included a large community auditorium. The portion of the school closest in this view is the 1916 building. (Photograph by Woodward, courtesy Sebring Historical Society.)

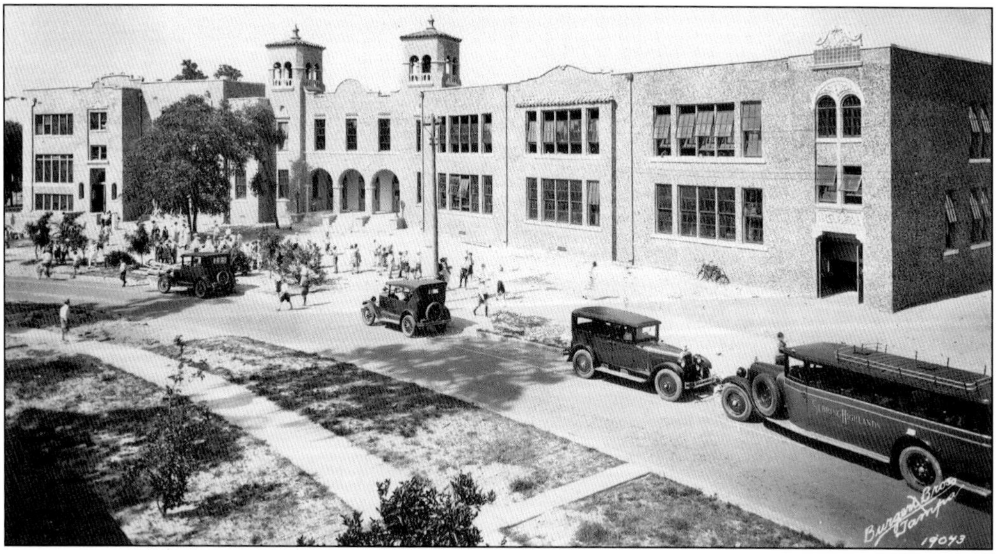

A band room was added to the school in 1940 to support the celebrated music program, and a gymnasium with a basement cafeteria was constructed in 1948. In 1955, the elementary grades moved to Woodlawn Elementary School. When the new Sebring High School was occupied in 1971, this building became Sebring Middle. Sadly, the building was razed in 1979. (Photograph by Burgert Brothers Tampa, courtesy Sebring Historical Society.)

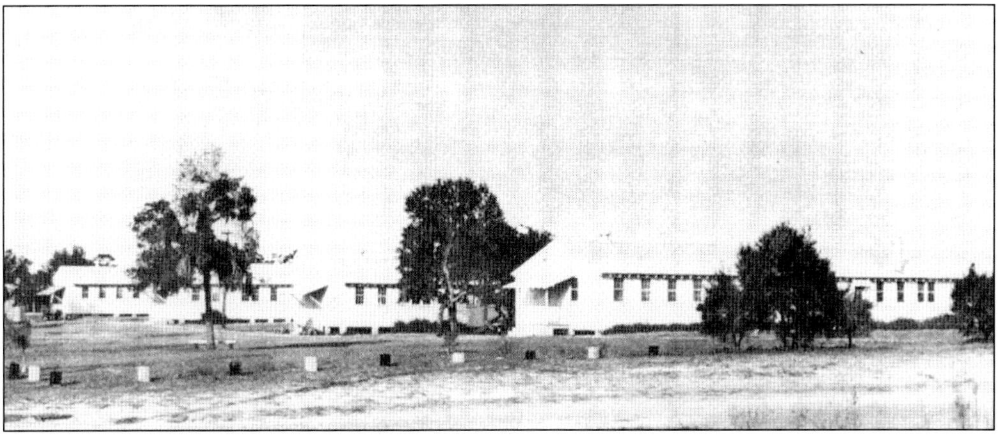

African American students attended school in Avon Park beginning in 1919, before a Sebring school was founded in 1922 on Lemon Avenue with teacher D. S. McNeil. Later moved to Zion Hill Baptist Church, Maxwell Saxon and C. C. Marion were principals in the 1930s. The E. O. Douglas High School, shown here, opened in 1941, and the first graduates in 1943 were Ralph Coleman, Robert Reed, Elnora Smith, and Jo Anna Watson. (Courtesy Sebring Historical Society.)

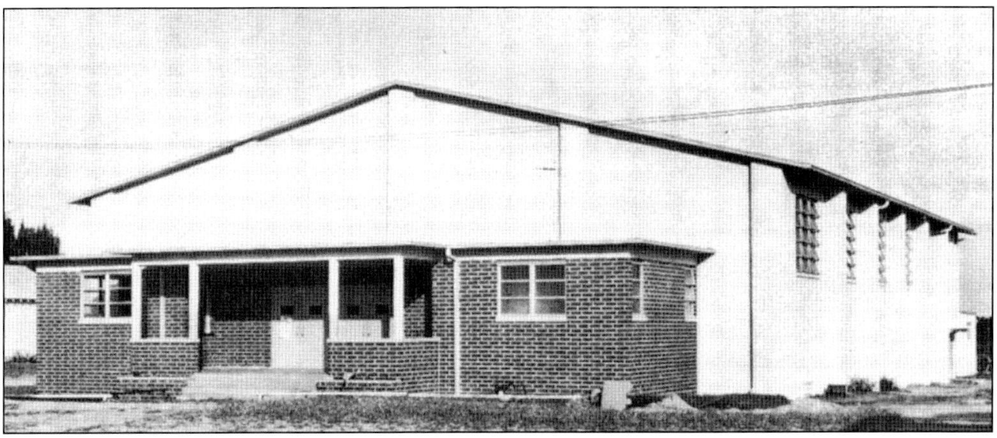

A library, science, and agriculture buildings, a multipurpose "gymnatorium," and two classroom buildings were constructed at E. O. Douglas High School in the 1950s. In 2002, Rev. Robert J. Walker recounted how the school band first marched in the Sebring Christmas Parade in 1952, playing "The Washington Post" march—a signal event in Sebring's history and in the lives of the 40 band members and their families. (Courtesy Sebring Historical Society.)

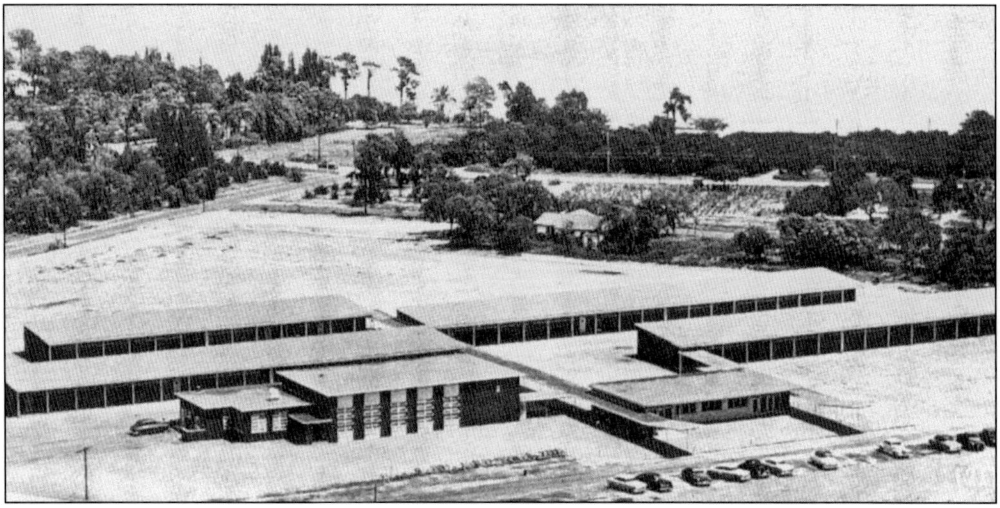

Woodlawn Elementary School was constructed north of downtown on Fielder Boulevard between Lake Jackson and Dinner Lake during 1954 and 1955, and welcomed its first students in grades one through six during the fall of 1955. The school contained 18 classrooms, an administrative building, a multi-purpose "cafetorium," a library, and facilities for speech correction and exceptional children. Additions were made in 1985 and 2001. (Courtesy Sebring Historical Society.)

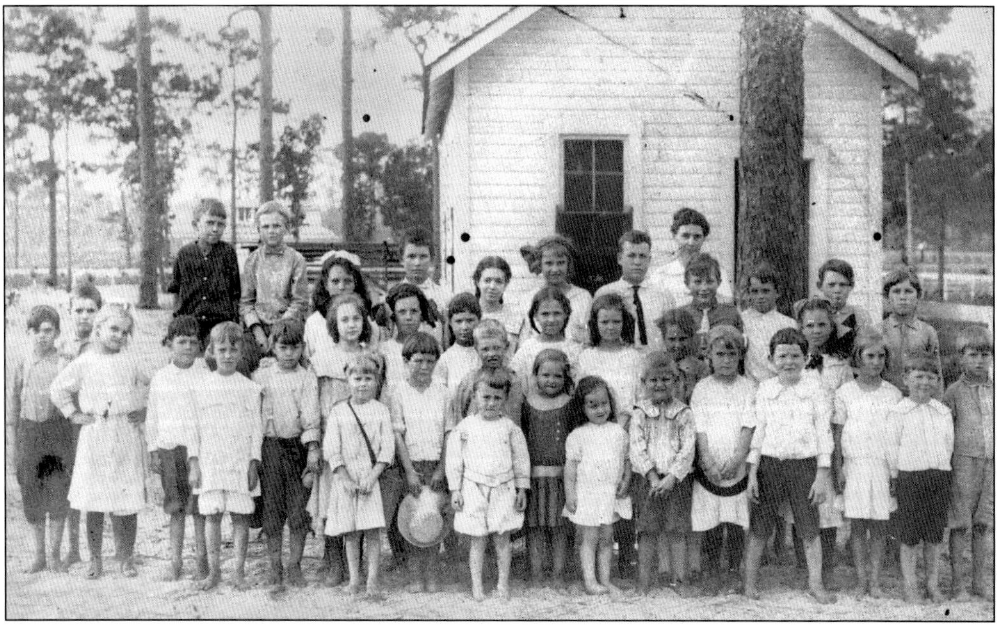

A group of 53 students attended the first small, wood-frame school in August 1912. The students were of all ages and were under the direction of teacher Sally Chapman, who received a salary of $65 per month. She was joined by Miss Michner in 1914 and a third teacher in 1915. The school had other transitory locations before the 1916 brick school was constructed. (Courtesy Sebring Historical Society.)

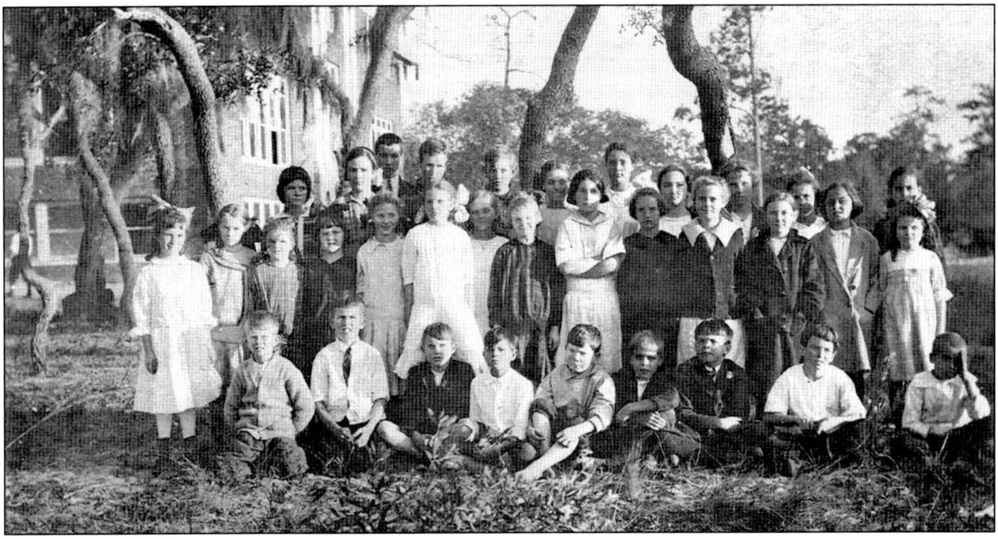

This *c.* 1916 school group poses near the new school. Pictured from left to right are (first row) Reuben North, Fred Newcomb, James Whidden, Glenn Pollared, Charles Hiers, Frank Warren, Herman Hansen, Harold Newcomb, and unidentified; (second row) Leila Sebring, two unidentified, Dorothy Singletary, unidentified, Geralda Whitehouse, Ruth Amy, four unidentified, Edna Capwell, unidentified, and Emma Whitehouse; (third row) four unidentified, Reid Bellew, two unidentified, Mildred Capwell, unidentified, Dorothy Sebring, and Dorothy Taylor. (Courtesy Sebring Historical Society.)

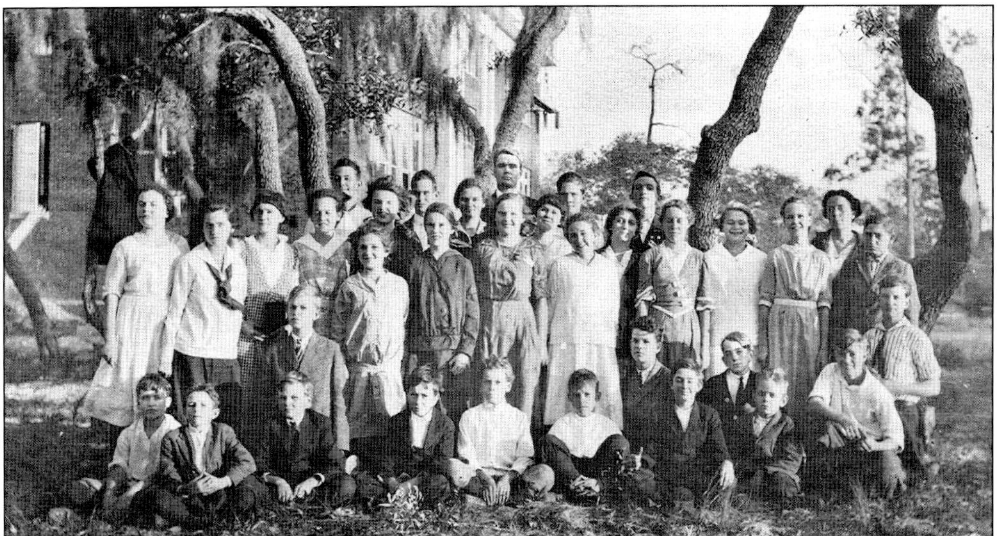

Another *c.* 1916 group of students poses in the same location. Pictured from left to right are (first row) Gerald Bee, Maurice Wright, Payne Sebring, Vernon LaFaile, John Warren, Perry Marsh, Paul Pollard, Eugene Sebring, Willie Palow, Percy Gearing, Richard Callahan, Orin Fuller, and Gerry Whitehouse; (second row) Naomi Warren, Olga Hanseri, Regina Marsh, Annie Mae Bellew, Leah Wright, ? Whidden, Leona Whitehouse, Anna Jones, Ethel Singletary, ? Callahan, Lulua Whitehouse, Maude Newcomb, Corinne Whidden, Annie Laurie Etheredge, and Mable Crump; (third row) unidentified, Lester Jennings, Mr. Putnam, and three unidentified. (Courtesy Sebring Historical Society.)

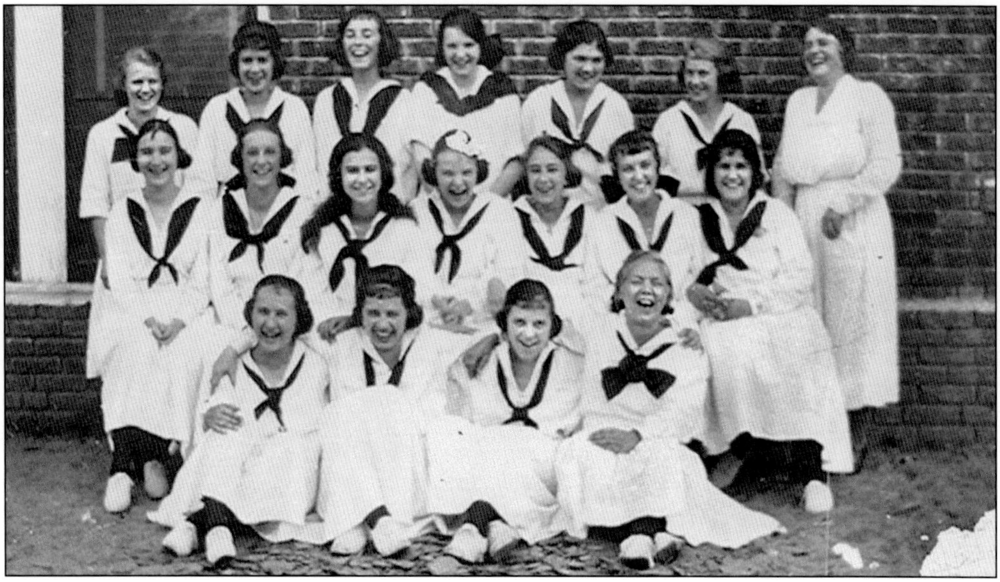

The Sebring Girls Glee Club was organized by high school music teacher Miss Drought. Seen here in March 1921, the voice culture club met on Monday evenings and performed during school play intermissions. The highlight of the season was their performance of the operetta "The Japanese Girl" to the musical accompaniment of Elizabeth C. Wright. The club also performed at Tuscawilla Park during 1921 Fourth of July festivities. (Courtesy Sebring Historical Society.)

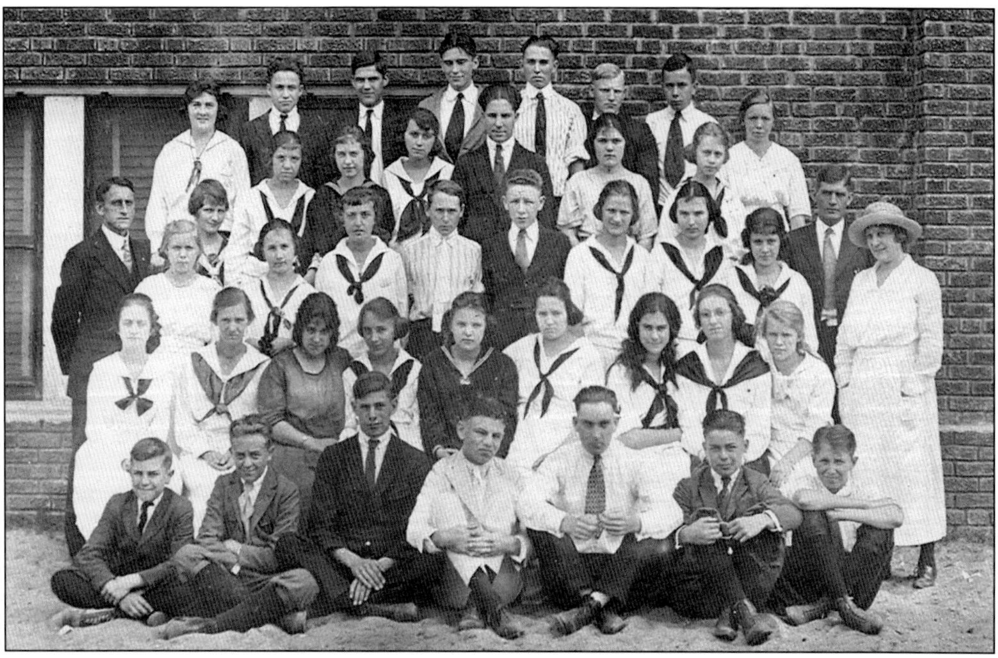

Members of the Glee Club are joined in this March 1921 photograph by their classmates. The only student identified is Allie Mae, the last girl on the right in the third row. This was an exciting time to be in Sebring, which would soon be in the midst of a spirited competition to be named the seat of newly formed Highlands County. (Courtesy Sebring Historical Society.)

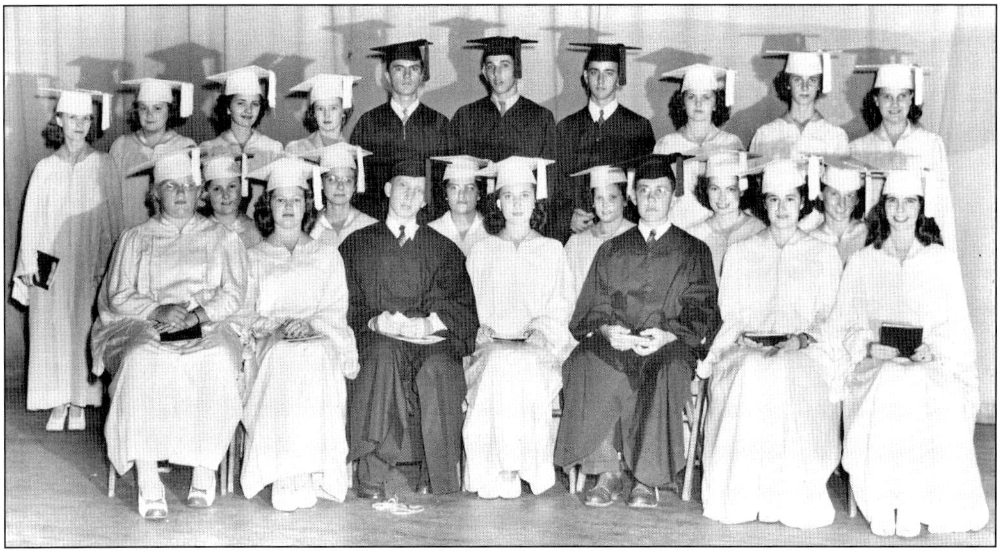

The Sebring High School class of 1944 included, from left to right, (first row) Verdelle Sebring, Wilma Butler, Jim McRae, Iris June Hart, Kenneth Johnson, Jamie Lee Whitaker, Geraldine Burton, Elizabeth Martin, Harold Long Jr., Erma Jean Hayes, Marilyn Stauffer, Faye Freeland, and Juanita Haskins; (second row) Dorothy Johnson, Ruth Foster, Shirley Sue Spooner, Dorothy Jean Mock, Billy Hunter, William Z. Carson, Edward Hollenberg, Louise Picket, Mary Leta Albritten, and Ruth Davis. (Courtesy Sebring Historical Society.)

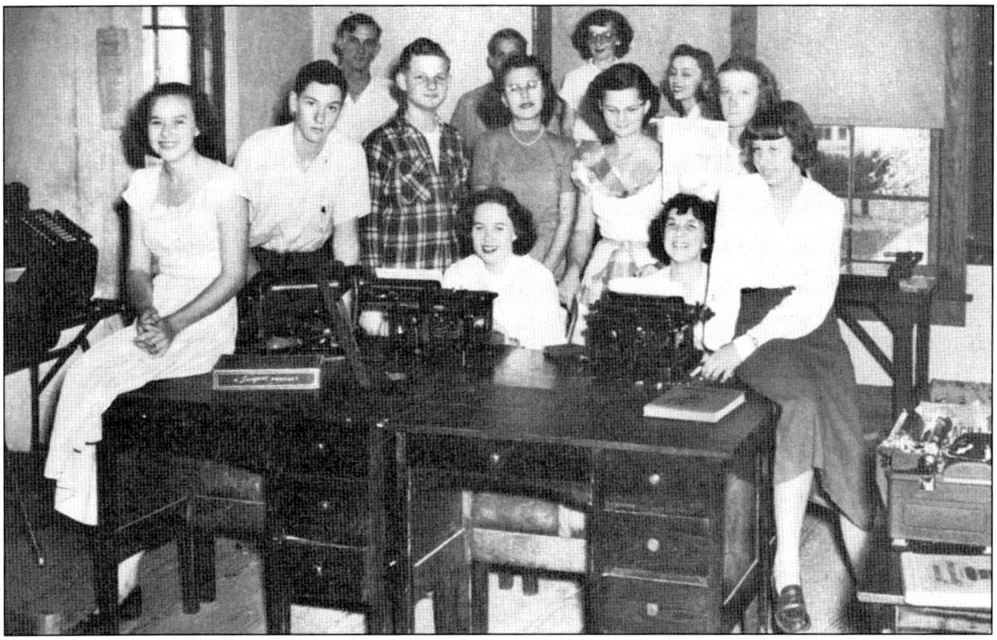

The 1949–1950 Sebring High School Journalism Club, pictured in the 1950 *Nan-Ces-O-Wee* yearbook, included Editor Jimmy Stevenson and Assistant Editor Shirley King, and members Jim Armistead, Edna Brown, Edward Carwithen, Sally Dalrymple, Zaida Davis, Allen Entz, Larry Hill, Peggy Howerton, Lynn Kelly, Donald McDonald, Guy McPherson, Sylvia Poer, Helen Stokes, Claggett Taylor, Deloris Taylor, Beverly Woodburn, and Delores Woodburn. The club sponsor was Mrs. Ingle. (Courtesy Sebring Historical Society.)

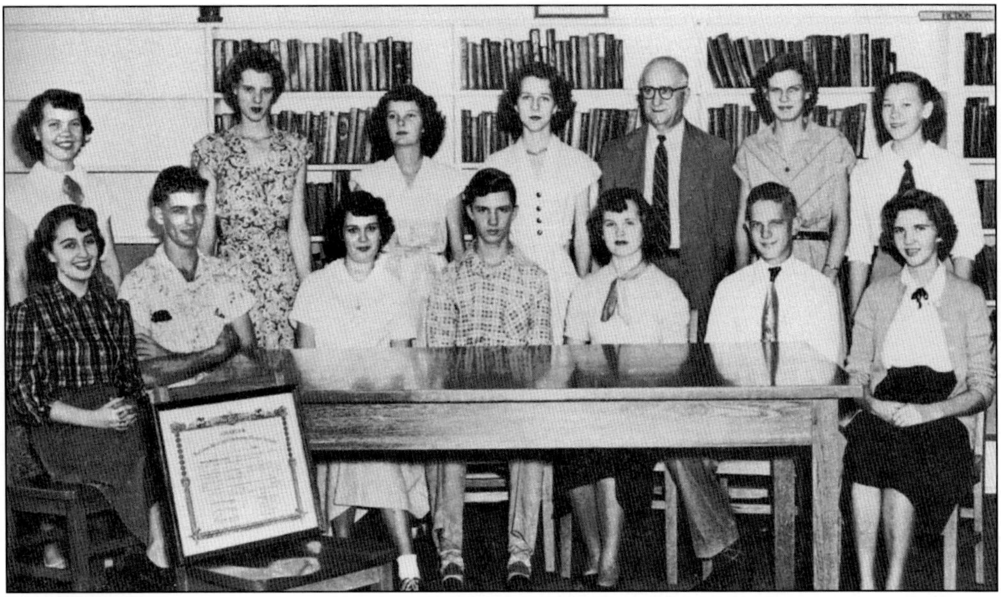

The 1950 *Nan-Ces-O-Wee* yearbook also depicted the Band Honor Society. Officers included Pres. Ramona Stauffer, Vice Pres. Billy Higgins, and Secretary/treasurer Margie Alsmeyer. Those pictured from left to right are (seated) Nancy Williams, Charles Rogers, Barbara Schumacher, Billy Higgins, Mary Belle Twitty, Bill Alsmeyer, and Mary Graham; (standing) Peggy McGee, Cheri Lynch, Velma Kendrick, Ramona Stauffer, Prof. Peter J. Gustat, Margie Alsmeyer, and Miriam Waters. (Courtesy Sebring Historical Society.)

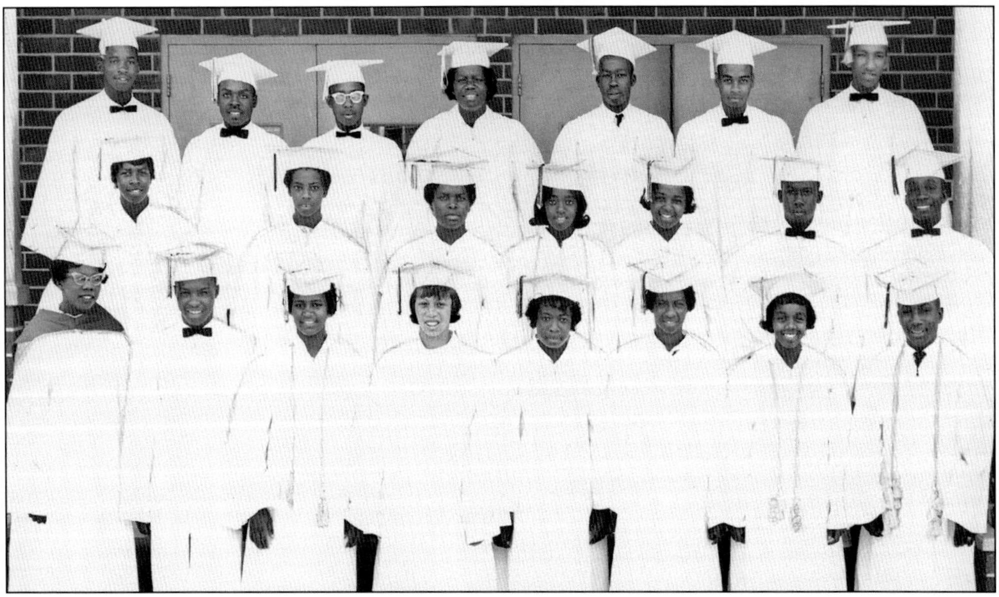

Among this 1960s E. O. Douglas High School graduating class were, from left to right, (first row) Ora Lee Hill, Willie Dan Flowers, Carol Annette Gainey, Mary Berry, Lorelee Kinsey, Catherine Brown, Patricia B. Lyons, and Moses Aaron; (second row) Myra Lee Holdman, Judith E. Welch, Ethel Mae Hall, Linda Lee Corey, Josephine Hall, and Richard Caldwell; (third row) Cleveland Williams Jr., David A. Washington, Walter Longstreet, Ethel E. Kerney, David E. Tate, Johnnie L. Singer, and Samuel L. Lawson. (Courtesy Sebring Historical Society.)

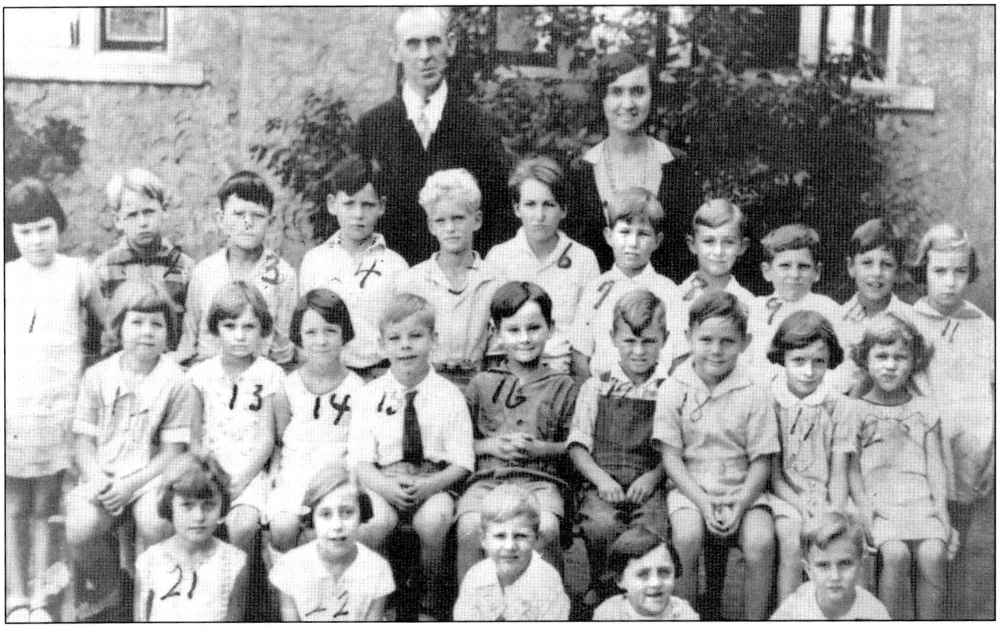

This 1929 photograph shows members of the class of 1940. Standing are Principal Samuel Long and teacher Esther Ridder. The students are numbered: (1) Venia Jean Campbell, (2) Paul Foster, (3) Frederick Pollard, (4) Jimmie Maxcy, (5) Jack Adams, (6) Ishmael Brown, (7) Earl Williams, (8) Weldon Emmett, (9) Howard Weems, (10) Clyde Collins, (11) Martha Durance, (12) Myrl Nell Ryall, (13) Thelma Varnadore, (14) Thelma Crews, (15) Gene Sebring, (16) Jake Butler, (17) Robert Ingle, (18) Billie Barker, (19) Virginia Updike, (20) unidentified, (21) Ruth ?, (22) unidentified, (23) David ?, (24) Marjorie Arkell, and (25) Patricia Kansinger. (Courtesy Sebring Historical Society.)

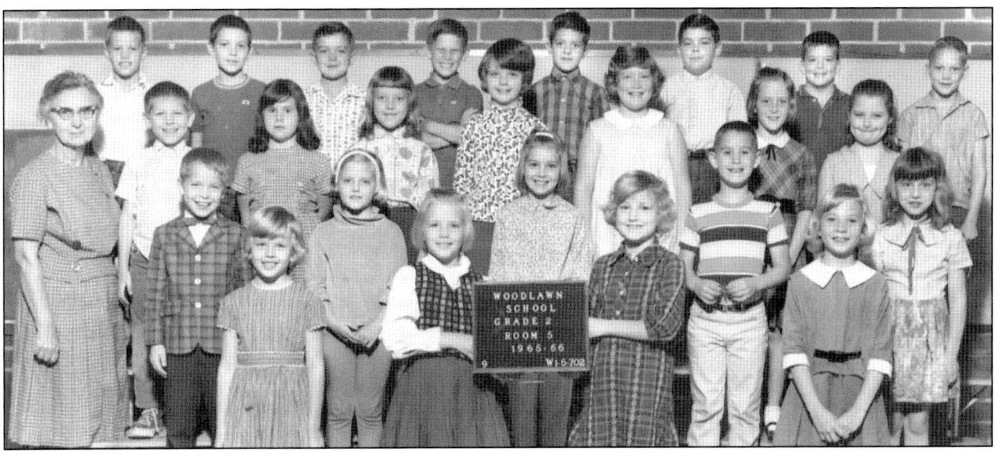

Thirty-six years later, in 1965–1966, Esther Ridder's Woodlawn Elementary School second-grade students included, from left to right, (first row) Diane Calhoun, Kay Browning, Tammie Lynn Robinson, and Tammy Sue Bennett; (second row) Peter Asciutto, Natalie Elizabeth Heacock, Susanne Bauer, Parke Slater, and Melissa Thompson; (third row) teacher Esther Riddler, Steve Jones, Diana Padgett, Mary Anne Handley, Teri Jane Hand, Susan Barnhurst, Carolyn Overbey, and Teresa Baker; (fourth row) Robert Emerson, Craig Shackelford, Ronald Nelson, Al Smith, Douglas Griffis, Wendell Haywood, Mark Wilkerson, and Terry Randall. (Courtesy Sebring Historical Society.)

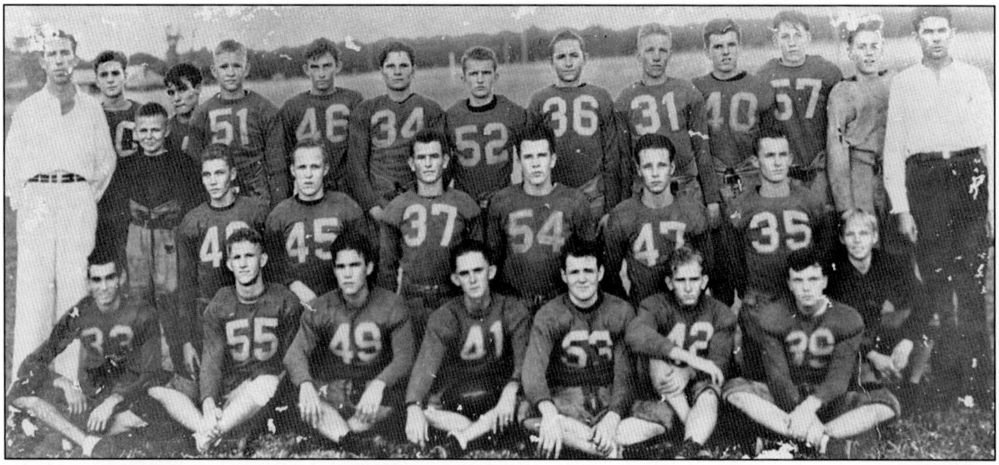

The 1933–1934 Sebring High School Blue Streaks football team included, from left to right, (first row) J. Bogle, R. Douglass, D. Sauls, J. Butler, ? Halaburton, W. Pollard, E. Harris, and ? Crawford; (second row) P. Marchand, J. Fulton, R. Grady, D. Baker, F. Howard, and C. Waldron; (third row) coach Jim Melton, unidentified, D. Mayo, E. Green, G. Douglas, H. McDonald, P. Roberts, T. Mayo, C. Foster, G. Crawford, R. Harris, J. Beaver, B. Starbuck, and coach Wilhite. (Courtesy Sebring Historical Society.)

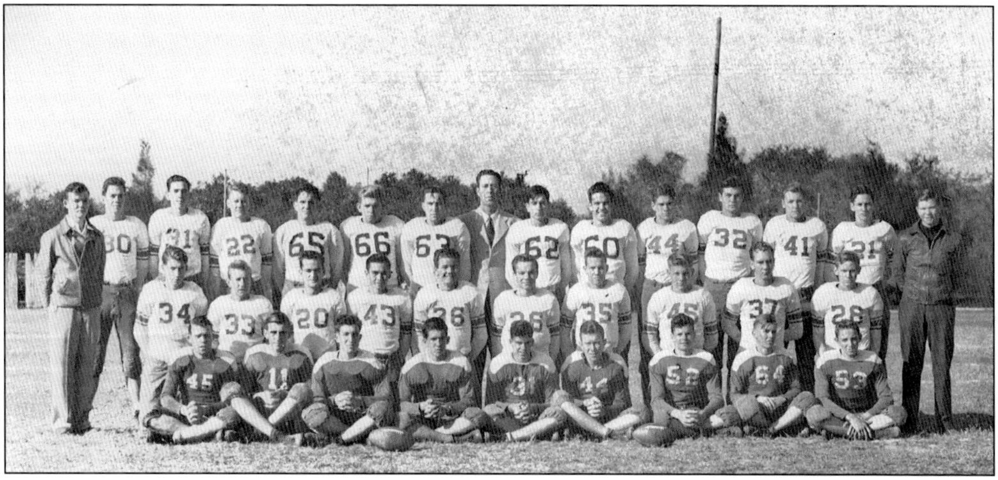

The 1944–1945 Blue Streaks included, from left to right, (first row) Bubba Cason; James Crawford; Stanley Kelsey; Wayne Taylor; Henry Eures; Robert Butler; Baird Green; Harry Swank; and Buddy Landrum; (second row) Legare Smoak; Carl Prescott; A. W. "Spizz" Pollard; Raymond Odom; Joe Barber; Hart Sebring; Billy Cason; Bobby Leaphart; Jeff Barrow; and Francis Twitty; (third row) Ira Gillis, the team's manager; Bob Silcox; Milton Stivender; Gene Mathis; Loyd Morgan; Loy Waldron; Buddy Wise; Mr. Melton, the team's coach; Jack Hancock; Wayne Carlton; Ted Shoemaker; Lenard Williams; Eugene Hamilton; Gerald Luther; and Eldredge Pollard. (Courtesy Sebring Historical Society.)

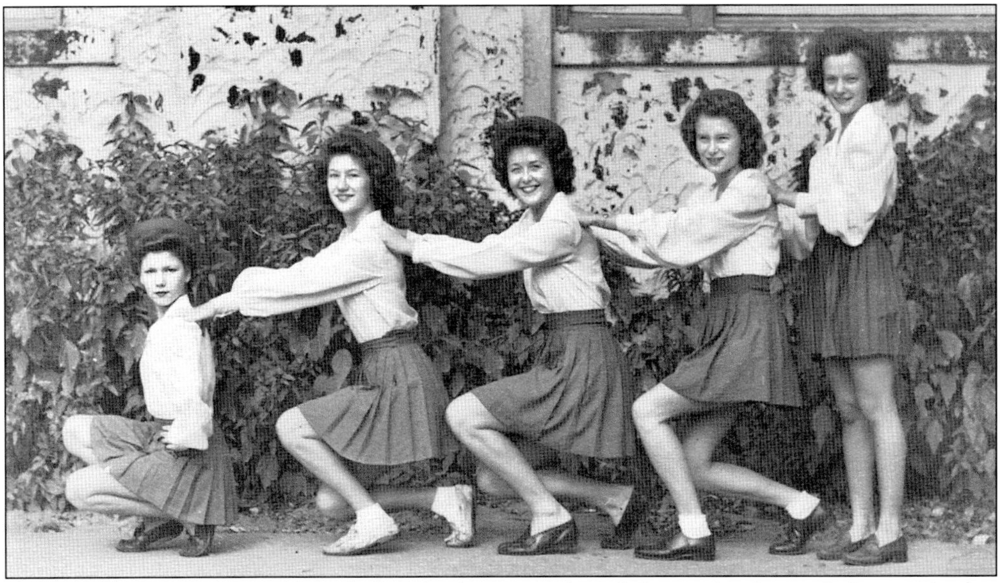

In 1945, the Sebring High School cheerleaders were, from left to right, Joann Roberts, Marilyn Poer, Ruth Cribb, LaVonne Peebles, and Mary Esther Johnson. The Blue Streaks's greatest rivals included the Avon Park Red Devils, the Lake Placid Green Dragons, and the Lake Wales Highlanders. (Courtesy Sebring Historical Society.)

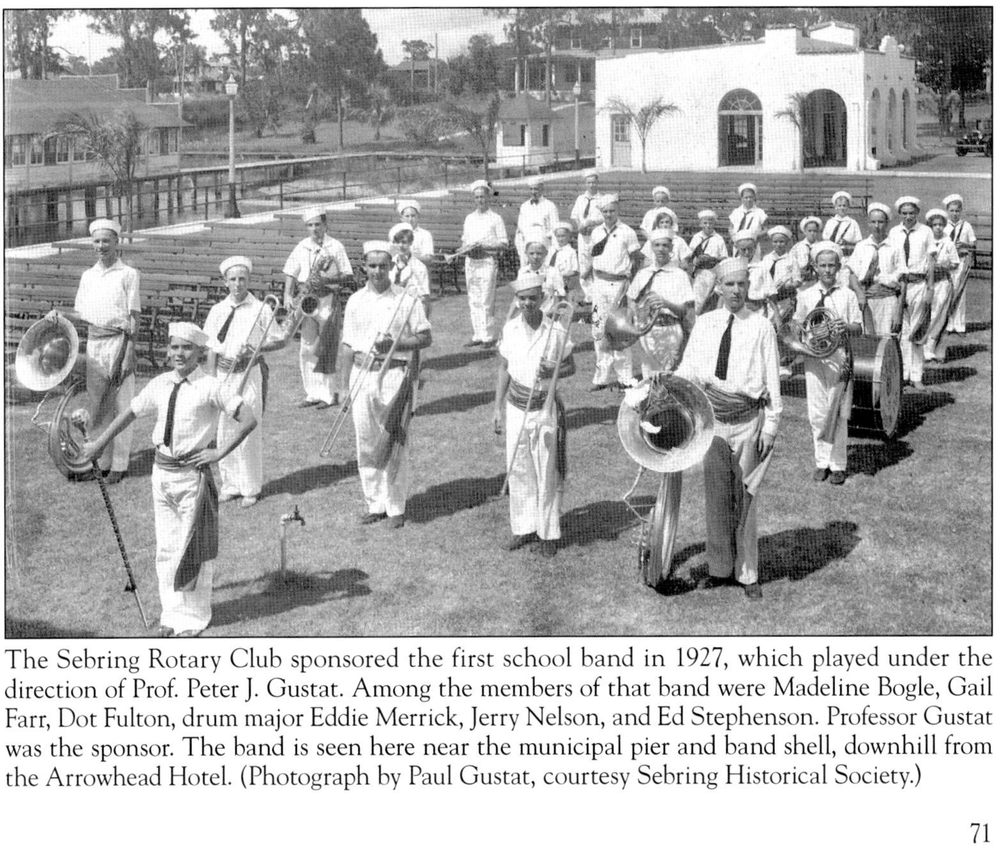

The Sebring Rotary Club sponsored the first school band in 1927, which played under the direction of Prof. Peter J. Gustat. Among the members of that band were Madeline Bogle, Gail Farr, Dot Fulton, drum major Eddie Merrick, Jerry Nelson, and Ed Stephenson. Professor Gustat was the sponsor. The band is seen here near the municipal pier and band shell, downhill from the Arrowhead Hotel. (Photograph by Paul Gustat, courtesy Sebring Historical Society.)

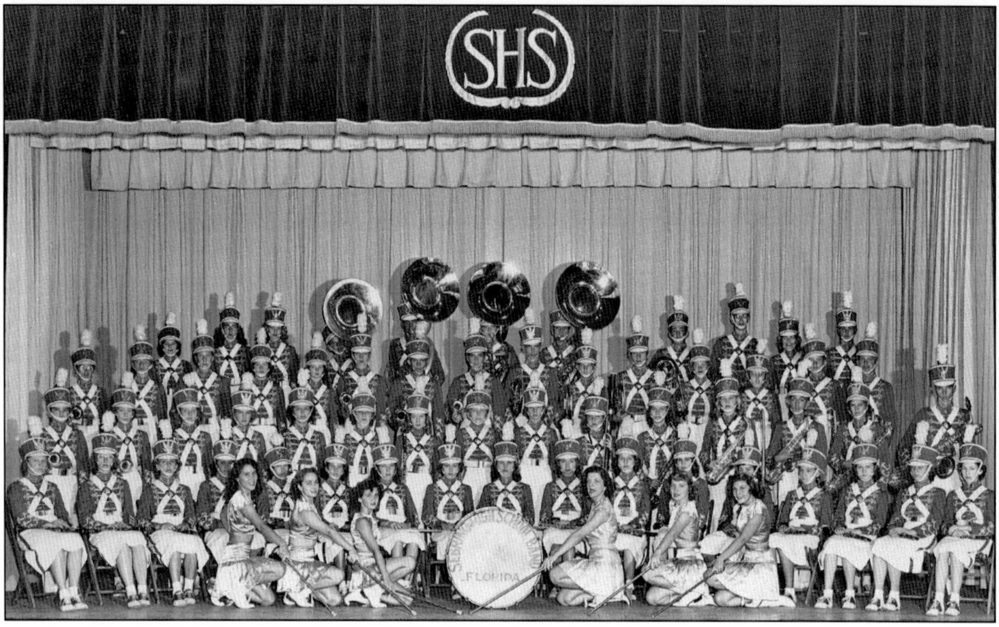

The Sebring High School band consistently earned superior ratings at state competitions, due in large measure to the outstanding direction of Prof. Peter J. Gustat, who was named "Father of Bands" in the state of Florida by the Florida Bandmasters Association. He and the band served as a model of excellence for other schools. The 1949 band is seen in the school auditorium. (Courtesy Sebring Historical Society.)

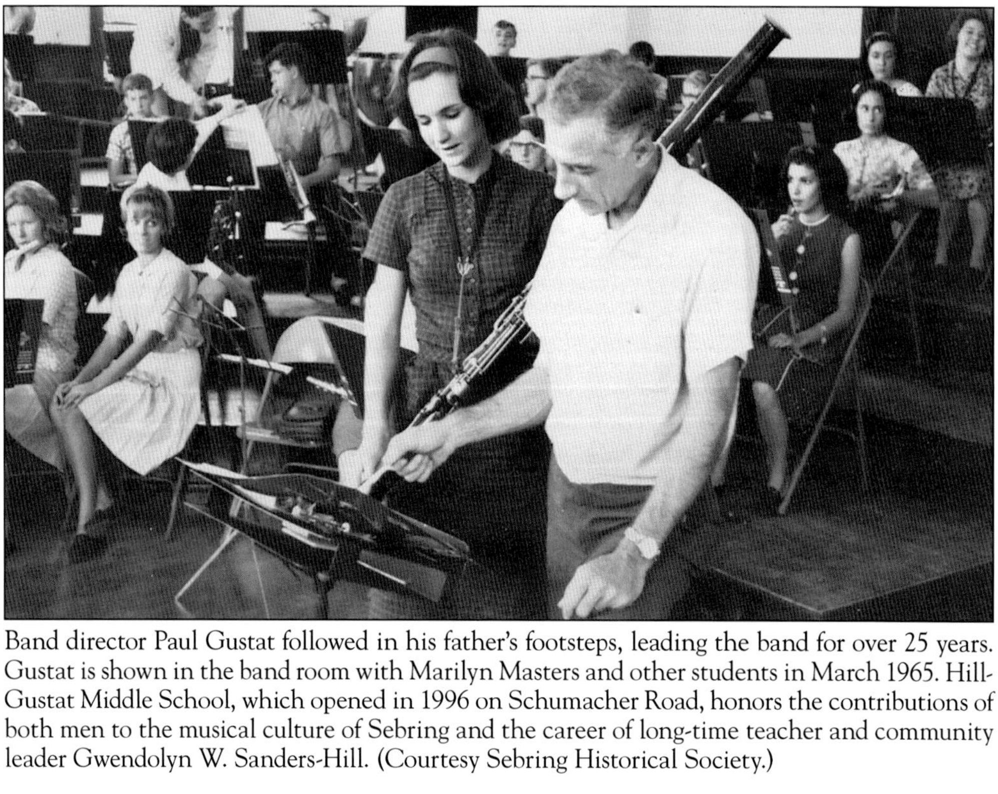

Band director Paul Gustat followed in his father's footsteps, leading the band for over 25 years. Gustat is shown in the band room with Marilyn Masters and other students in March 1965. Hill-Gustat Middle School, which opened in 1996 on Schumacher Road, honors the contributions of both men to the musical culture of Sebring and the career of long-time teacher and community leader Gwendolyn W. Sanders-Hill. (Courtesy Sebring Historical Society.)

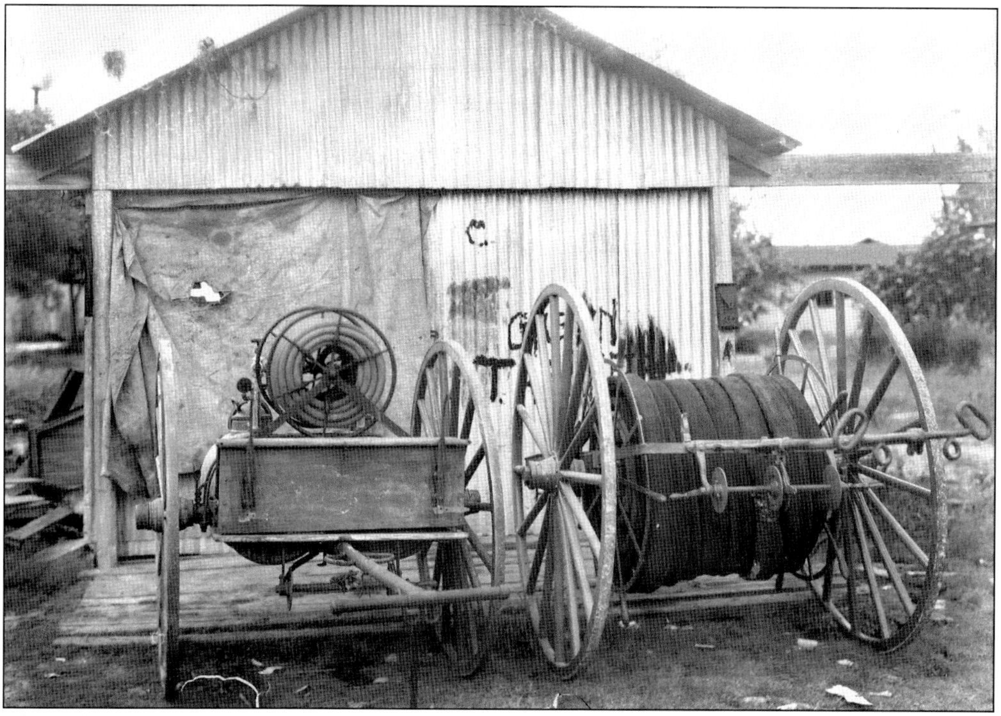

The Sebring volunteer fire station was constructed on East Center Avenue in 1914 to house equipment purchased by George E. Sebring the previous year. This early equipment included two hand-drawn reels with 800 feet of 2.5-inch hose from the Eureka Fire Hose Company. Aaron Withers served as the first fire chief; the first major fire loss was Cason's Hotel on South Commerce Avenue in 1914. (Courtesy Sebring Historical Society.)

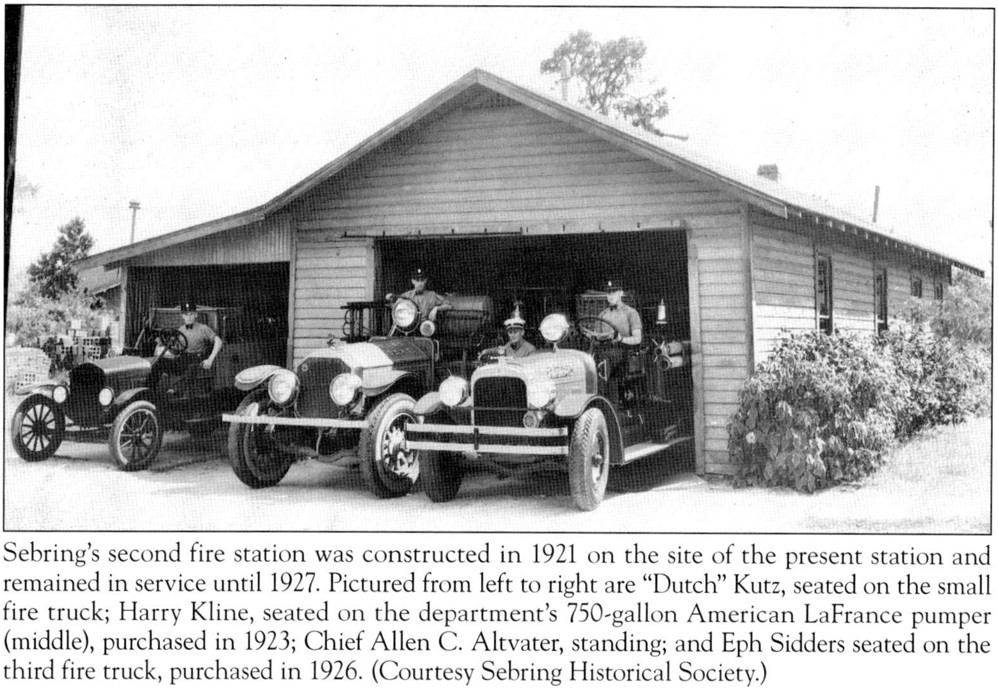

Sebring's second fire station was constructed in 1921 on the site of the present station and remained in service until 1927. Pictured from left to right are "Dutch" Kutz, seated on the small fire truck; Harry Kline, seated on the department's 750-gallon American LaFrance pumper (middle), purchased in 1923; Chief Allen C. Altvater, standing; and Eph Sidders seated on the third fire truck, purchased in 1926. (Courtesy Sebring Historical Society.)

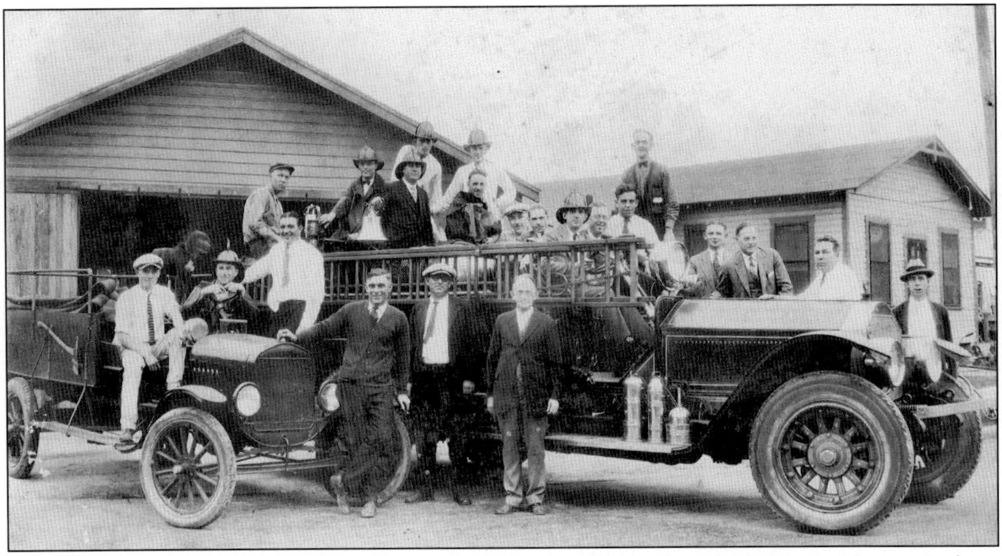

Most of the firemen in this February 27, 1924, photograph are identified: Spencer Jones, Gideon Yeager, and Allen C. Altvater's dog, Speed, on the small truck; Allen C. Altvater and Art Young in front of the small truck; Ben McGee, Brandon Jones, Payne Sebring, Roseo Yeager, Josh Spooner, and Stanley Capwell on the large truck; and Chal Lighthiser, C. F. Saunders, Eph Sidders, and P. G. Gearing seated with Ken Johnson, B. A. Cope, Bert Fields, and Charles Beresford on the far step. (Courtesy Sebring Historical Society.)

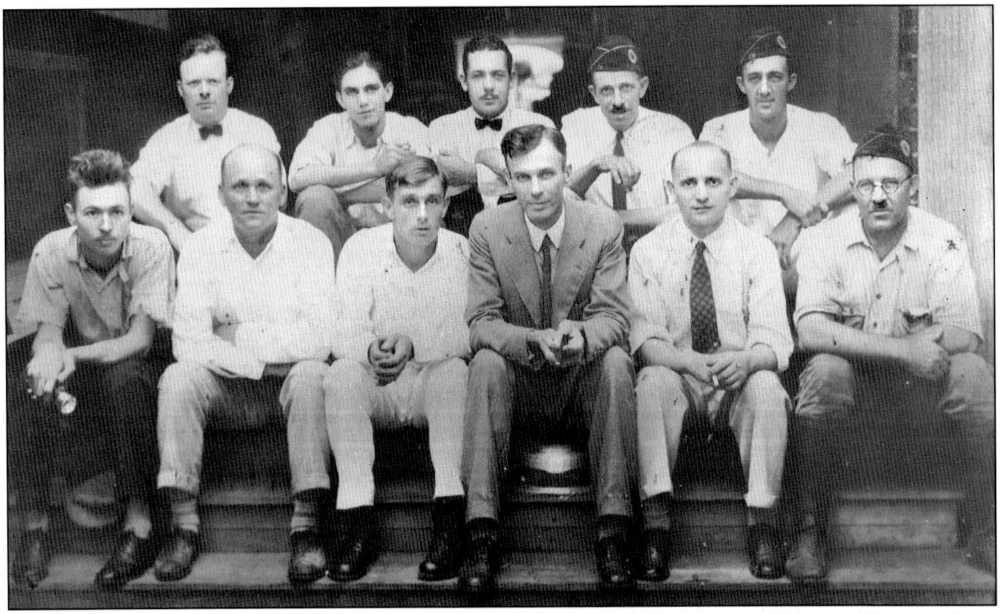

The Great Miami Hurricane of September 1926 decimated the town of Moore Haven where the dike was overrun by the Lake Okeechobee storm surge. The Sebring firefighters led rescue efforts in Moore Haven. The relief crew included, from left to right, (first row) Ernest Roberts, Glenn Skipper, Allen C. Altvater, Dr. J. W. Mitchell, Mike Kahn, and H. G. Eastwood; (second row) "Red" Cleaver, N. N. Van, Ed Spear, George Wyandt, and O. C. White. (Courtesy Sebring Historical Society.)

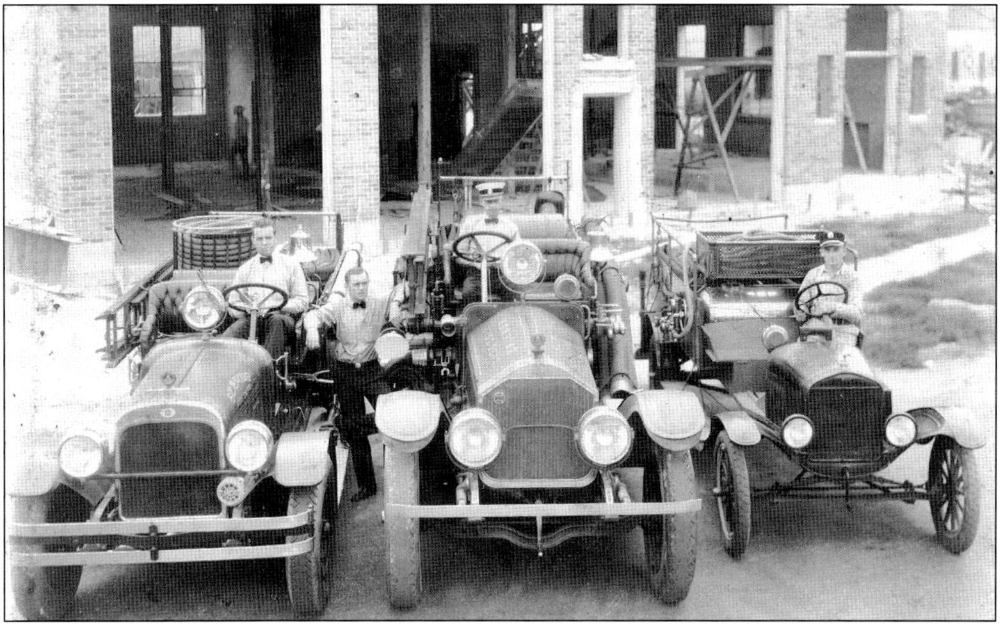

Construction was nearly complete on the Central Fire Station on North Mango Street in 1927 when four members of the Sebring Fire Department recreated their 1921 pose with the fire fighting apparatus (see page 73). Pictured from left to right are Eph Sidders, Allen C. Altvater, Harry Kline, and "Dutch" Kutz. Designed by architect William J. Heim, the station was added to the National Register of Historic Places in 1989. (Courtesy Sebring Historical Society.)

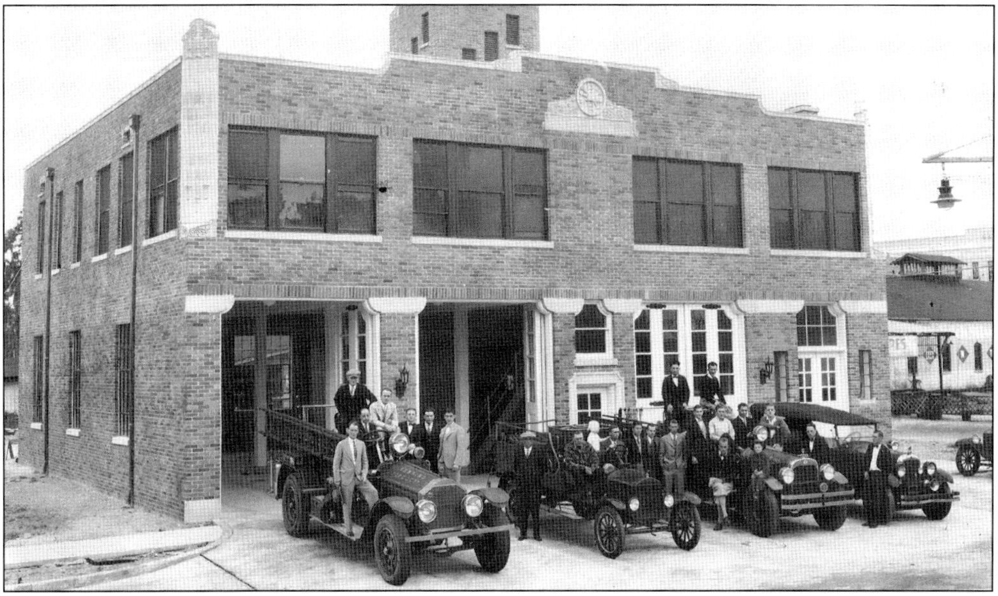

At the Central Station in 1927 were (first truck from left) Al Butler, Harry Kline, P. G. Gearing, Kenneth Johnson, and Ford Heacock; (second truck from left) Art Young (standing), Harry Raymond, Billy Jones, Spencer Jones, Stan Wyandt, Walter Ivings, and Doug Estes; (third truck from left) Payne Sebring (seated on running board), Al Keifer, "Dutch" Kutz, Eph Sidders, O. W. Chapman, and Roscoe Yeager, and Laurie Williams on the back. Allen C. Altvater was leaning against the car. (Courtesy Sebring Historical Society.)

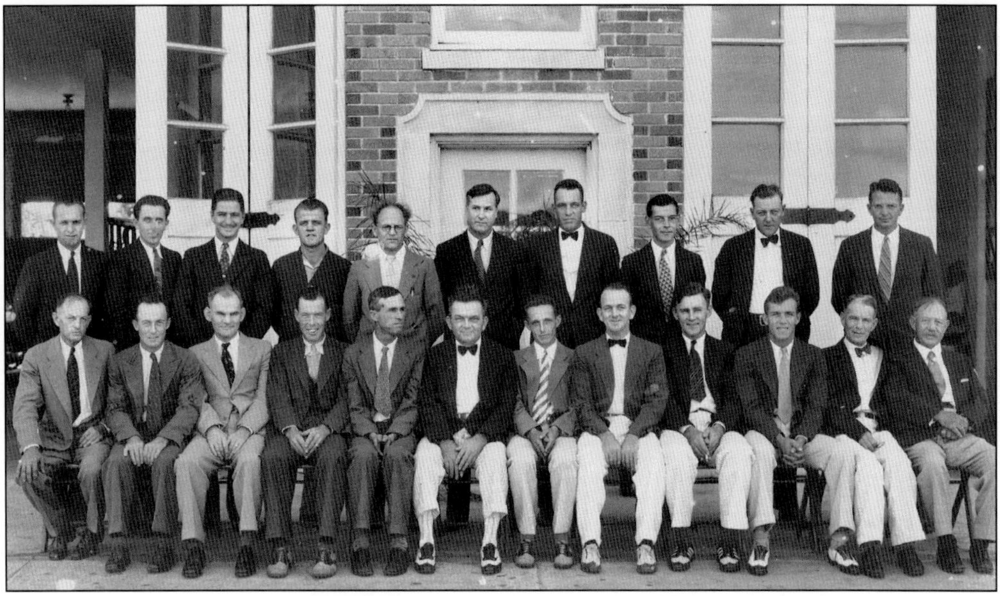

The 1933 Sebring firemen included, from left to right, (first row) B. A. Cope, Joe Long, Playford "Skeet" Naylor, Hal Long, Spencer Jones, Jack Williams, Joe Lighthiser, P. G. Gearing, Joe Stiles, Jack Parker, Al Butler, and C. F. Saunders; (second row) Ray Morgan, "Gatchell" Burton, Stan Wyandt, O. W. Chapman, Jimmy Ball, Brandon Jones, George Hicks, Norman Lane, Harry Raymond, and Ray Vinton. (Courtesy Sebring Historical Society.)

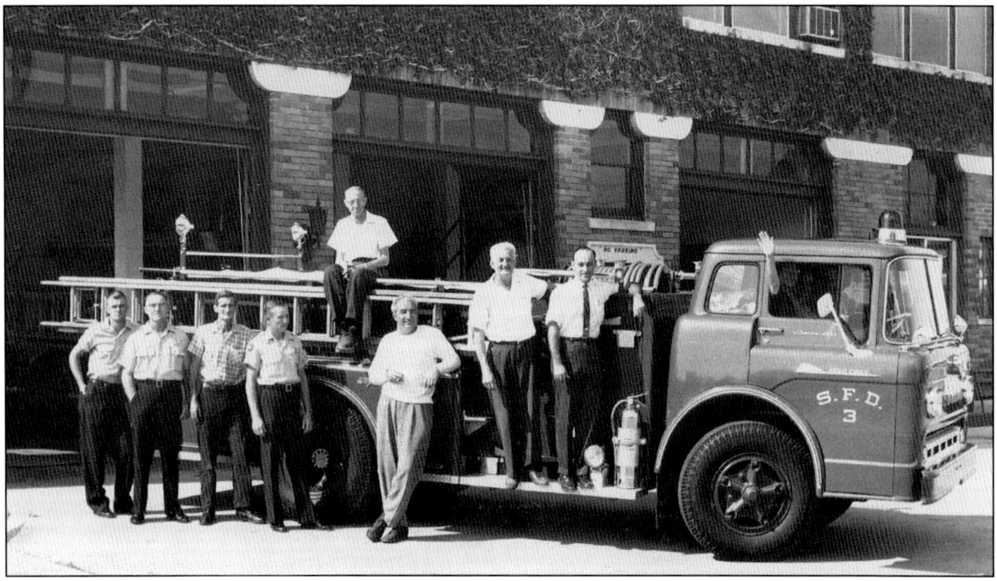

The Sebring Firemen, Inc., was formed in 1930 as a civic organization designed to support the mission of the department, including the promotion of local athletics. Membership was not restricted to firefighters and has included many local leaders. This late-1950s image includes (from left to right) Gary Lanier, Thurman Haywood, unidentified, Red Carter, Clarence Schaeffer, Ben Eastman, Bean Brummell, Haywood Taylor, and four unidentified in the cab. Schaeffer, who worked at the chamber of commerce, is the only one pictured who was not a firefighter. (Courtesy Sebring Historical Society.)

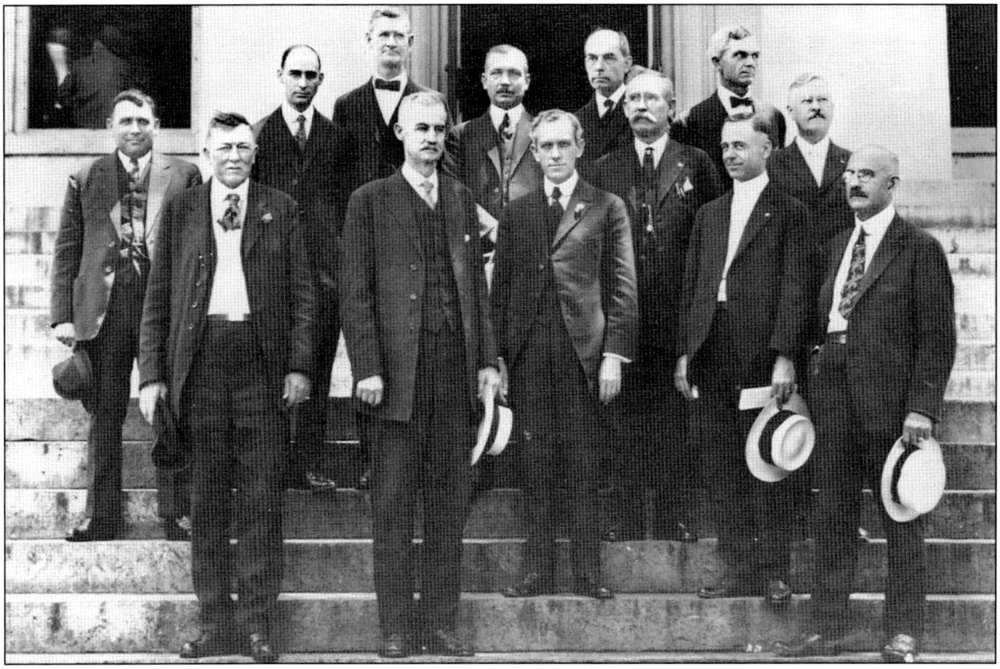

Highlands County was formed in April 1921 from part of DeSoto County. Members of the Division Committee were, from left to right, (first row) former governor Albert W. Gilchrist, Senator Cooper (Punta Gorda), Gov. Carey Hardee, Capt. W. H. Johnson (Punta Gorda), E. J. Etheredge (DeSoto City), and George E. Sebring. Among those pictured on the second row were Jack Taylor (Lake Placid), D. W. Stephenson (Moore Haven), Charlie Carlton (Wauchula), Chester Blount (Punta Gorda), A. G. Smith (Wauchula), and two unidentified. (Courtesy Sebring Historical Society.)

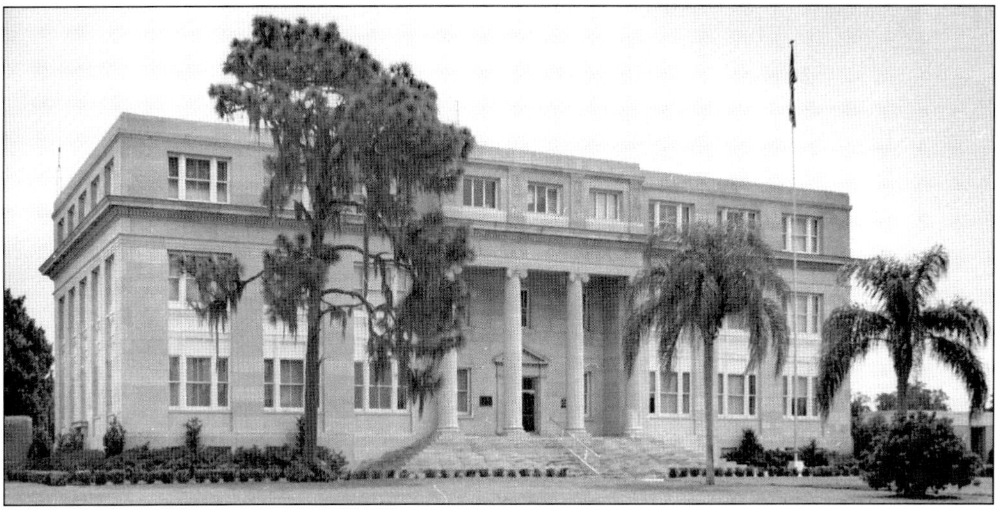

As the county seat, Sebring needed a courthouse to substantiate its new status. The classical Revival–style Highlands County Courthouse, designed by Fred Bishop, was completed in 1926 on the north side of South Commerce Avenue. Highlands County covers over 1,028 square miles and is the 15th largest of Florida's 67 counties. (Courtesy Sebring Historical Society.)

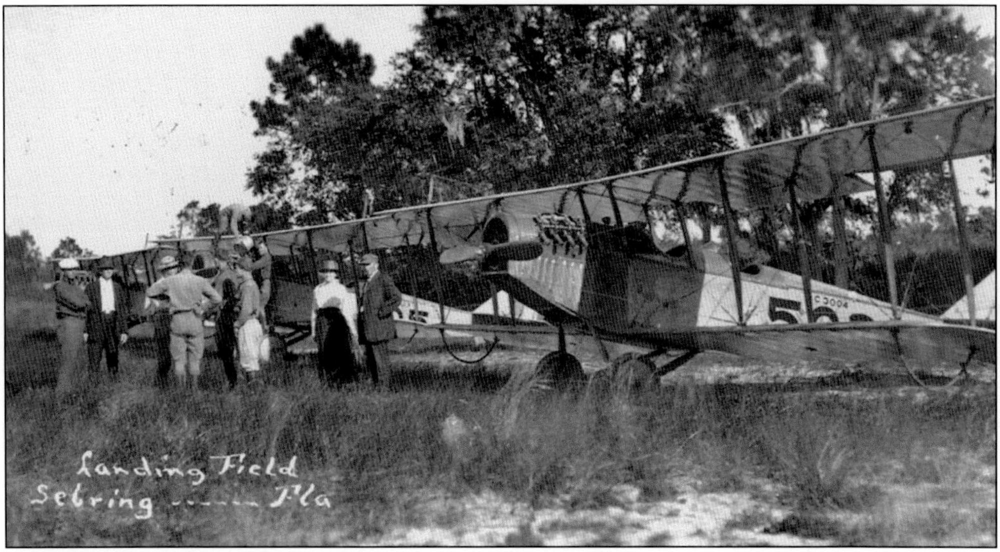

Fliers gas up one of three Curtiss Jenny biplanes at Sebring's landing strip, probably in the 1920s. The Jenny was a World War I training plane, carried the first U.S. Air Mail, and was popular among barnstormers for many years. The famous "Inverted Jenny" error airmail stamps (1918) featured the Curtiss JN-4. (Courtesy Sebring Historical Society.)

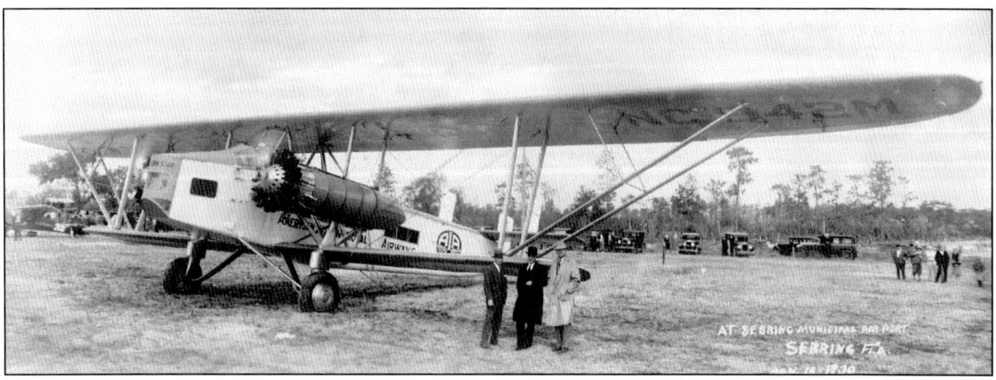

This American International Airways biplane was in town on January 16, 1930. The Sebring Municipal Airport was located west of Lake Jackson on Hammock Road between what are now U.S. Highway 27 and Lakewood Road, a site large enough to warrant a guard during World War II. Today the Sebring Regional Airport is located seven miles southeast of Sebring at the former Hendricks Field site. (Courtesy Sebring Historical Society.)

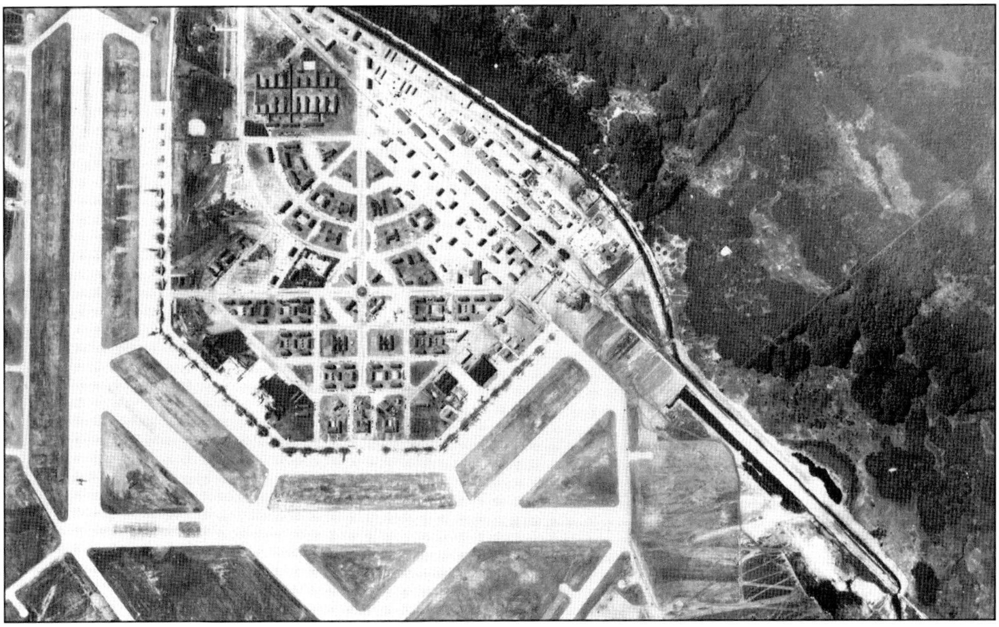

In 1940, with the United States' involvement in World War II on the horizon, local leaders lobbied Congress to establish a military training camp. Hendricks Field, a B-17 Army Air Force base seen here in 1942, was situated on 9,200 acres. Over 9,000 servicemen were stationed at Hendricks Field during the height of the war, and when the base was decommissioned in 1946, a number of servicemen settled in the community. (Courtesy Sebring Historical Society.)

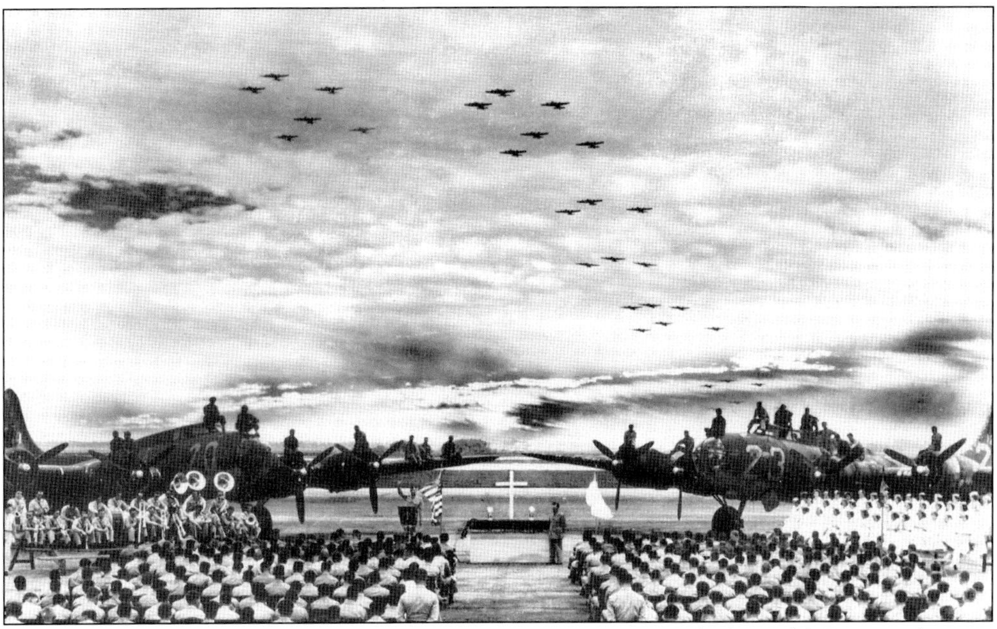

Servicemen gathered for the Easter 1944 sunrise service at Hendricks Field. During the war, the municipal pier served as an entertainment venue for the USO, and the entire city worked toward making the military and their families welcome. The proximity of the base gave increased awareness of the need for bond sales, scrap metal drives, and other efforts to support the war effort. (Photograph by Marge MacNeil, courtesy Sebring Historical Society.)

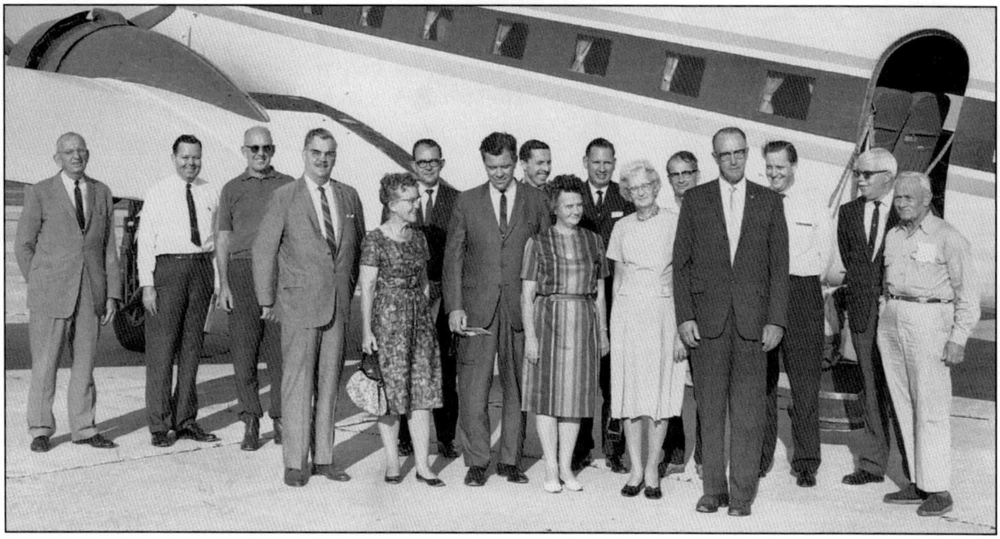

The first commuter airline flight to and from Sebring was flown in 1958. Not all of those shown in this photograph are identified, but those known include, from left to right, (first row) Dr. Hubolt of the Sudan Interior Mission, Mrs. Hubolt, and Allen C. Altvater; (second row) Forrest Lloyd, Ken Grady, Donald Pillinger, Ernie Breed, Al Roepstorf, and Roy Alexander. (Courtesy Sebring Historical Society.)

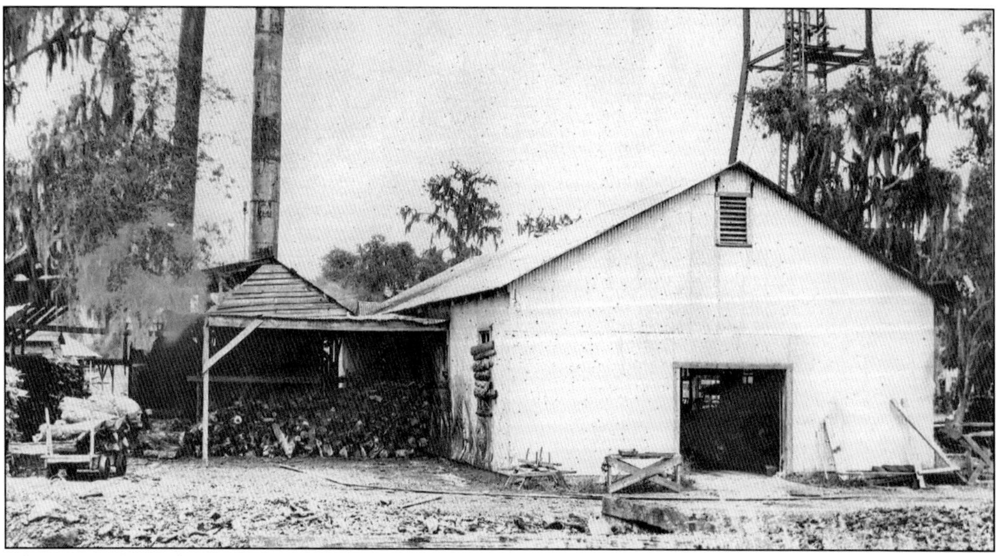

The city's first electrical power plant was located at the end of North Pine Street and North Commerce Avenue near the first railroad depot. The Sebring Light and Water Company was financed by George E. Sebring, and electricity was available from 6:00 p.m. to 11:00 p.m. each evening. Increased demand, especially for nighttime electrical service, culminated in the purchase of the utility company by the city in 1923. (Courtesy Sebring Historical Society.)

Six

Business and Agriculture

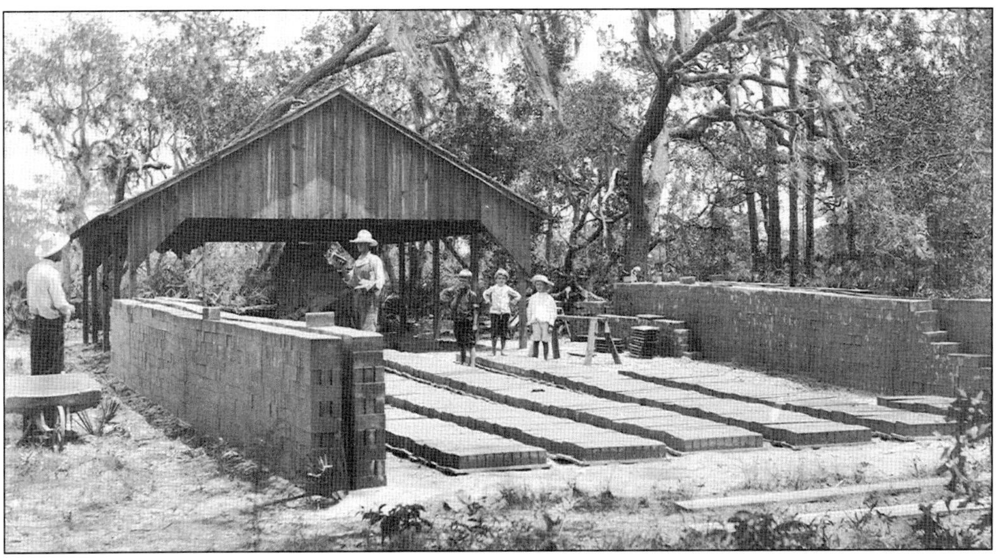

I. L. Jenkins opened his brick plant in May 1912 on the Atlantic Coast Line Railroad right-of-way. According to John F. Newcomb, one of the first to observe the workings of the new plant, the Arrowhead Hotel was the first building to use Jenkins's air-dried bricks the next month in its foundation. The three youngsters in this photograph are, from left to right, Landis Jenkins, and Fred and Harold Newcomb. (Courtesy Sebring Historical Society.)

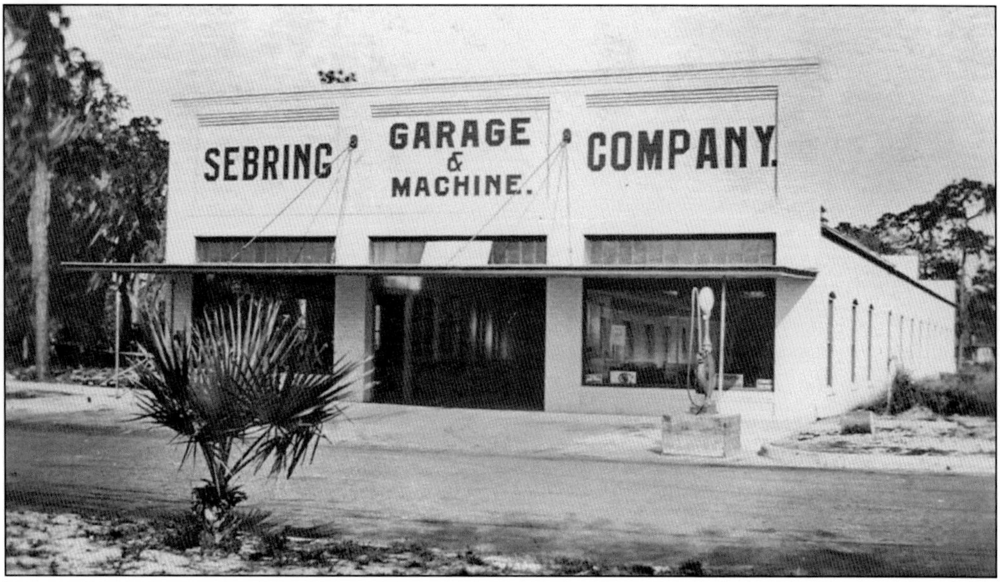

The Sebring Garage and Machine Company was located on North Ridgewood Drive between North Mango Street and the Circle. In 1924, the garage sold Overland Touring cars for $495. This photograph was taken before 1923 when the Hainz Building was constructed immediately south of the garage. See pages 32 and 33 for photographs of the garage adjacent to the Hainz Building. (Courtesy Sebring Historical Society.)

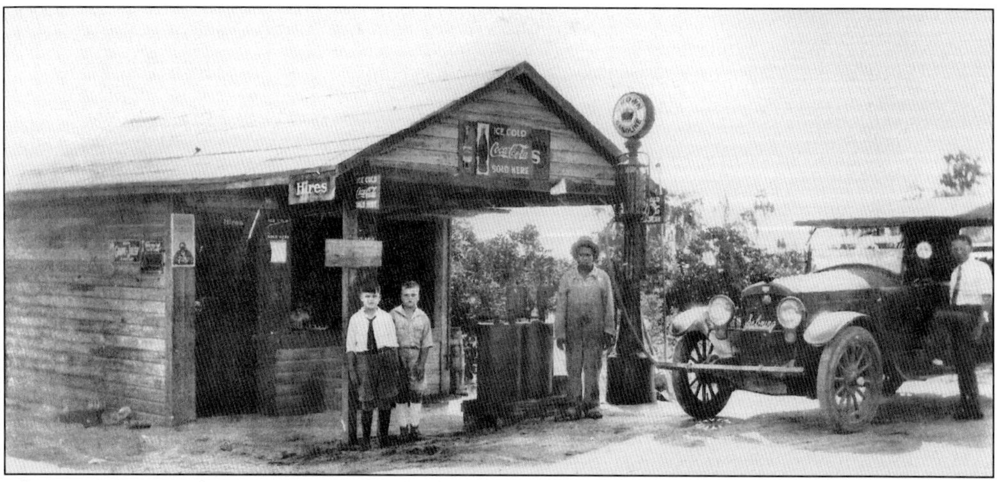

The open-air Dowling Gas Station, which sold Crown Gasoline from aboveground barrels, is shown in this *c.* 1925 image. The Dowling family also owned Dowling and Newsome Realtors. The youngsters at left are (from left to right) Grafton Geddes Dowling Jr. (1915–2001) and Joab Mauldin Dowling (1917–1992), both of whom practiced law in South Carolina for many years. The car has a decorative "Sebring" sign on the grill. (Courtesy Sebring Historical Society.)

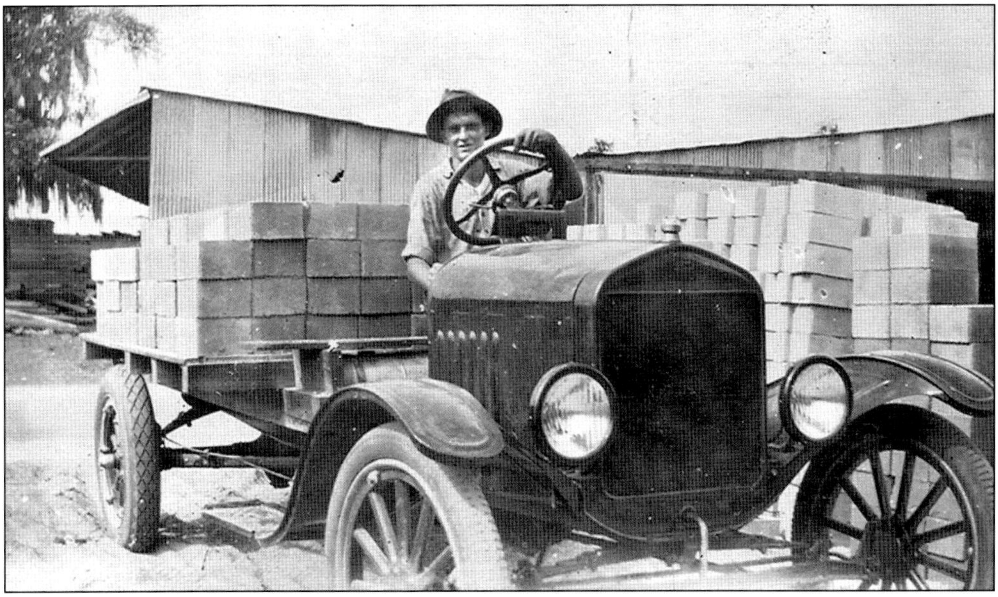

Vern Cunningham is seen behind the wheel of a Ford Model T truck belonging to Milt Baker's block plant, which in 1926 was located at the north end of Pine Street. Among Baker's many other enterprises were his grocery store, the Ohio Movie Theater, and a Nash automobile agency. He was active in local governance as a member of the town council from 1936 to 1939. (Courtesy Sebring Historical Society.)

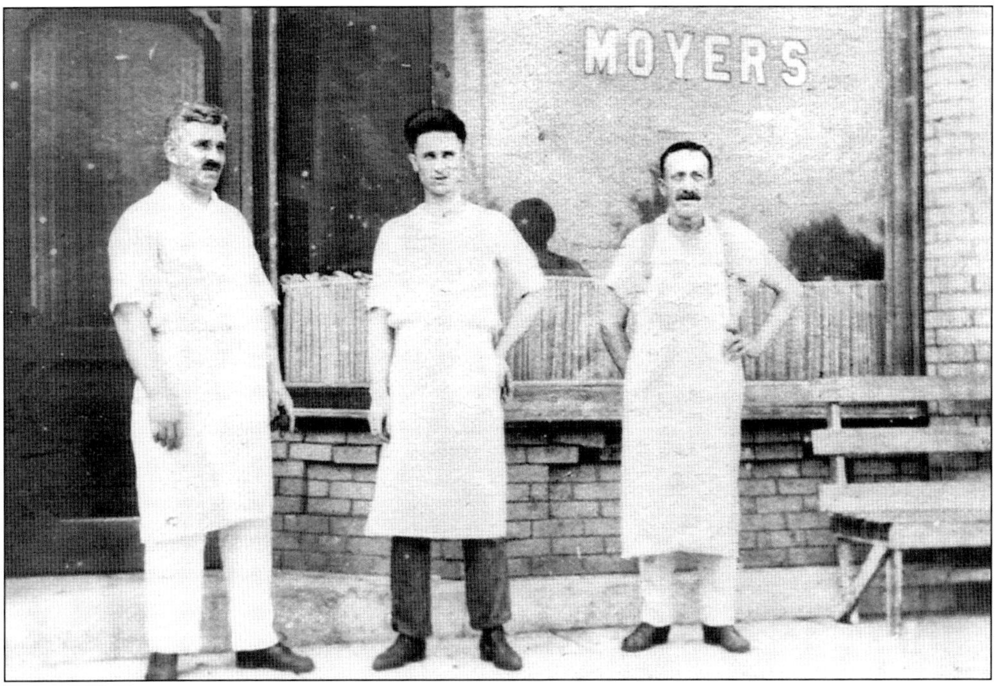

Moyers Café was located in downtown Sebring. The family also owned Moyers Garage in the old Ohio Theater building (1922) at the corner of South Ridgewood Drive and Magnolia Avenue. In the 1930s, Moyers Garage sold Sinclair H-C Gasoline and Good Rich tires, and serviced Pontiac automobiles. (Courtesy Sebring Historical Society.)

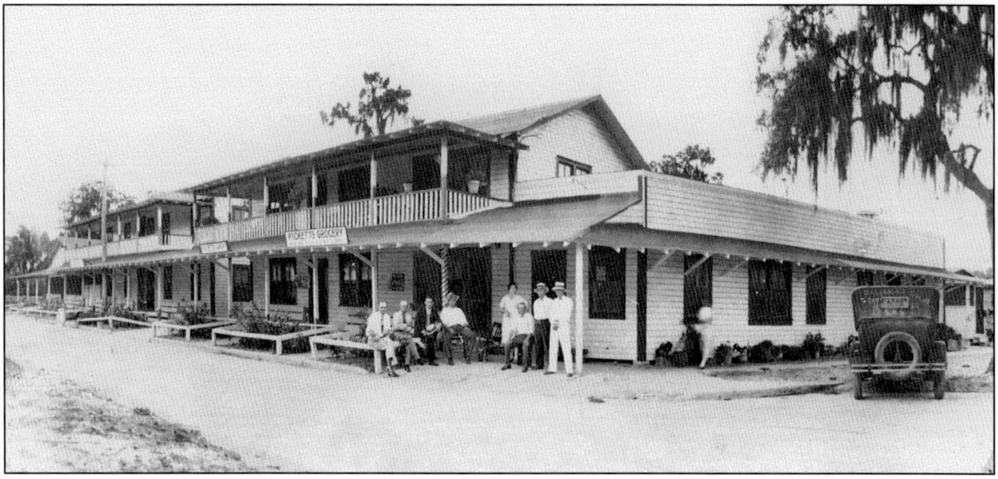

Pickett's Grocery and Boarding House was built in 1926 on Orange Street. In July 2001, Louise Pickett Smoak reminisced in *The Historian* about growing up in her parents' boarding house, which included "two two-storied buildings with 16 smaller houses in the back." John S. and Claribel Spencer Pickett operated the venture together, and after his 1928 death, Claribel supported her family with the business. (Courtesy Sebring Historical Society.)

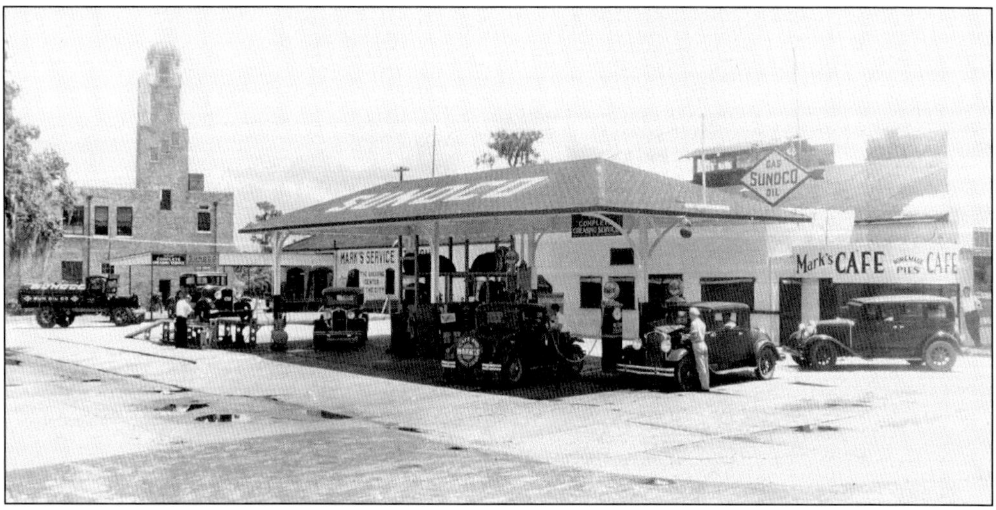

Situated at the corner of North Ridgewood Drive facing North Mango Street, Mark's Service Station—"The Greasing Center of the City"—and Mark's Café, featuring homemade pies, were close to the post-1927 action. The Central Fire Station is clearly visible in the distance, and the Sebring Garage and Machine Company building is at far right. (Courtesy Sebring Historical Society.)

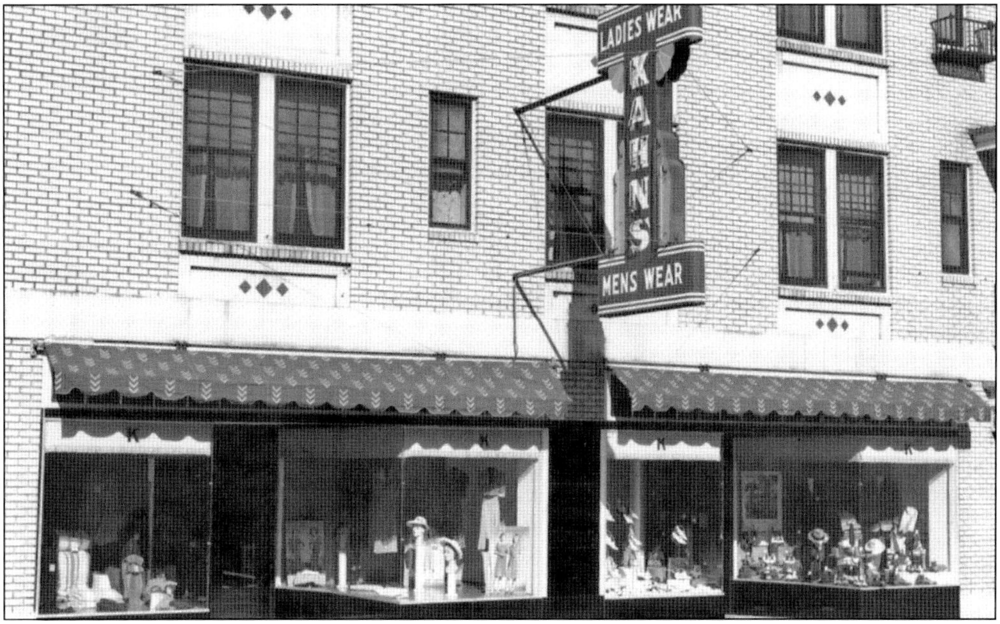

Kahn's Department Store, for many years, was the largest and most complete upscale department store in town. A double-front store in the Nan-Ces-O-Wee Hotel, it was owned by Michael "Mike" and Sadie Kahn, who arrived from Georgia in about 1921. The Kahns were founding members of Temple Beth Israel, and organized a Passover Seder for servicemen from Hendricks Field and the Avon Park Base in the 1940s. (Courtesy Sebring Historical Society.)

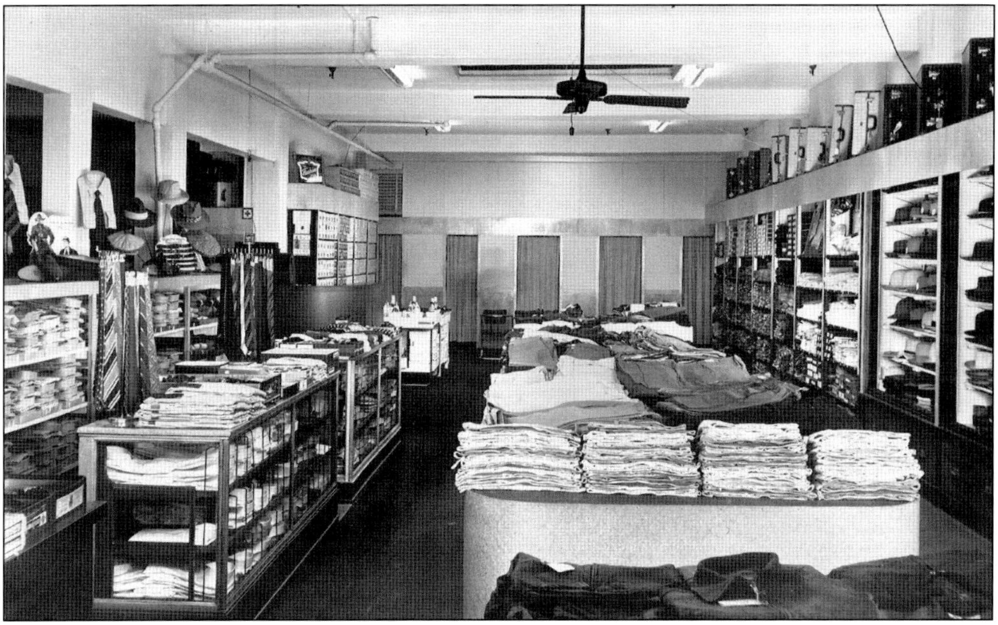

The men's section of Kahn's is shown in this image from 1940. Abraham Jacob (A. J.) "Bucky" Kahn managed the store from 1949 until it closed in the mid-1960s. Bucky was a member of the Sebring Lions Club for 48 years and a past district governor. Mike and Sadie Kahn's other children included Leon, Marvin, and Ruth Kahn Davis; all were successful and held in the highest regard. (Courtesy Sebring Historical Society.)

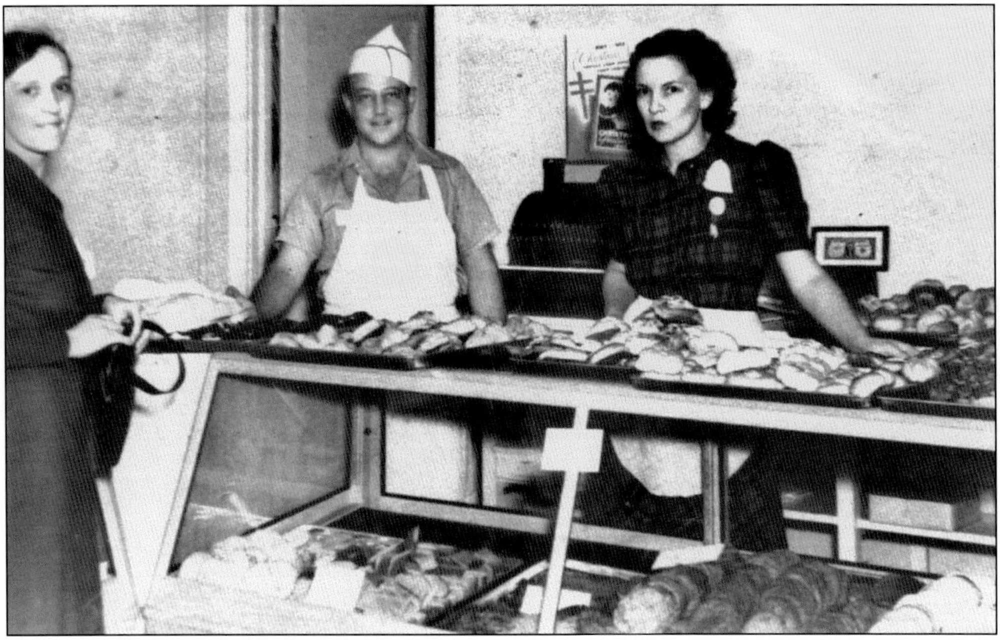

Muff's Bakery was owned from the early 1920s by Bill Muff. His sons Harris (a member of the Sebring Fire Department in the 1920s) and Anvil did not remain with him in the business and eventually moved from Sebring. This photograph from 1940 shows Anvil Muff and his wife in the bakery with customer Ruth Amy (Mrs. Payne) Sebring. (Courtesy Sebring Historical Society.)

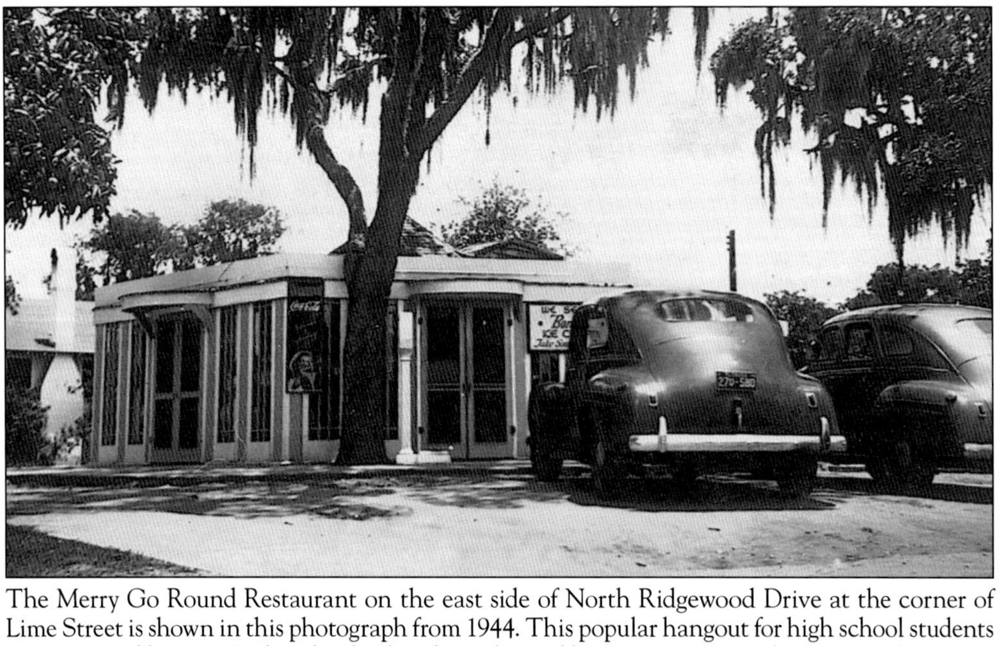

The Merry Go Round Restaurant on the east side of North Ridgewood Drive at the corner of Lime Street is shown in this photograph from 1944. This popular hangout for high school students was managed by Mrs. Barlow; her husband ran the Gulf gas station across the street and Barlow's Taxi service. (Photograph by Ted Shoemaker, courtesy Sebring Historical Society.)

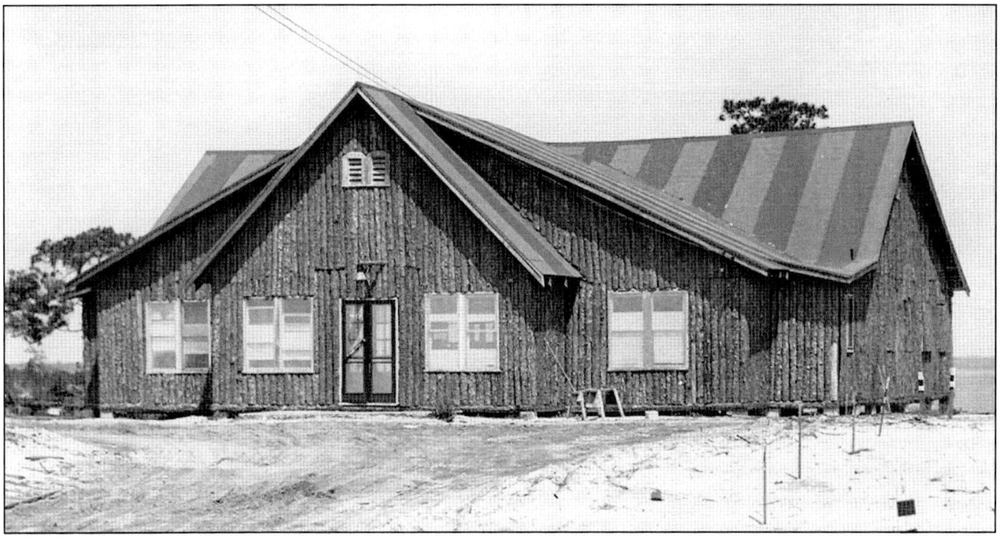

In 1936, George Lilly's dance hall and tavern was located on Lakeview Drive along the south shore of Lake Jackson on property now home to the VFW Club. During World War II, the tavern was a popular spot for military personnel and locals, who enjoyed music provided by high school students and musicians from Hendricks Field. (Courtesy Sebring Historical Society.)

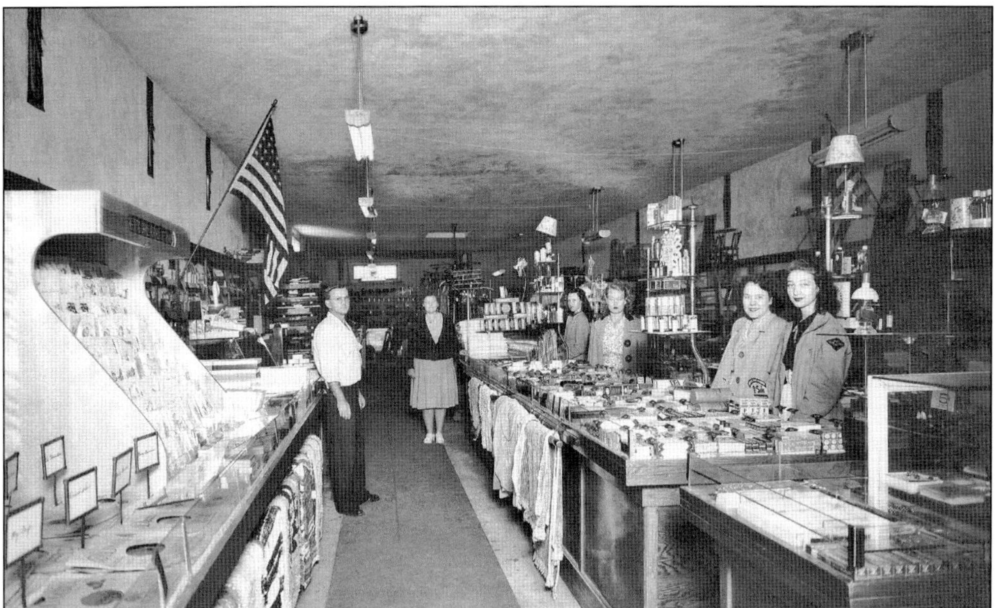

The well-stocked Peters Five and Dime Store was located on North Ridgewood Drive. This photograph was taken on January 5, 1945, and shows the staff, (from left to right) Mr. Peters, Mrs. Peters, Myrt Foster, unidentified, Betty Foster Witt, and Muriel Odell Phelps McGee. This week featured a 1¢ sale on Colgate Tooth Powder. (Courtesy Sebring Historical Society.)

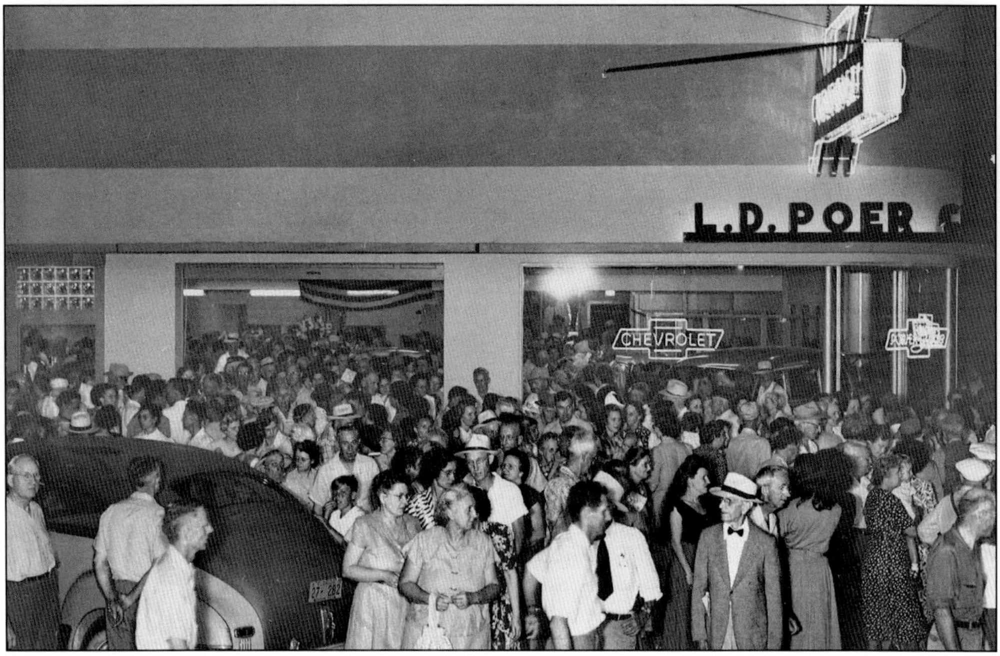

A crowd gathered for the grand opening of L. D. Poer's Chevrolet dealership at North Ridgewood Drive and North Pine Street in May 1950. The dealership had been in business since at least the early 1930s. Poer was active in local governance, serving on the city council from 1940 to 1943. This building is still standing. (Courtesy Sebring Historical Society.)

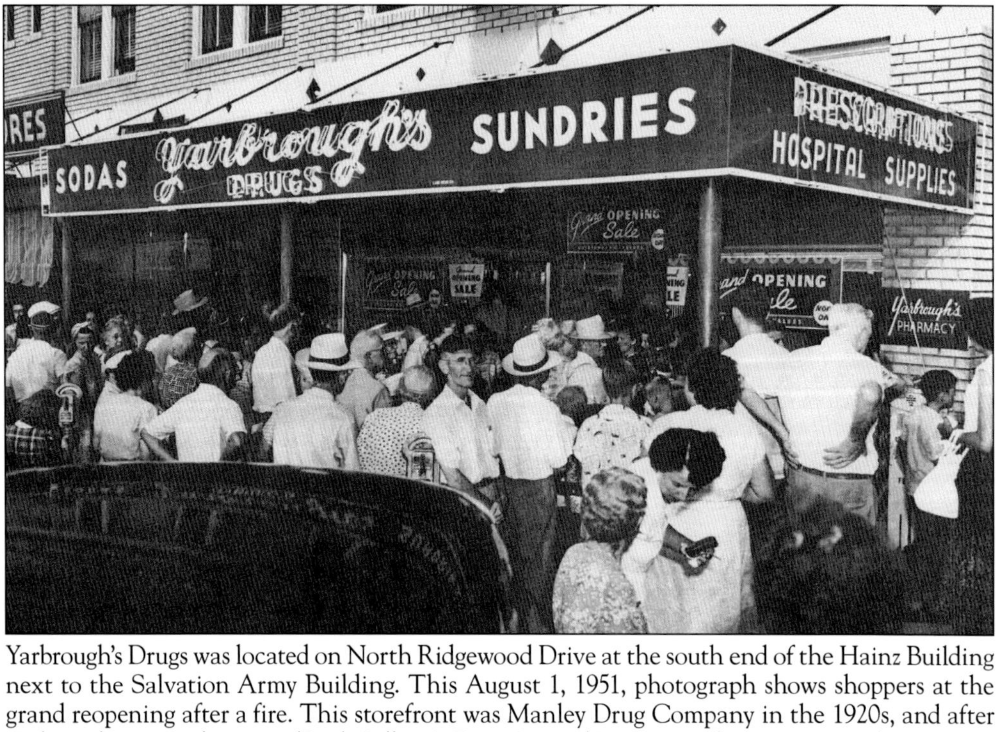

Yarbrough's Drugs was located on North Ridgewood Drive at the south end of the Hainz Building next to the Salvation Army Building. This August 1, 1951, photograph shows shoppers at the grand reopening after a fire. This storefront was Manley Drug Company in the 1920s, and after Yarbrough's, it was home to (Roy) Gilbert's Drug Store. (Courtesy Sebring Historical Society.)

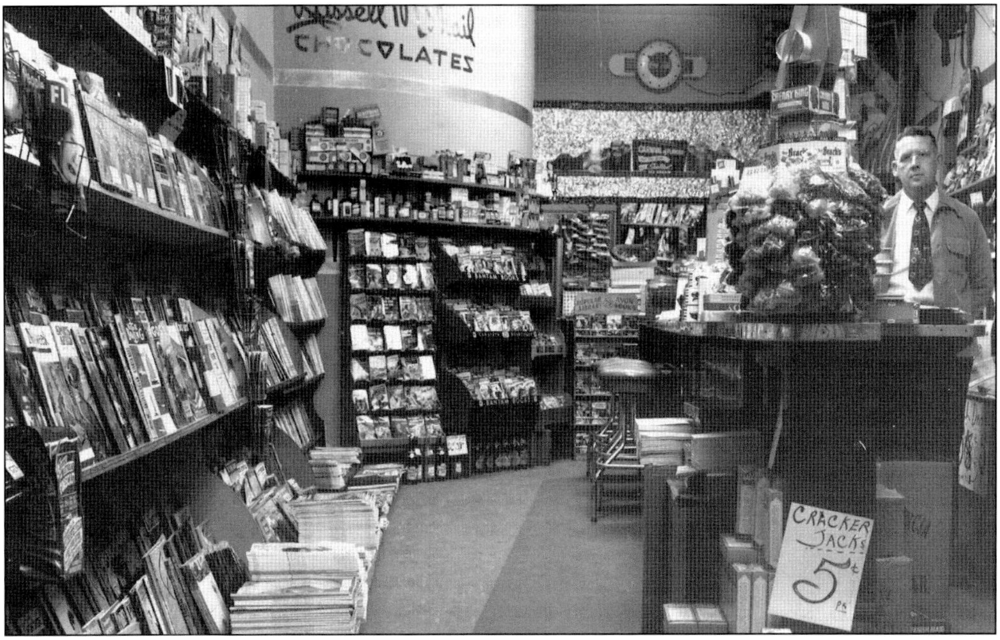

Noah B. "Bill" Graybill (1912–1985) is seen in the Sweet Shop on the Circle in Sebring adjacent to the Circle Theater in this photograph from early 1951. The newsstand was conveniently located and catered to those with a sweet tooth. Graybill was an active member of the Sebring Firemen, served on the city council in 1958 and 1959, and managed the Sebring Air Terminal. (Photograph by Ted Shoemaker, courtesy Sebring Historical Society.)

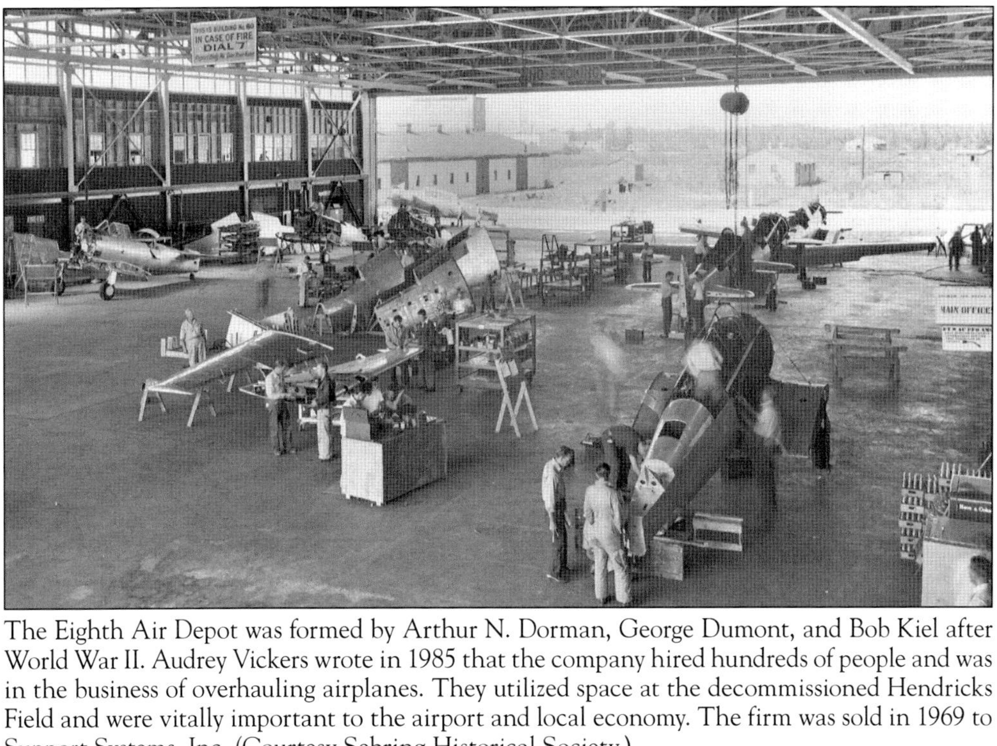

The Eighth Air Depot was formed by Arthur N. Dorman, George Dumont, and Bob Kiel after World War II. Audrey Vickers wrote in 1985 that the company hired hundreds of people and was in the business of overhauling airplanes. They utilized space at the decommissioned Hendricks Field and were vitally important to the airport and local economy. The firm was sold in 1969 to Support Systems, Inc. (Courtesy Sebring Historical Society.)

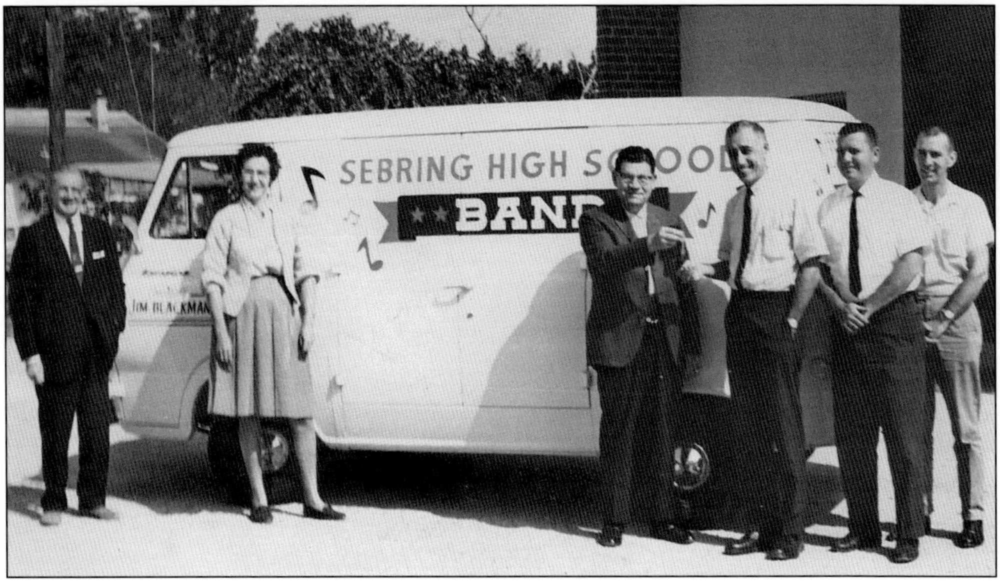

Jim Blackman operated the local Ford dealership beginning in the mid-1950s. Blackman was supportive of local school groups, and in the 1960s, he donated a van to the Sebring High School band. Shown from left to right are Raymond Clarke, Joan Masters, Jim Blackman, band director Paul Gustat, Wally Cox, and Joe Poff. (Courtesy Sebring Historical Society.)

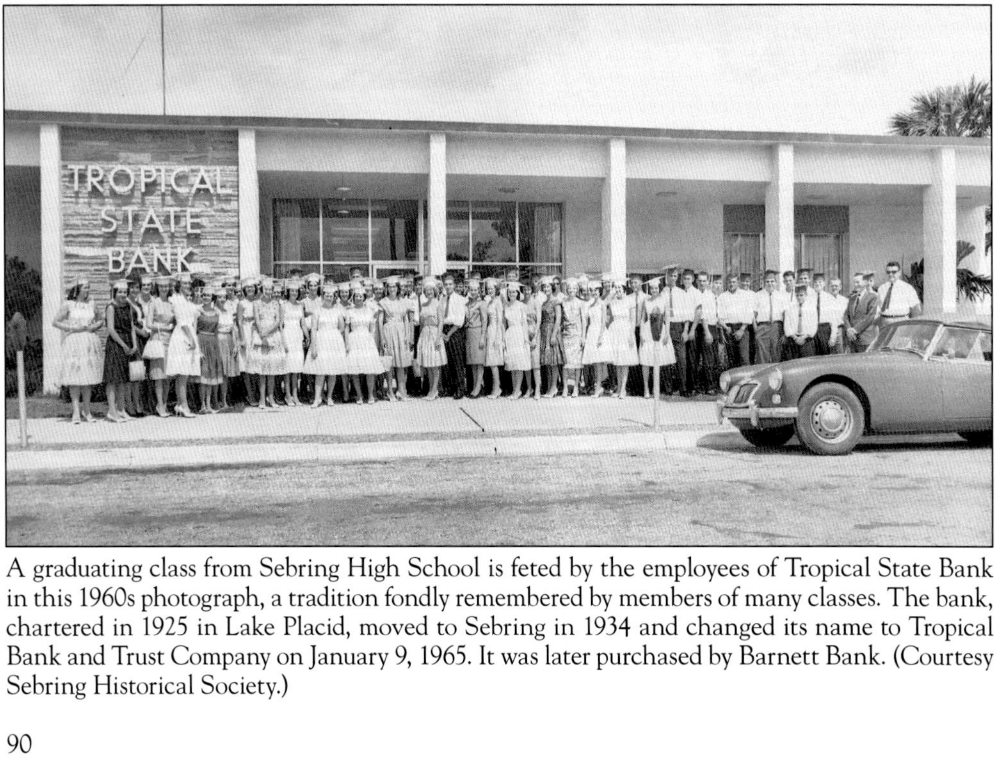

A graduating class from Sebring High School is feted by the employees of Tropical State Bank in this 1960s photograph, a tradition fondly remembered by members of many classes. The bank, chartered in 1925 in Lake Placid, moved to Sebring in 1934 and changed its name to Tropical Bank and Trust Company on January 9, 1965. It was later purchased by Barnett Bank. (Courtesy Sebring Historical Society.)

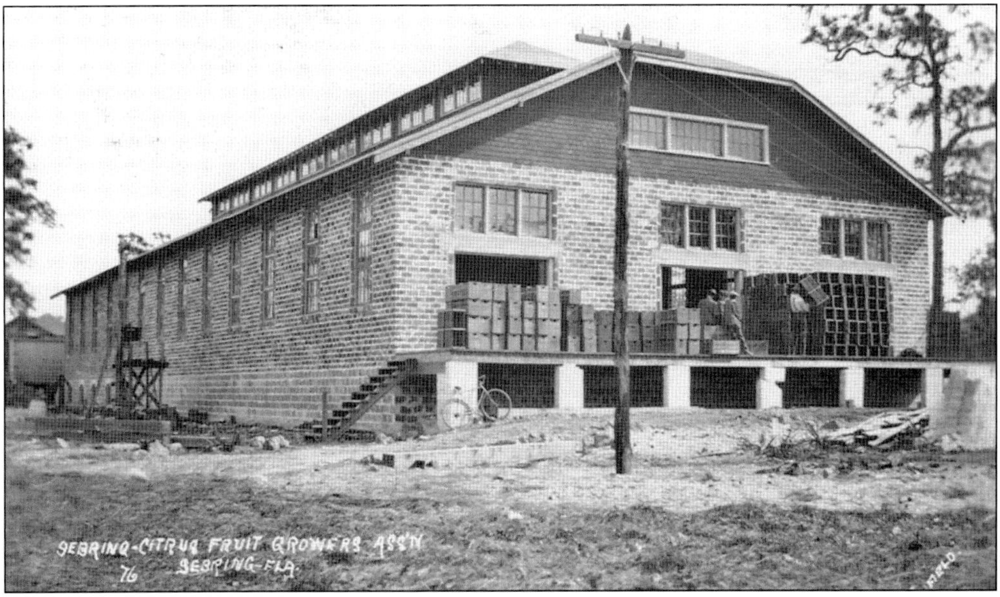

Established in 1918, the cooperative Sebring Citrus Fruit Growers Association packinghouse was integral to the local citrus industry. Sebring was surrounded by groves, and eventually Highlands County was to become the center of the state's citrus industry. The plant burned in October 1923 with damages estimated at $75,000. (Photograph by Field, courtesy Sebring Historical Society.)

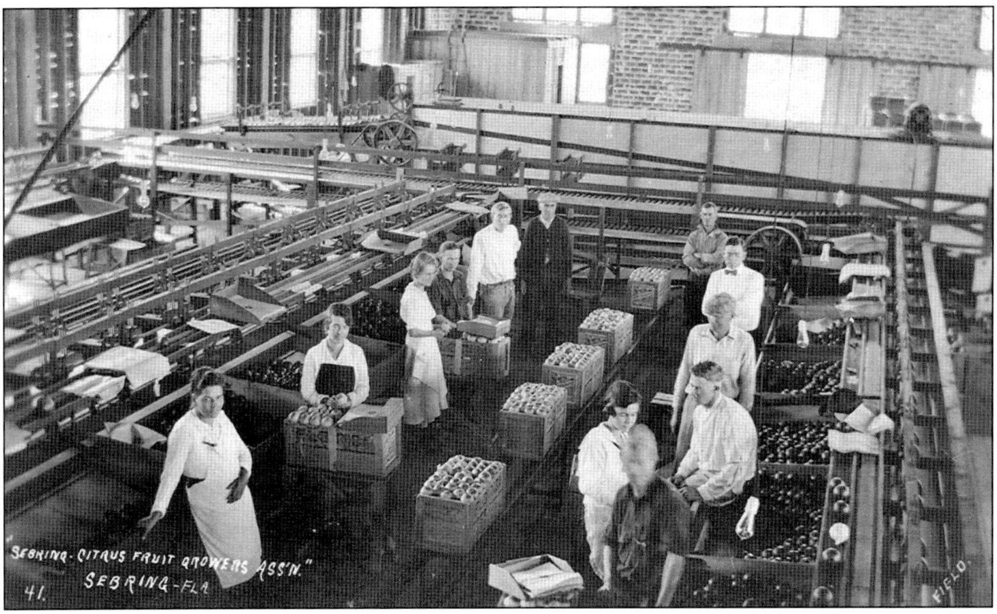

The interior of the Sebring Citrus Fruit Growers Association packinghouse was the scene of this c. 1920 photograph. Incoming fruit was sorted by size and quality, and the best were individually wrapped in printed tissue paper. Colorful citrus crate labels were promotional and informative, indicating the origin and quality of the citrus. The Sebring Sealdsweet brand label featured an illustration of Kenilworth Lodge. (Photograph by Field, courtesy Sebring Historical Society.)

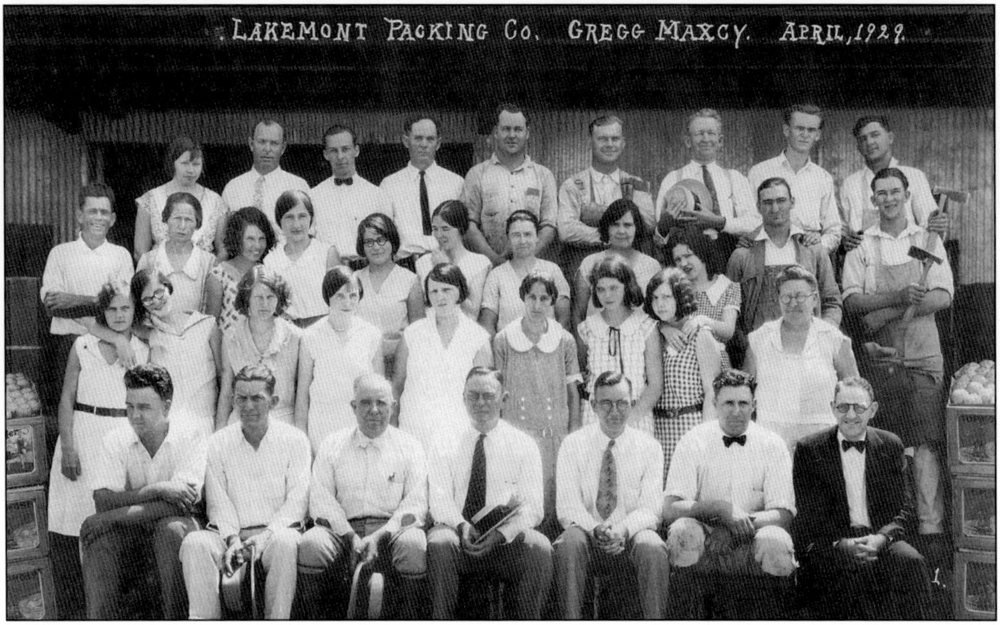

Employees from the Lakemont Packing Company are shown in April 1929. Gregg Maxcy, a member of a prominent central Florida citrus family, owned the company. In 1932, Lakemont packaged fruit under the Perfect Number 7 label. A label used by both Lakemont and the Sebring Citrus Growers was Speed brand. Gregg Maxcy also sold fruit under the Ladye and Leader brands. (Courtesy Sebring Historical Society.)

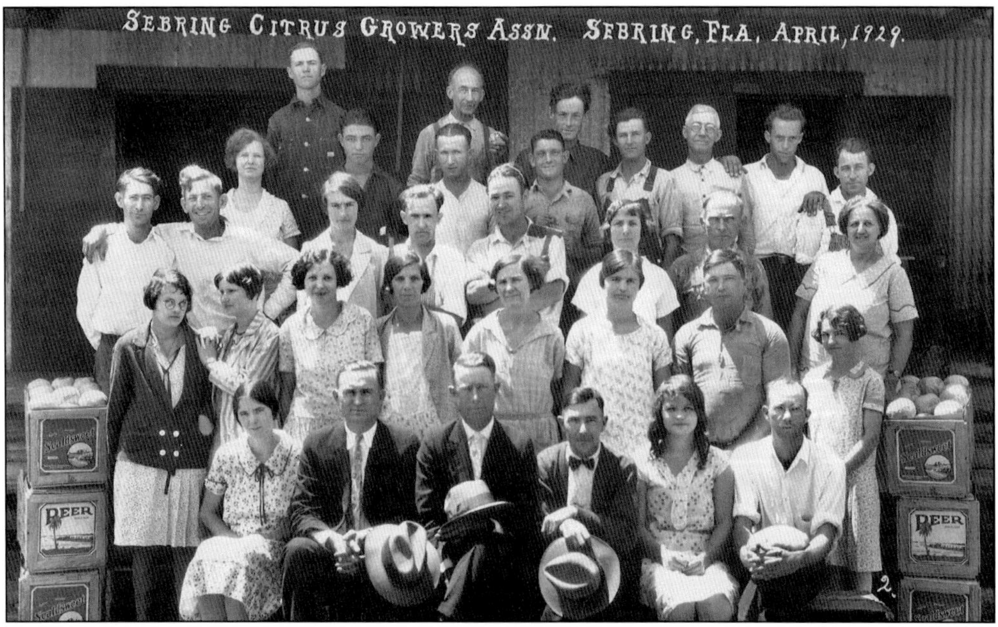

This image shows members of the Sebring Citrus Fruit Growers Association in April 1929, which at this time was affiliated with Gregg Maxcy. In *The Seventy-Five Years of Sebring*, Tim Hurner wrote that "Citrus has been the premier agricultural crop in Highlands County. The acreage has almost doubled over the past twenty five years, with most of that increase coming in the sixties and early seventies." (Courtesy Sebring Historical Society.)

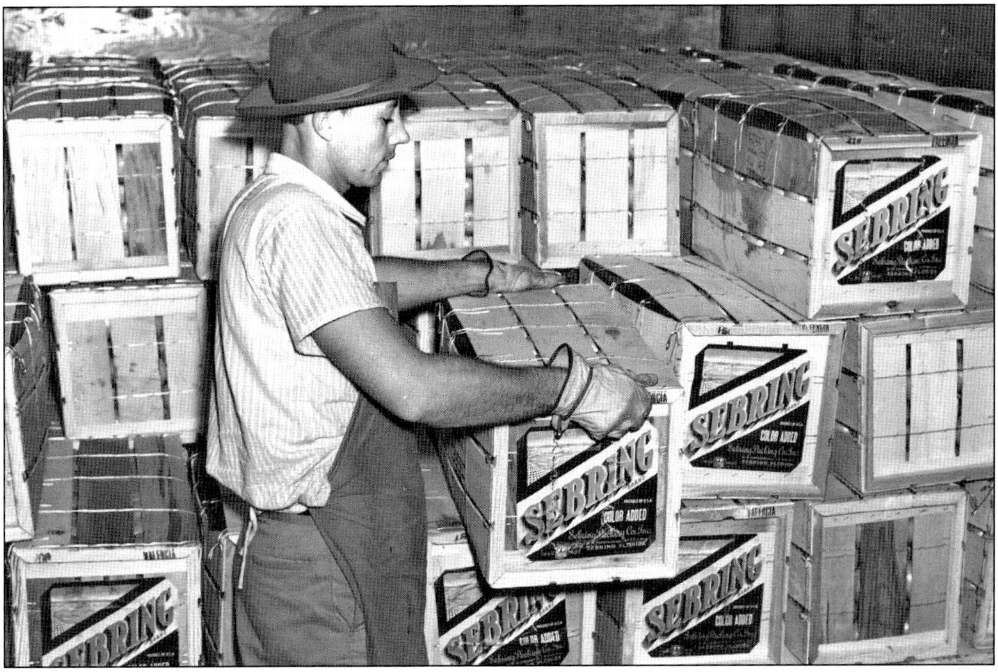

Payne M. Sebring and Leland Keck organized the Sebring Packing Company in 1942, the same year the Florida Citrus Exchange closed the Sebring Fruit Growers Association cooperative, which had been in operation since 1918. The new company, headquartered on Pear Street, provided a stable outlet for local growers to market their fruit. This photograph shows boxes of Valencia oranges stacked for shipping. (Courtesy Sebring Historical Society.)

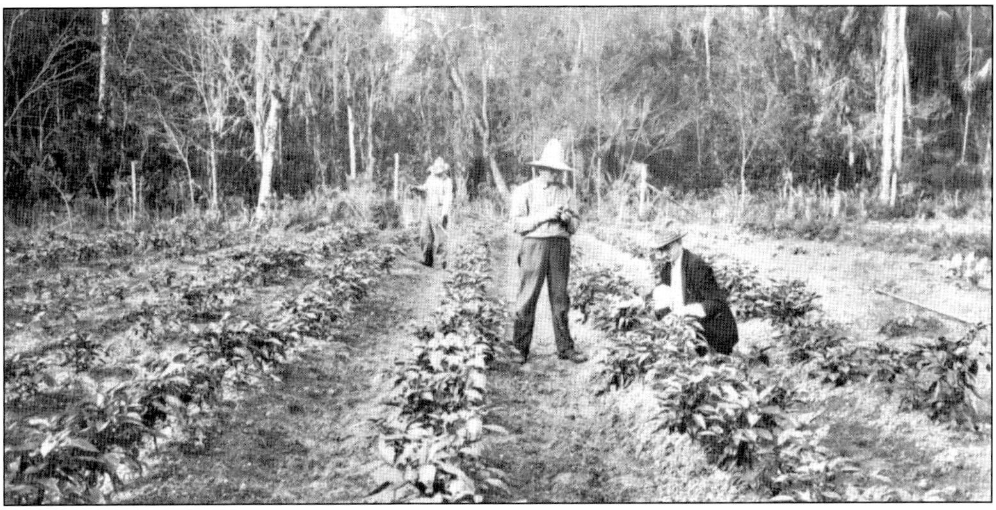

Citrus was not the only agricultural product grown in Highlands County. The wide variety of produce included avocados, cabbage, caladiums, celery, Easter lilies, peppers, pineapples, tomatoes, winter beans, and many more. This December 16, 1926, view shows Jesse Vaughn (center) in his pepper patch with Louis Alsmeyer (right), Highlands County's agricultural agent from 1926 to 1944. Alsmeyer also managed an agricultural fair near Lakemont with A. L. Butler in the 1920s. (Courtesy Sebring Historical Society.)

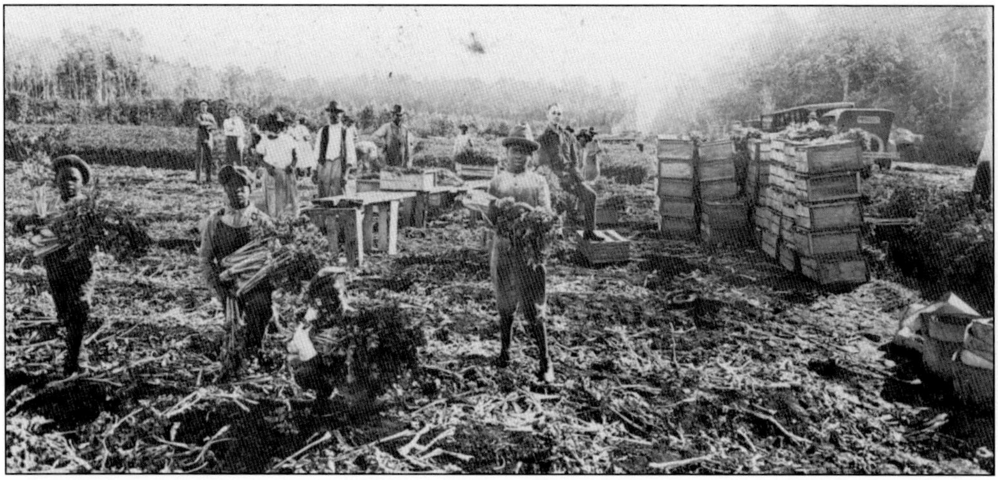

A celery farm crew pauses for a photograph in the 1920s near Sebring. In the 1930s, Rex Beach operated a celery farm, one of his many agricultural interests. The gladiola and Easter lily farm he and his wife, Edith Greta Crater Beach, owned was especially profitable, earning an estimated $1 million. (Courtesy Sebring Historical Society.)

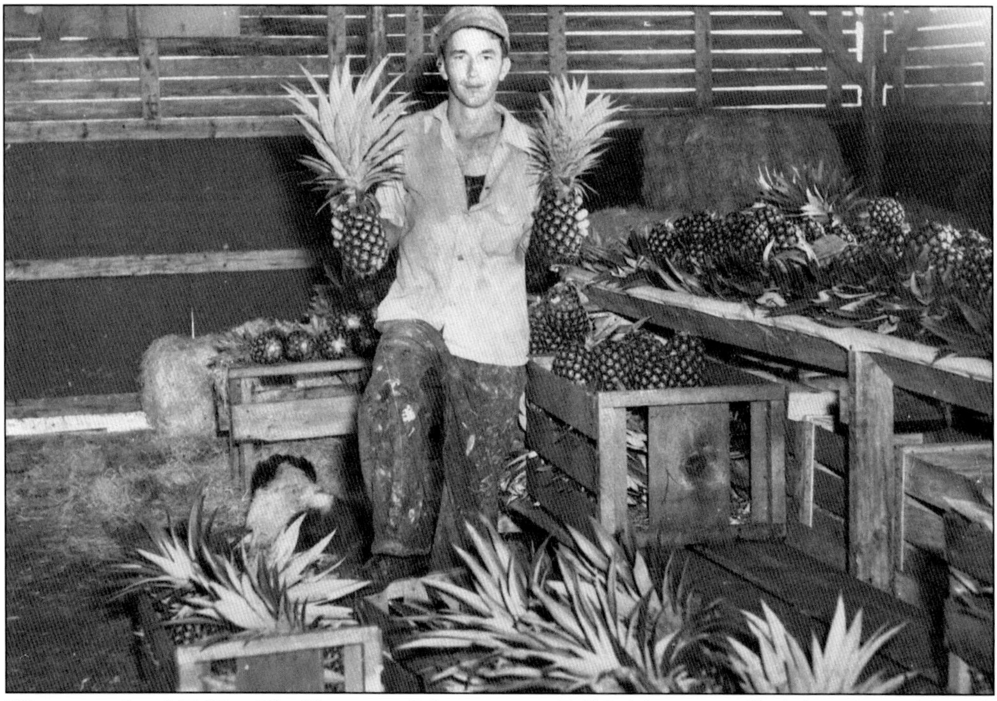

Writing in April 2007 in *The Historian*, Sebring native Bill Schlosser recalled that the Radebaugh pineapple farm was "about where Alan Jay Chevrolet is today. Then a little south of that was Grotewold Pineapple field." According to Allen C. Altvater, "one of the Gearing boys had a lot on North Lakeview planted solidly in pineapples and on all four sides, signs, complete with skull and crossed bones, warned 'These pineapples are poison.' " (Courtesy Sebring Historical Society.)

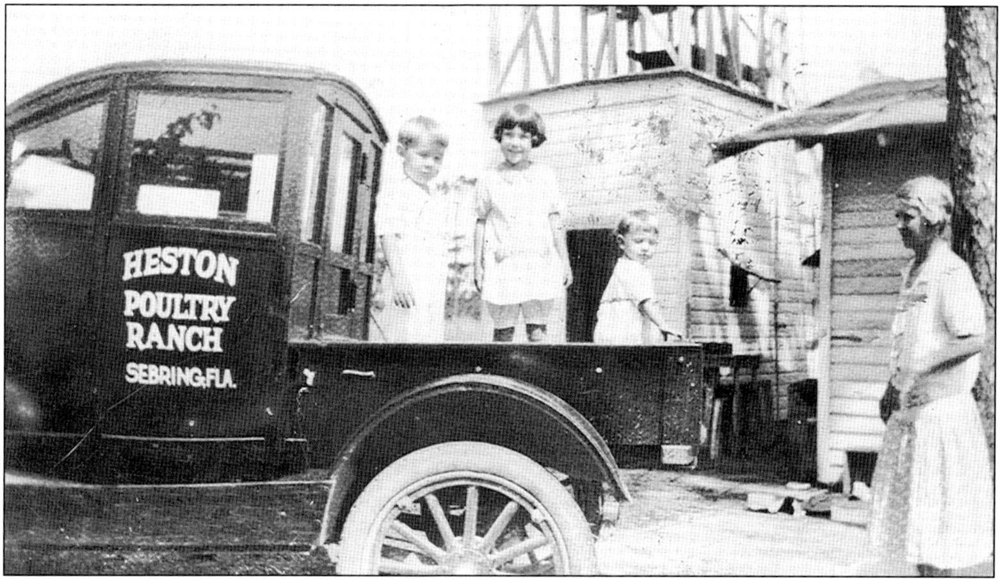

In 1927, the Heston Poultry Ranch truck was full of young helpers. As early as 1936, the South Florida Motor Company supplied heavy-duty farm equipment to the Sebring area, including tractors, harrows, sprayers, and irrigation equipment. The company was owned by Smith J. Rudasill and his son Smith Jr., who served many terms as mayor. (Courtesy Sebring Historical Society.)

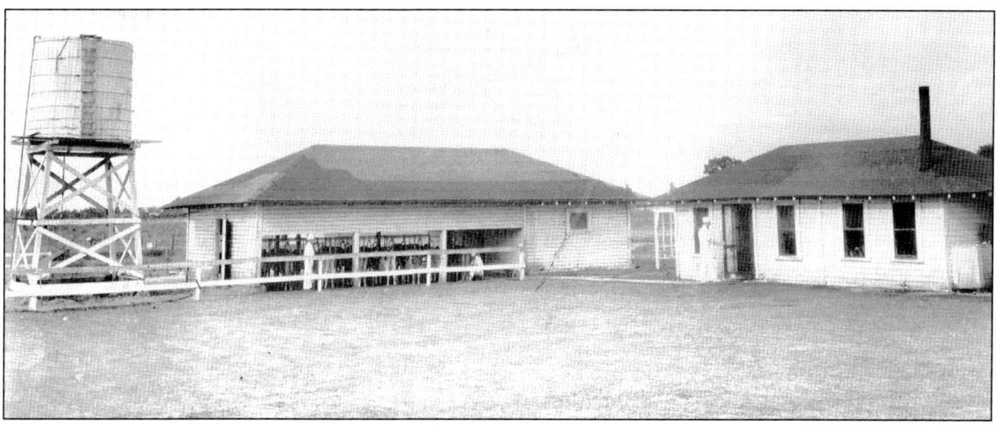
This photograph shows Oscar Spivey's Kenilworth Dairy, located close to present-day Villa Road on the east side of Lake Jackson. According to the Greater Sebring Chamber of Commerce, over 60 percent of present-day Highlands County lands are used for cattle grazing, a total of some 425,000 acres. Annual gross sales exceed $31 million. (Photograph by E. G. Burton and Son, courtesy Sebring Historical Society.)

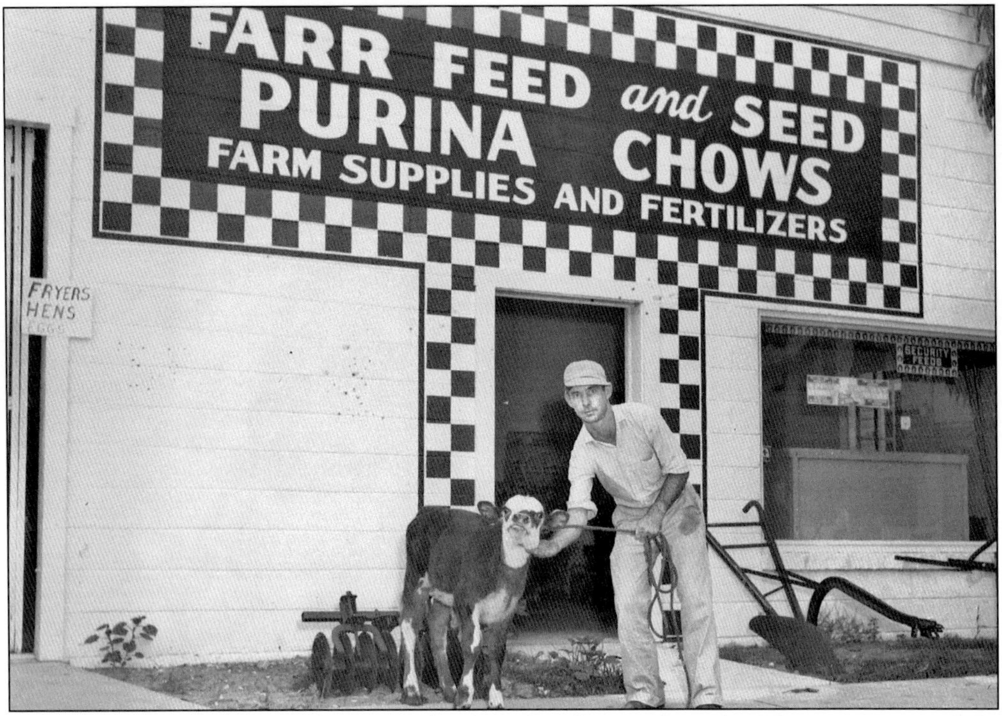

Owner Ted Farr is shown outside Farr Feed and Seed, perhaps in the 1950s. The store supported the local agricultural community, including crop farming and the livestock trade. It sold fryers, hens, and eggs, and advertised Security Feeds poultry feed, manufactured by a company in Knoxville, Tennessee. The Sebring Feed Store was located on South Commerce Avenue and was established in 1940. (Photograph by Ted Shoemaker, courtesy Sebring Historical Society.)

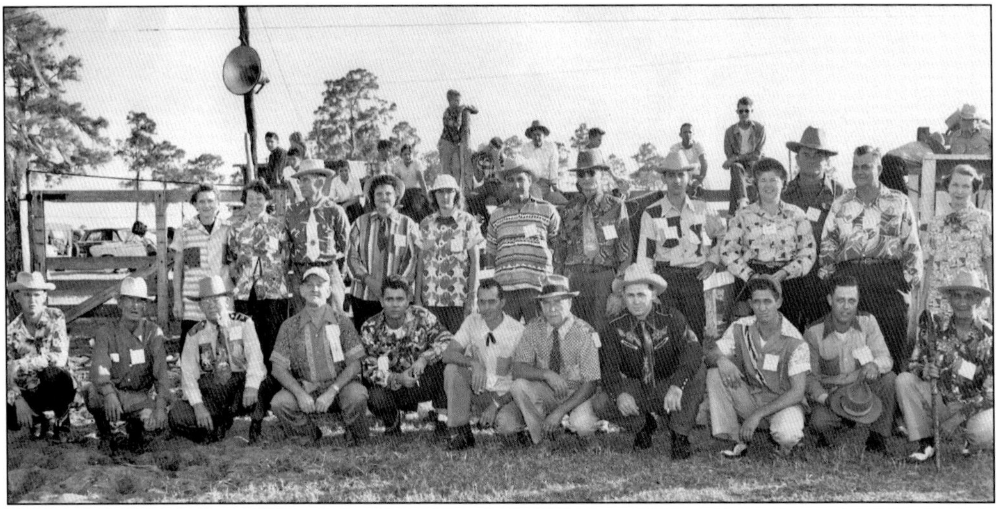

The 1951 Highlands County Cattlemen Association Round-Up was a big event. Attendees included, from left to right, (first row) B. Waggaman, ? Stokes, G. V. Hudson, P. G. Gearing, A. Munson, three unidentified, J. McKenzie, and two unidentified; (second row) unidentified, Maebelle Abney, Broward Coker, two unidentified, E. H. Norris, unidentified, Bucky Kahn, Dot Sauls, Jimmy Creel, Fisher Sauls, and unidentified. B. G. Collier is in the far upper right. (Photograph by Ted Shoemaker, courtesy Sebring Historical Society.)

Seven

Recreation

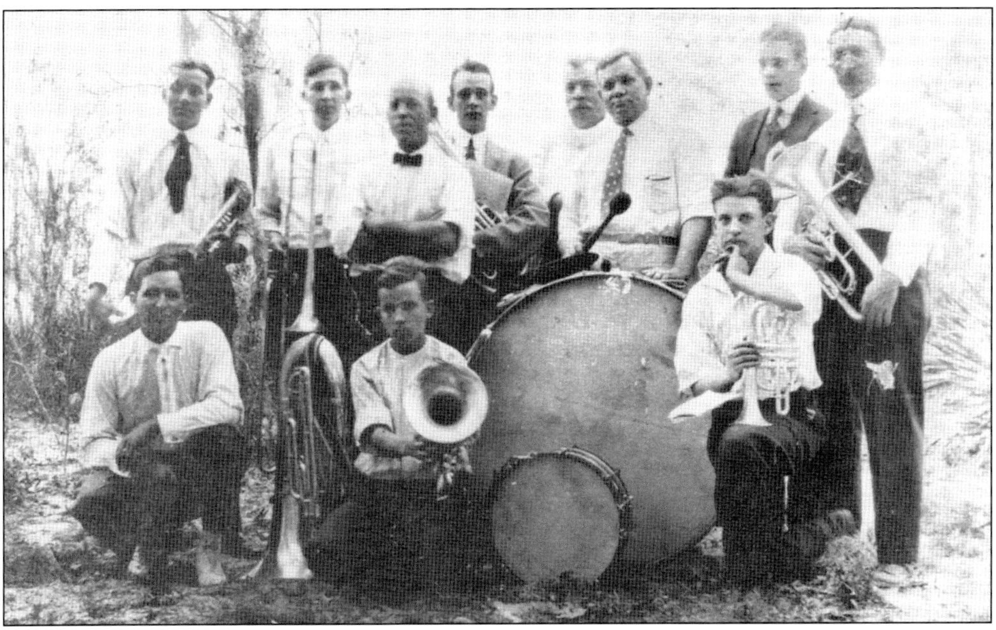

Sebring's first town band is seen here in around 1912. Pictured from left to right are (first row) A. I. Young, Paul Pollard, and George Whitehouse; (second row) Guy Ruhl, Walter Zachary, Ben Pollard, Ray Gearing, George Crump, G. A. Rule, Herbert Gearing, and Tommy Whitehouse Sr. Allen C. Altvater reported that a Mr. Kuhlman brought the first violin to Sebring, and it could be heard nightly with guitar accompaniment nearly half a mile from his home. (Courtesy Sebring Historical Society.)

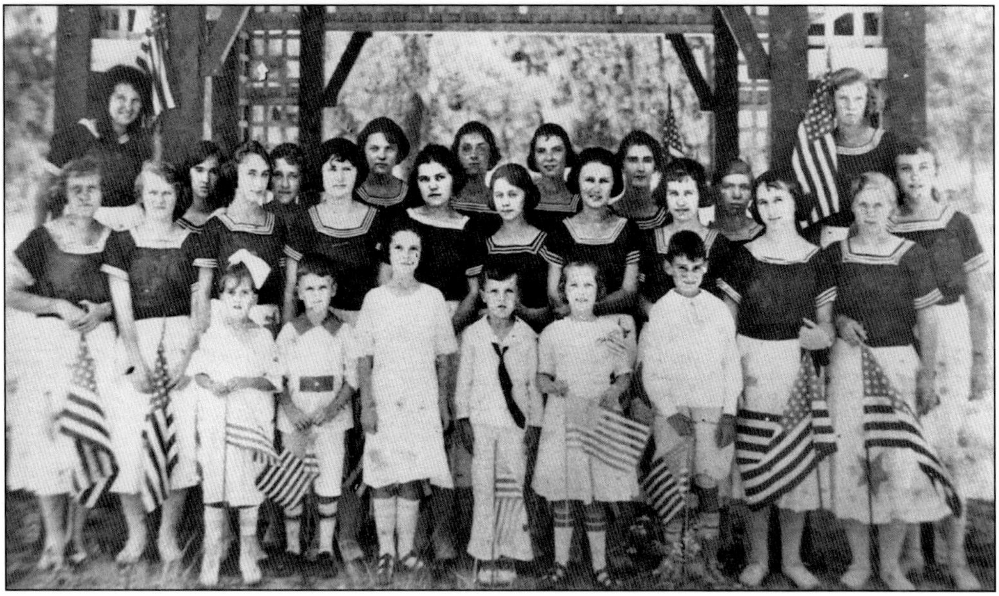

The Rah-Rah Girls (and boys) gathered for the 1921 Fourth of July festivities in Tuscawilla Park. Pictured are (first row) Mary Beth Heacock, Bobby McClure, Eva Butts, Austie Heacock, "Toddy" Butts, John Lake Bogle, "Sunny" Saunders, and Martha Swank; (second row) Mary Estes, Ruth Swank, Anna Bogle, Leona Whitehouse, Ellen Heacock, "Martee" Saunders, Charlotte Varena, Helen Moyer, and Ava Leatherman. Among those in the third row were Emma Whitehouse, Emelie Auslund, Rose Graham, Gerelda Whitehouse, Elizabeth Harbaugh, Anna Ausland, Mary Swank, and Marjorie Michner. (Courtesy Sebring Historical Society.)

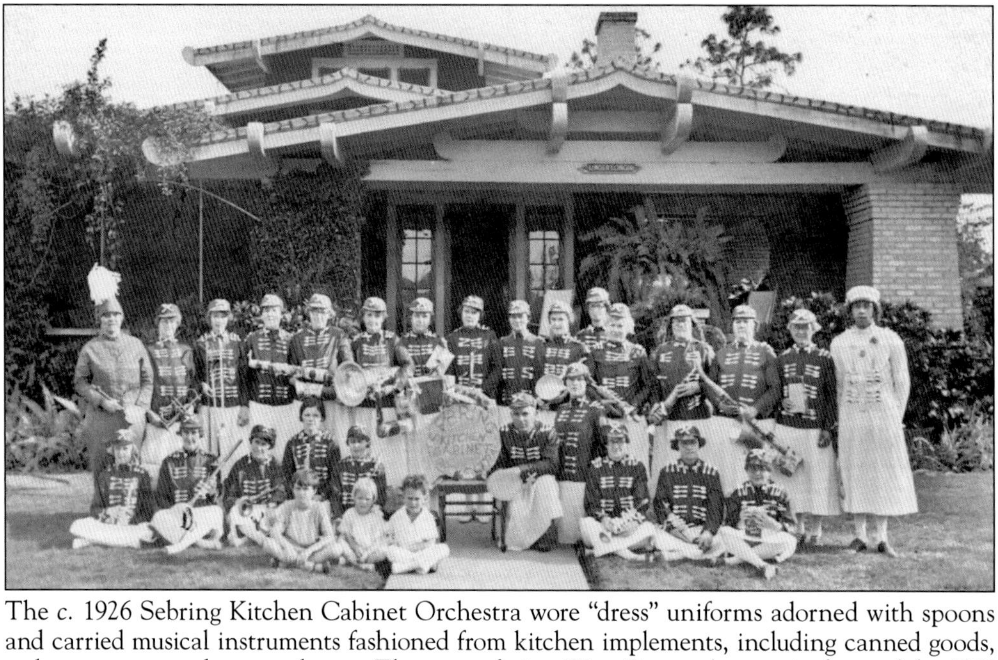

The c. 1926 Sebring Kitchen Cabinet Orchestra wore "dress" uniforms adorned with spoons and carried musical instruments fashioned from kitchen implements, including canned goods, a cheese grater, and pots and pans. They were facing West Center Avenue in front of the 1917 Edward L. Hainz house, also shown on page 41. Orchestra leader Lyall E. Wortman is at far right next to his mother, Ora Etta Wortman. (Courtesy Sebring Historical Society.)

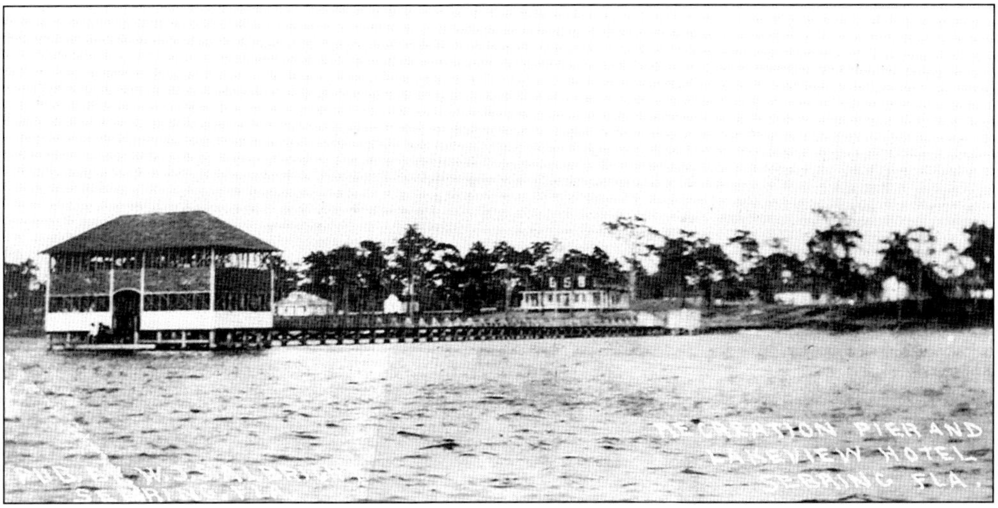

The 1912 municipal pier was one of the Sebring Real Estate Company's first major public works projects. Located at the end of West Center Avenue, the 300-foot pier featured a two-level pavilion and swimming and boating areas. The hotel identified in this Sewell Albright photograph as the Lakeview Hotel was better known as the Arrowhead Hotel. The Henning House and the Chamberlain cottage are also visible. (Courtesy Sebring Historical Society.)

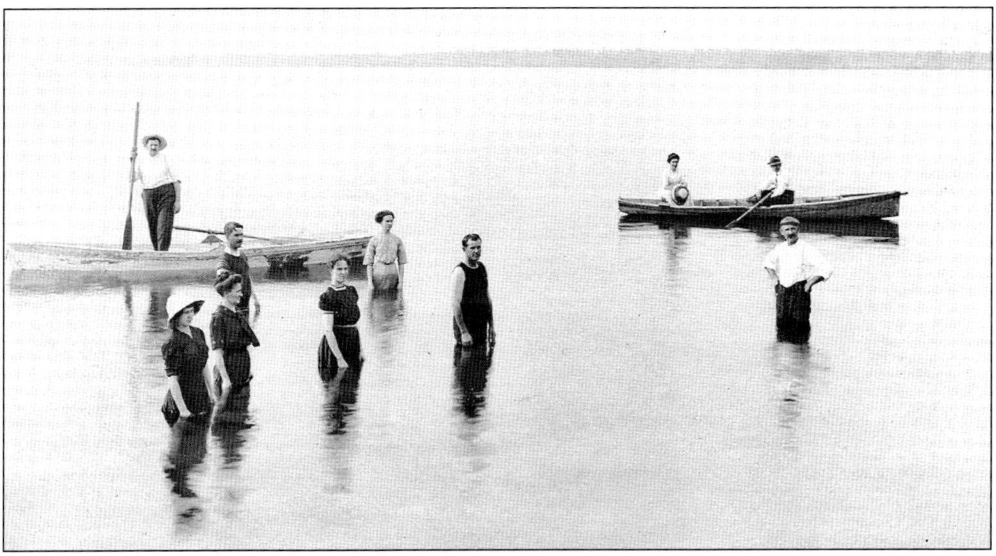

Pioneer settlers took a dip in Lake Jackson near the new municipal pier on January 25, 1912. Those identified include, Annie Riley (fifth from left), Aaron Withers (seventh from left), and George E. Sebring (standing, tenth from left). Lake Jackson is more than 3,400 acres in size and for a time was renamed Rex Beach Lake in honor of the late local author; the name did not stick. (Courtesy Sebring Historical Society.)

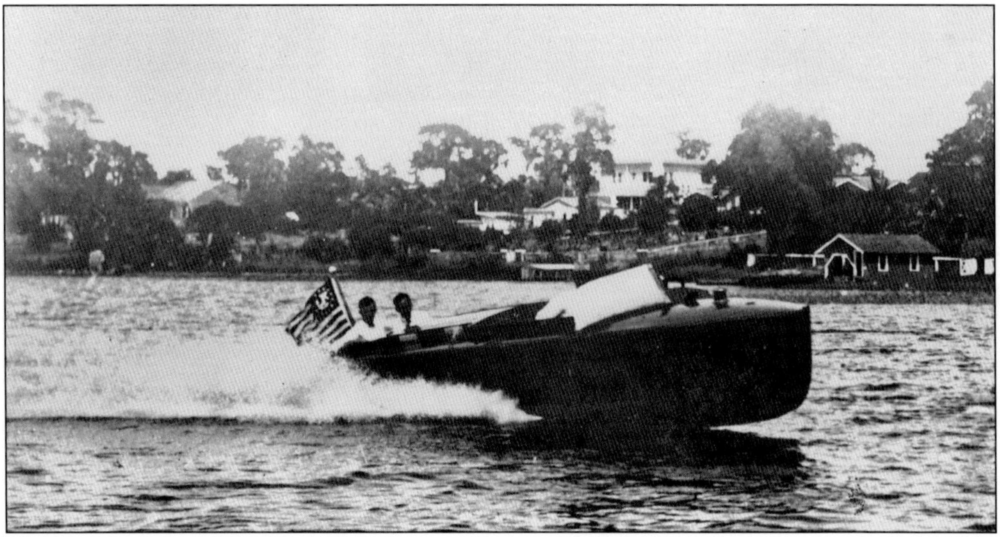

Seen in an early view is Dan Andrews's speedboat along what appears to be the east shore of Lake Jackson. Andrews was a versatile musician, able to play the piano, trumpet, banjo, and more. Little Lake Jackson, at 137 acres, is accessible through a short canal at the south end of Lake Jackson. Harder Hall stands on the north shore of this smaller body of water. (Courtesy Sebring Historical Society.)

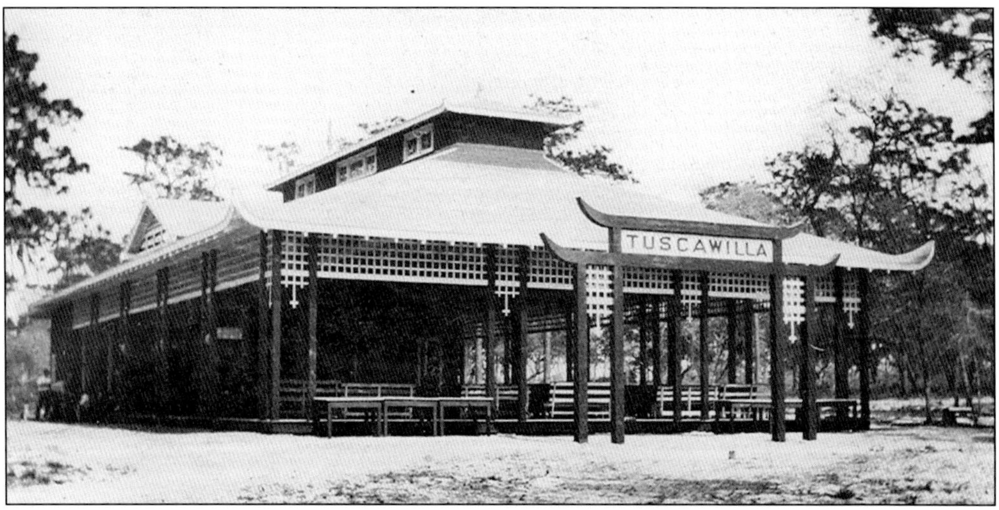

Tuscawilla Park was a city block donated by the Sebring family for a public recreational and meeting venue. In 1921, the city built an open-air pavilion here, which according to *The Way It Was in Early Sebring History*, was the site of "high school plays, study group classes, graduation exercises, basketball games, piano recitals, church services, political rallies," and other events until it was destroyed by fire in 1940. The site is presently occupied by city hall. (Courtesy Sebring Historical Society.)

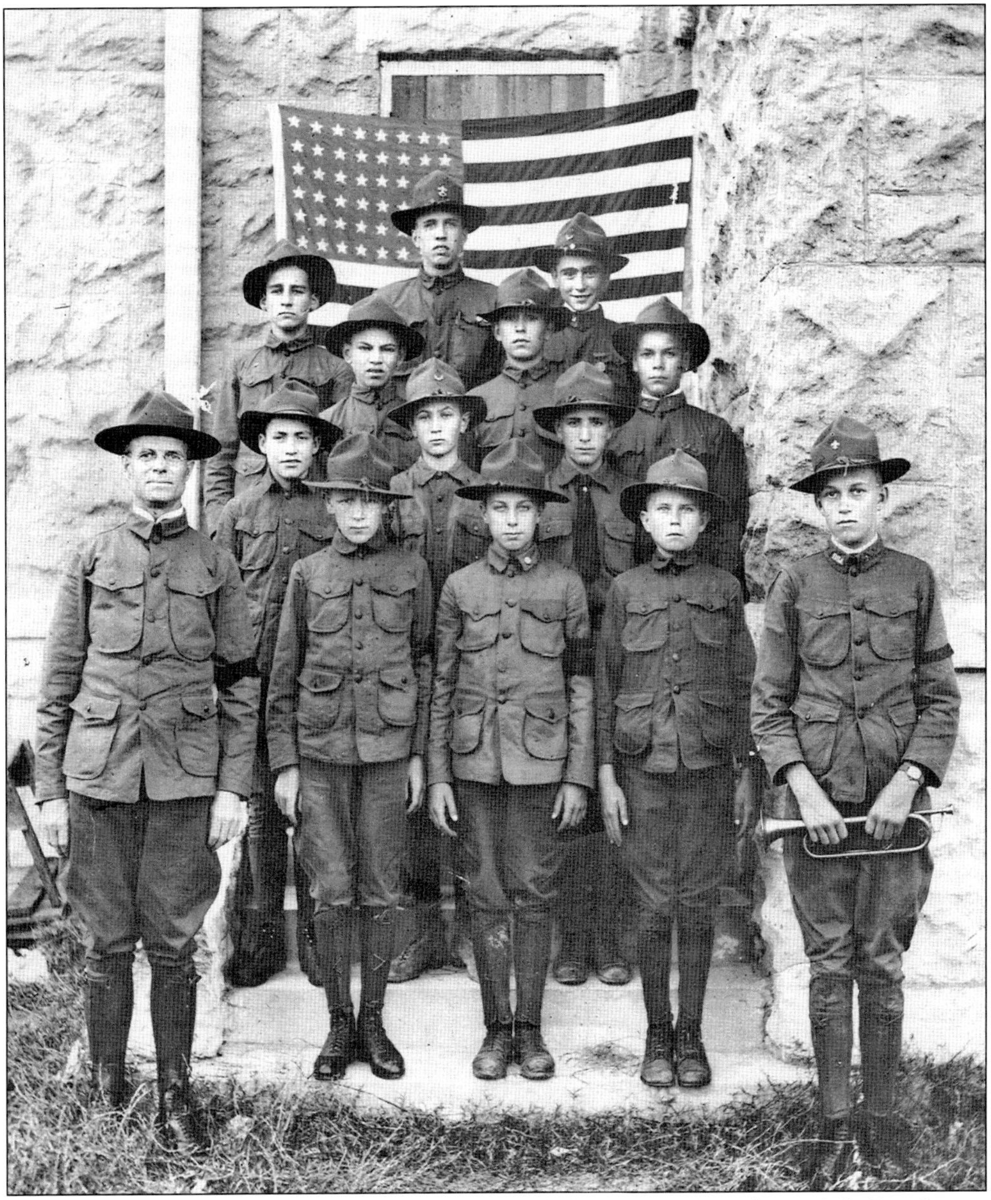

Boy Scout Troop No. 1 is shown in this photograph from 1916. As early as 1918, Boy Scouts were involved with volunteer firefighting drills, two years before other local drills were initiated. Among the members identified are Alfred Verona, Gerald Bee, Elbert Collier, Harris Muff, Floyd Schumacher, Jimmy Etheridge, Clagett Taylor, and H. Orvel Sebring Jr., with Payne Sebring holding a bugle at far right. This was likely taken at the First Methodist Church building, which was constructed that year; another period photograph in the Sebring Historical Society collection shows Boy Scouts standing along South Pine Street adjacent to the Methodist Church. Gerald Bee, Harris Muff, H. Orvel Sebring Jr., and Floyd Schumacher were later members of Sebring High School's first basketball team in 1921. Other team members were Ford Heacock, David Lane, Lloyd Leopold, Guy Miller, George Swank, and John Warren, with principal Homer Wakefield as coach. (Courtesy Sebring Historical Society.)

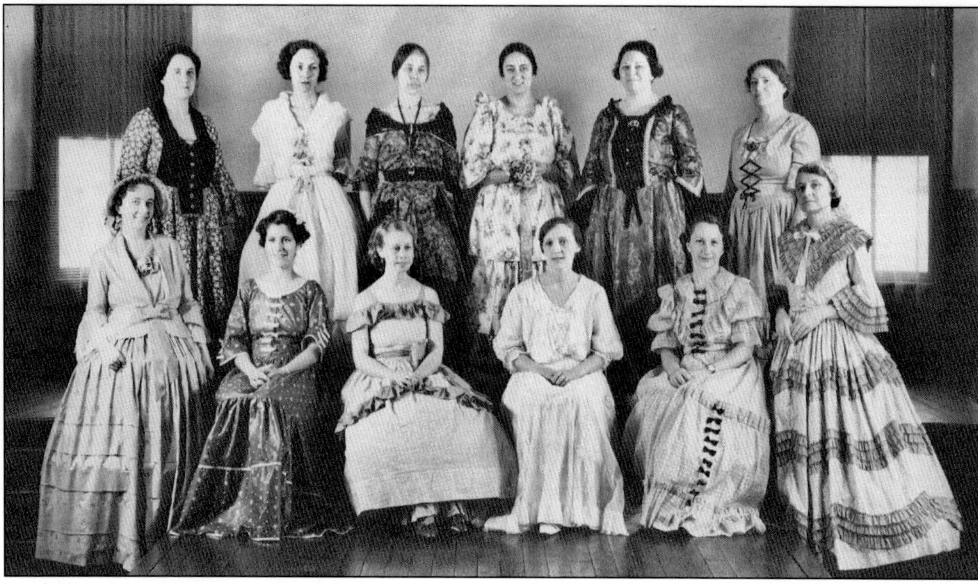

Members of the Staff and Book Club, which was organized on December 4, 1931, modeled early American finery in this *c.* 1930s photograph. Pictured from left to right are (first row) Theon Sebring, Faith Parker, Martee Heacock, Ruth Sebring, Sunny Weaver, and Jennie Gustat; (second row) Mary Frances Percy (organizer and first president), Charlotte Naylor, Anna Laurie Taylor, Maxine Martin, Vail Weems, and Peggy Laxton. (Courtesy Sebring Historical Society.)

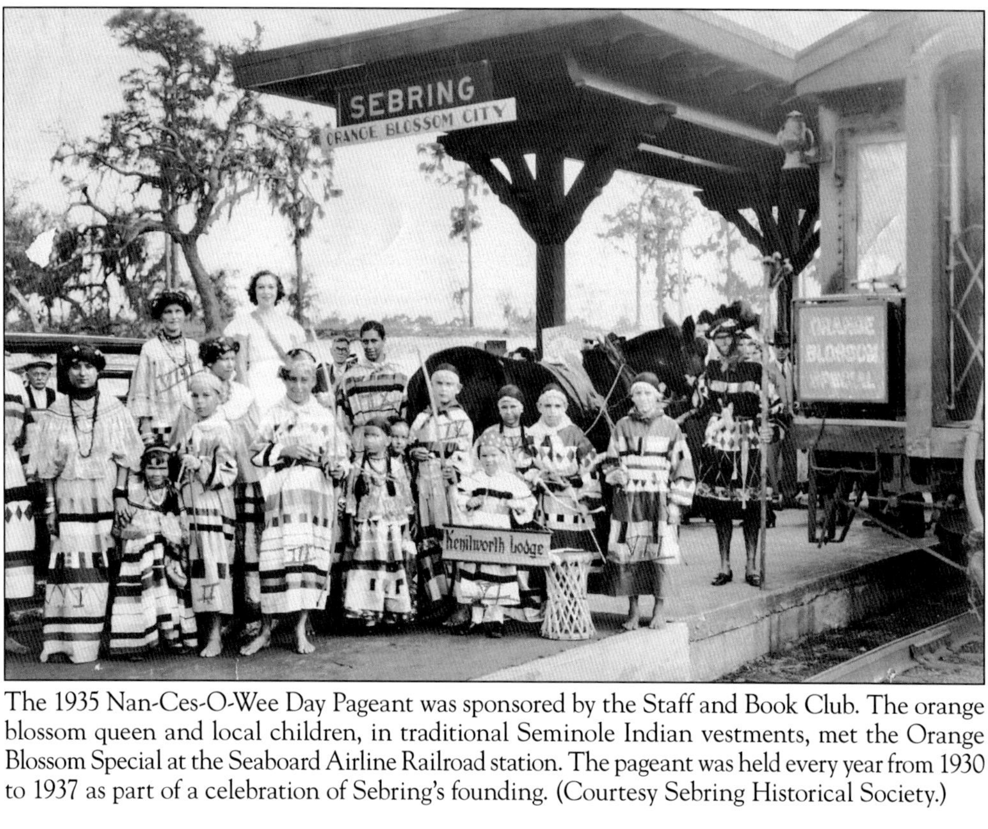

The 1935 Nan-Ces-O-Wee Day Pageant was sponsored by the Staff and Book Club. The orange blossom queen and local children, in traditional Seminole Indian vestments, met the Orange Blossom Special at the Seaboard Airline Railroad station. The pageant was held every year from 1930 to 1937 as part of a celebration of Sebring's founding. (Courtesy Sebring Historical Society.)

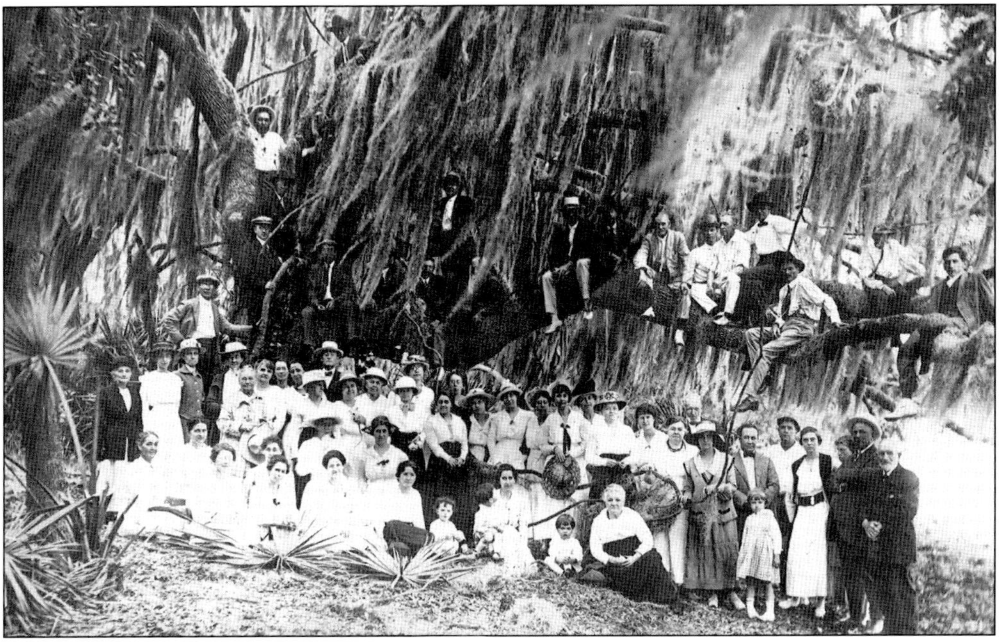

A spectacular Spanish moss–laden oak formed the backdrop for this 1919 Milt Baker photograph of a large fish fry and picnic gathering at Lake Josephine. The lake is actually three connected bodies of water totaling over 1,300 acres in size just south of Sebring at Kuhlman. (Photograph by Milt Baker, courtesy Sebring Historical Society.)

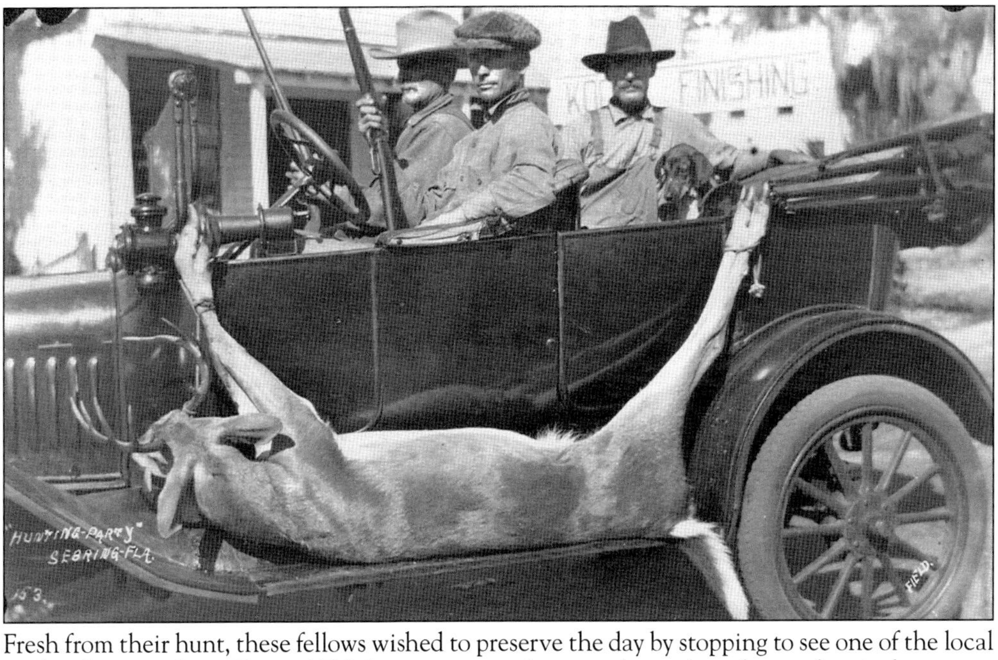

Fresh from their hunt, these fellows wished to preserve the day by stopping to see one of the local studio photographers. This *c.* 1920s hunting party photograph may have been taken in downtown Sebring; a sign for Kodak Finishing can be seen. Little is known about Field, Kugler Photo, or Woodward, but their marvelous photographs tell us much about early Sebring. (Photograph by Field, courtesy Sebring Historical Society.)

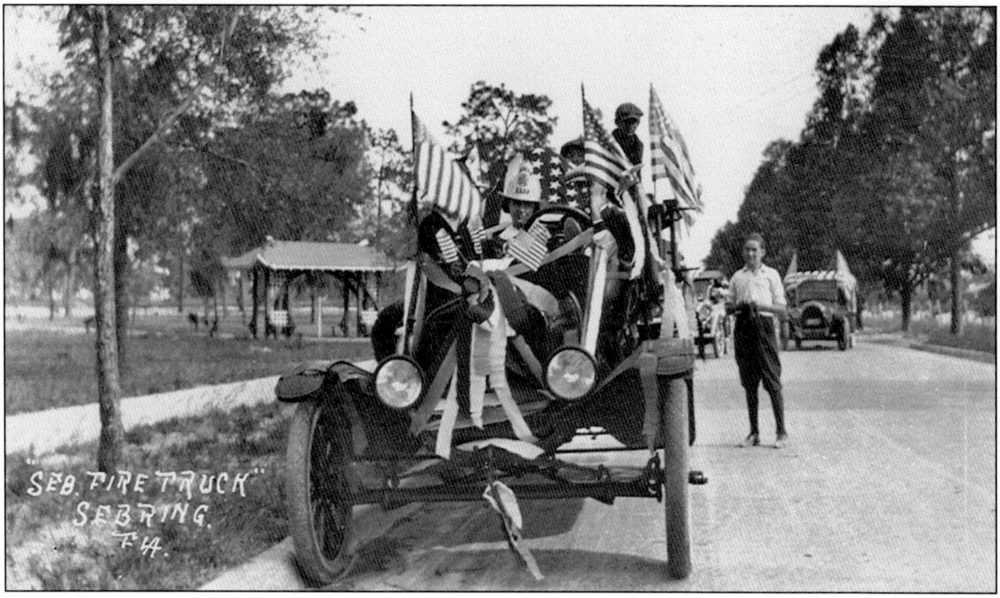

The Sebring Fire Department truck and other vehicles were decorated in a patriotic theme near Tuscawilla Park, in a photograph believed to date from July 4, 1921. On that day, the city turned out for a flag raising on the Circle, a procession to the new park, addresses by area dignitaries, the presentation of the new county flag, and an afternoon baseball game between Frostproof and Sebring. (Photograph by Field, courtesy Sebring Historical Society.)

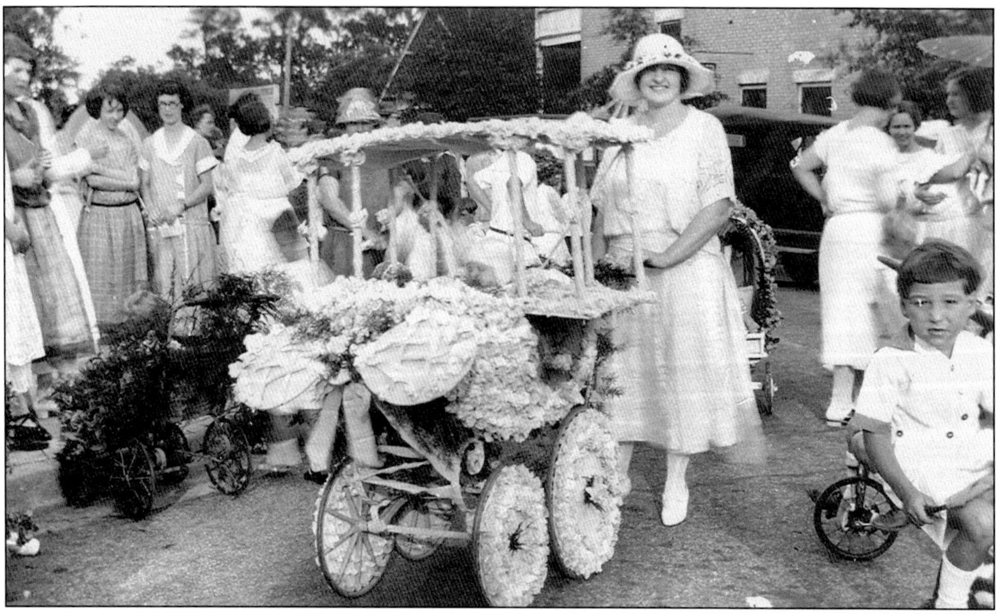

Sebring's inaugural May Day festivities were sponsored by the Woman's Club in 1924. The *Sebring White Way* reported that the "parade of decorated baby carriages, doll carriages, express wagons, sulkies, velocipedes, kiddie cars, and bicycles" was particularly popular. First prize among baby carriages was a tie between those of George E. Sebring III and Gideon George Jaeger Jr., both of which were decorated as airplanes. (Courtesy Sebring Historical Society.)

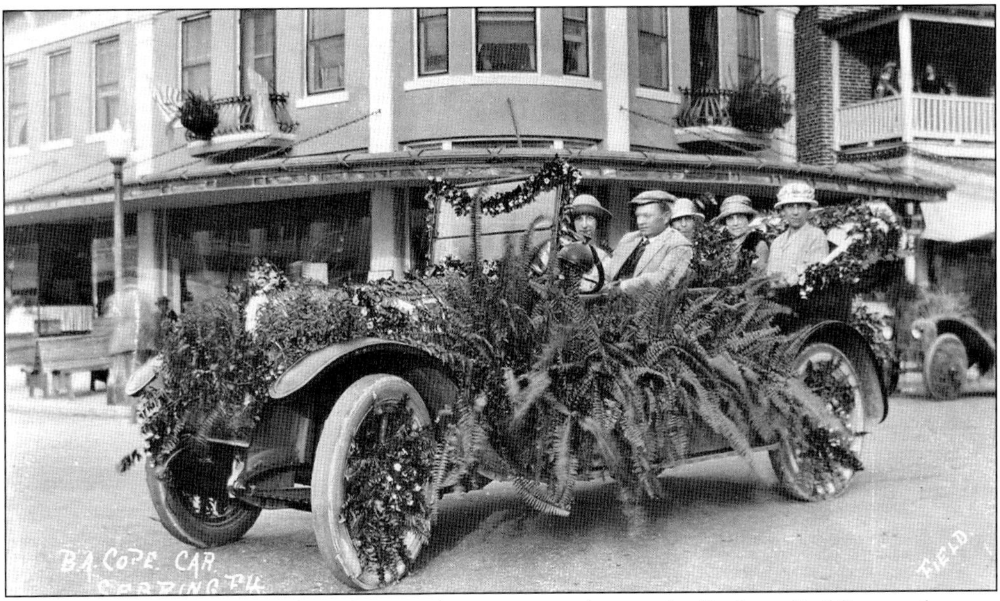

B. A. and Lois Cope drove their decorated car in a parade past the Buckeye Building, perhaps as part of the 1924 May Day festivities. Seated in the back was Eva Sebring Norris, sister of George E. Sebring and mother of Lois Cope. Cope was active in the Epworth League, and on April 27, 1924, she led a discussion entitled "Institutes and What they Are." (Photograph by Field, courtesy Sebring Historical Society.)

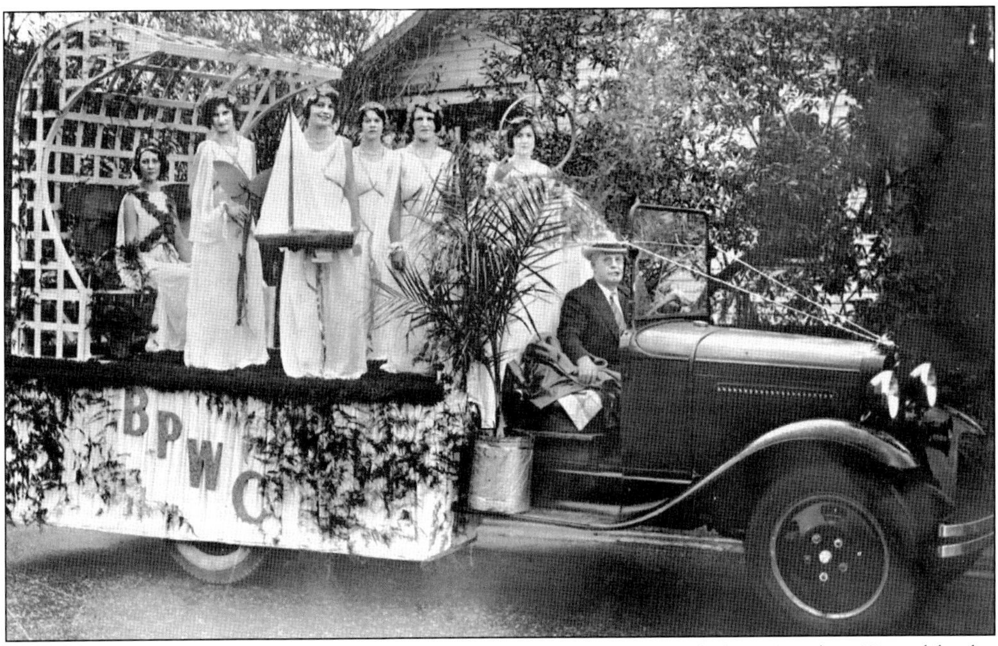

The Sebring Business and Professional Women's Club was founded in April 1927 and had a clubhouse on Oak Avenue across from the Sebring Hotel. The club formed a baseball team—the White Wings—which played against Avon Park that August. This photograph is believed to show the club's 1930 Nan-Ces-O-Wee Day parade float. Nell Hoffman was seated, Helen Hoperich held a model boat, and Ray Paschal was the driver. (Courtesy Sebring Historical Society.)

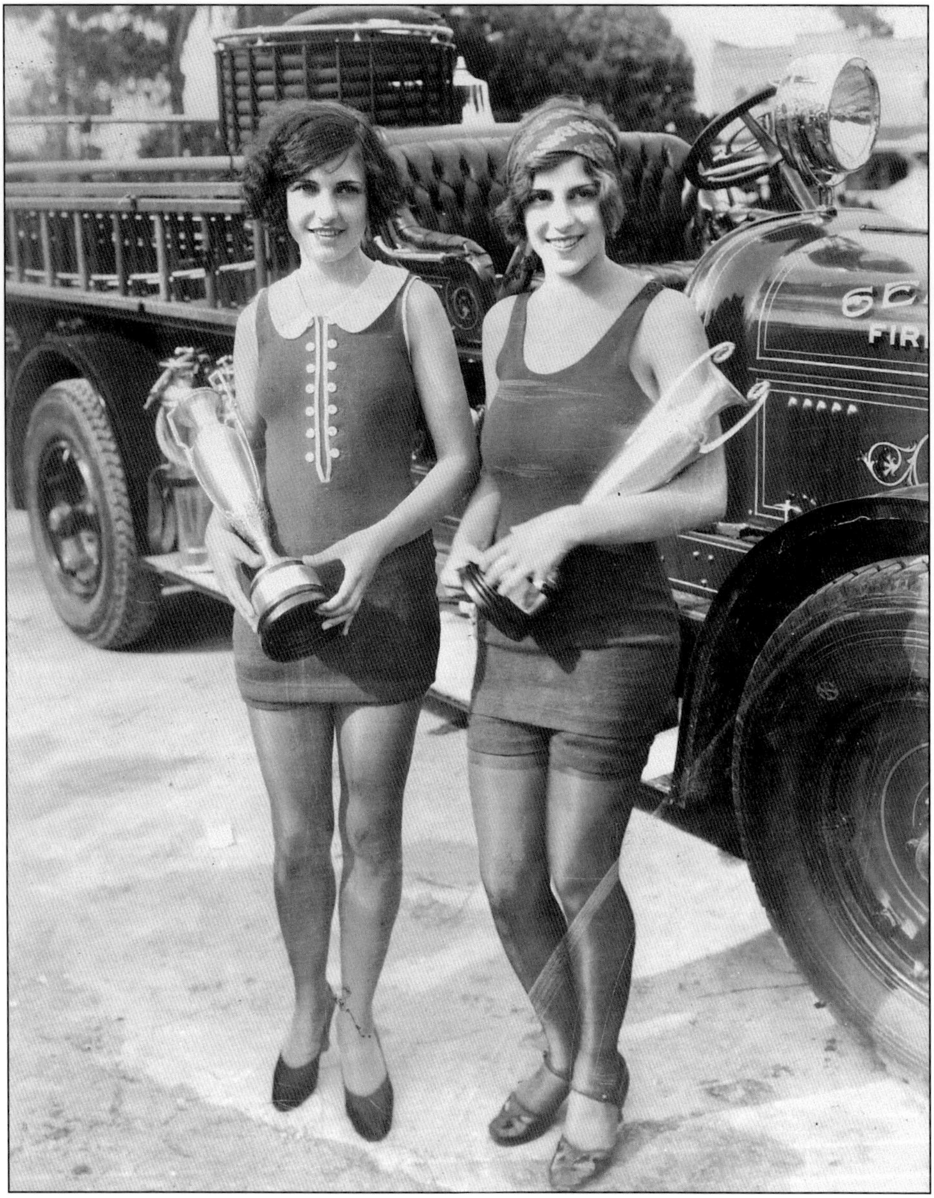

Lois Starbuck (left) and Virginia Woods (right) were participants in the Sebring Fire Department's Miss Flame beauty pageant on July 4, 1926, an event that attracted hundreds of people to Sebring. The fire truck behind the pair was purchased that year. It appears to be in the municipal pier parking lot, approximately where today's public library is located with the Masonic Temple (1921) visible in the distance. In April 2004, Carole Goad wrote about the importance of the department in *The Historian*. "The Sebring Fire Department is legendary in its service to this community. In 1929, Sebring firefighters decided to build an athletic field [Firemen's Field]. For this purpose, they incorporated, forming the Sebring Firemen, Inc. Going into debt, they acquired the present site, which was an abandoned orange grove at the intersection of Kenilworth Boulevard and Highlands Avenue. . . . the High School began using this facility as their athletic field, and have called it home ever since." The Sebring Firemen, Inc., helped establish the Florida Fire College in 1930 and established the Highlands County Fair in 1937. (Courtesy Sebring Historical Society.)

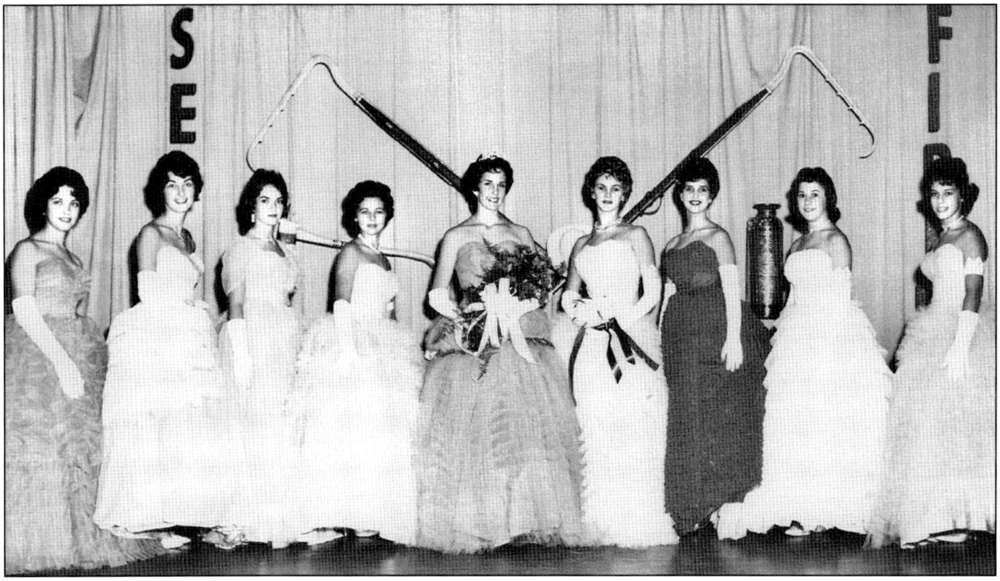

Beverly Carroll, in the center, was Miss Flame in 1962. An impressive display of firefighting tools, including a pair of Pompier ladders, formed the backdrop. These hooked ladders are no longer in use but were utilized by firefighters to scale the outside of buildings one or two floors at a time using windowsills for support. (Courtesy Sebring Historical Society.)

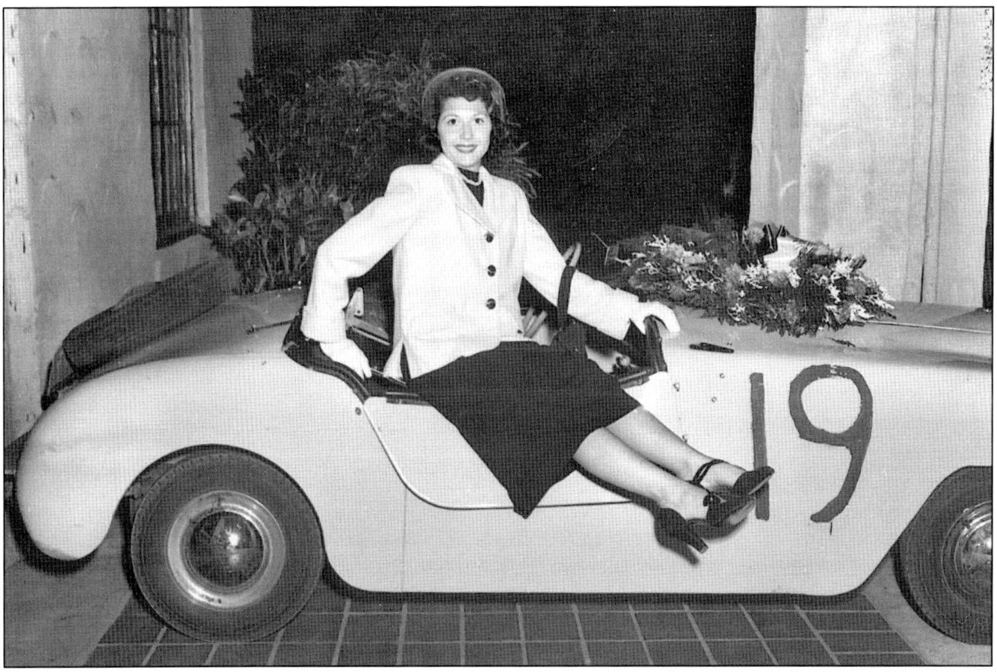

The December 31, 1950, six-hour Sam Collier Memorial race was the inaugural race at the Sebring Airport, followed by an award banquet at Harder Hall. Janice M. Shoemaker is seen on the winning stock Crosley Hot Shot at the hotel entrance. The car was driven by Ralph "Bobby" Deshon and Fritz Koster, and owned by Vic Sharpe. The first 12-hour race was in 1952. (Photograph by Ted Shoemaker, courtesy Sebring Historical Society.)

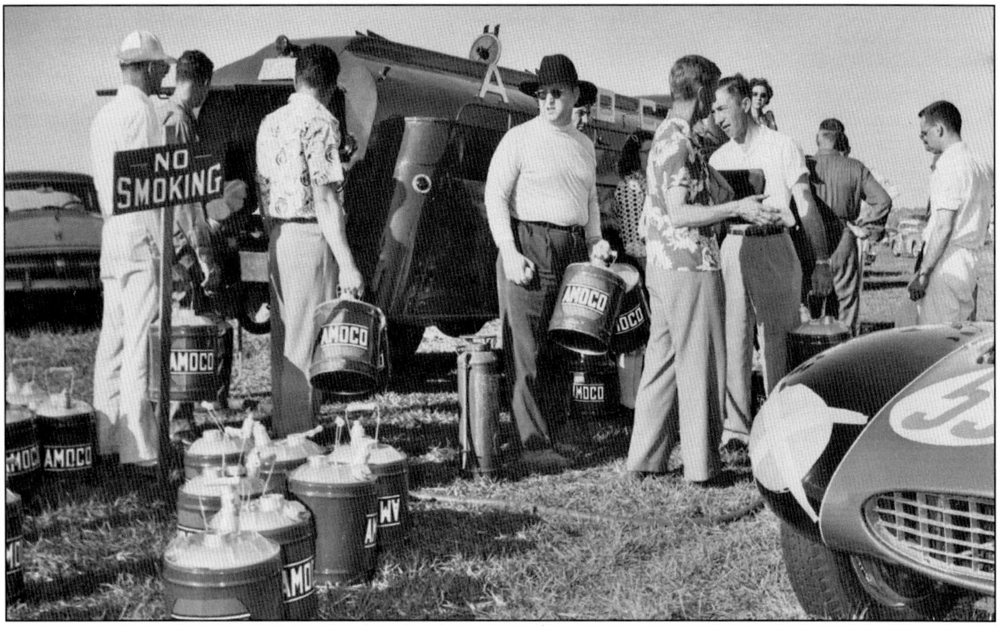

Modern risk managers might cringe at this view, which shows crew members dispensing fuel directly from an Amoco fuel truck into cans in 1955. The fuel was subsequently poured into a washtub, which drained into the race car, allowing more than one can to be emptied at once. No smoking, indeed! The 1955 overall winners were Mike Hawthorn and Phil Walters in a Jaguar. (Photograph by Ted Shoemaker, courtesy Sebring Historical Society.)

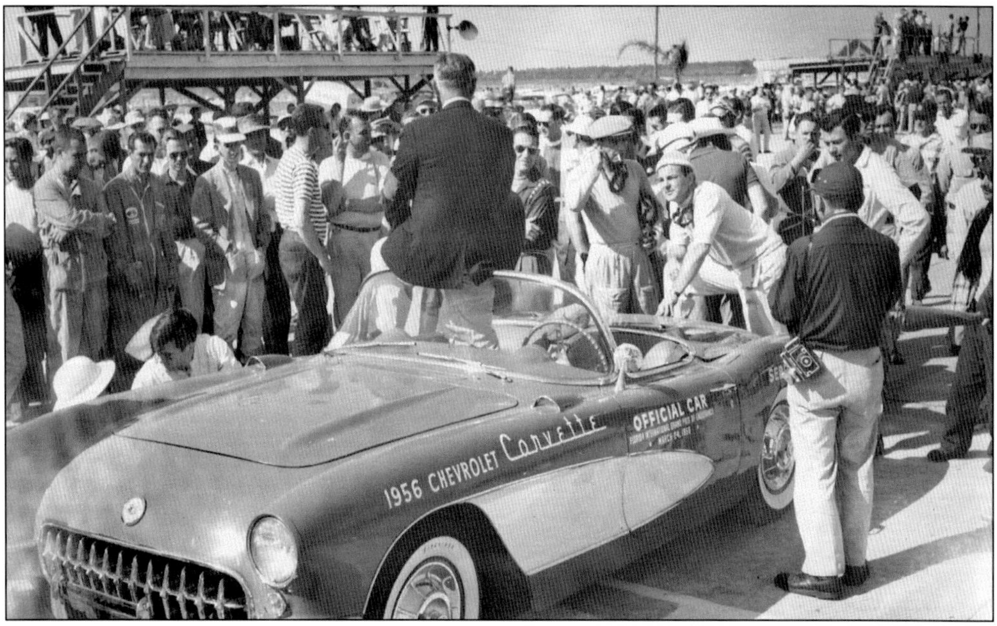

Russian Alec Ulmann was founder of the Twelve Hours of Sebring race. Here he is seen speaking with the drivers prior to the March 24, 1956, race, seated atop a Corvette, the official car of the "Florida International Grand Prix of Endurance." Ulmann, an aeronautical engineer by training, authored *The Sebring Story* in 1969, a history of the race and its drivers. (Photograph by Ted Shoemaker, courtesy Sebring Historical Society.)

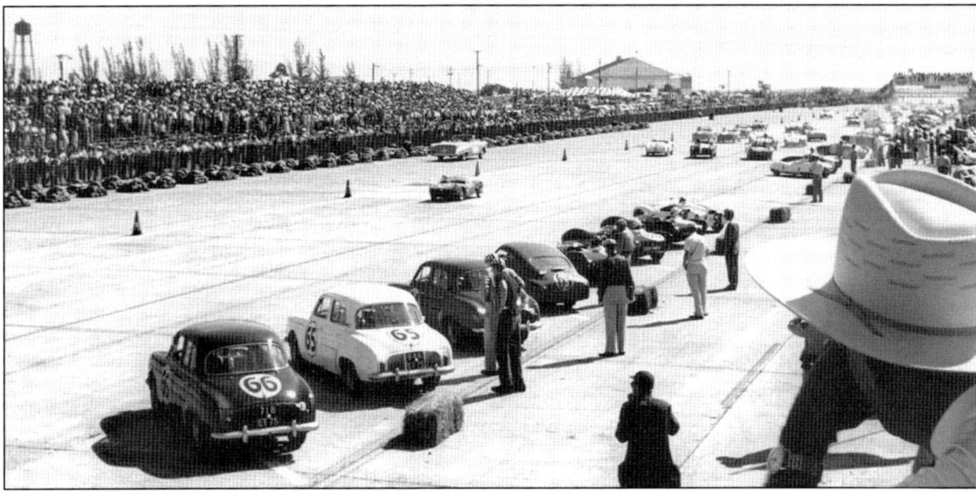

Seen on March 23, 1957, the exciting Le Mans start was used through 1969. At the race start, drivers sprinted to their waiting cars and began around the 5.2-mile circuit. Since 1970, a rolling start has been used with grid positions determined by qualifying speeds. Races were also judged by the complex Index of Performance, which rewarded consistency over pure speed. (Photograph by Ted Shoemaker, courtesy Sebring Historical Society.)

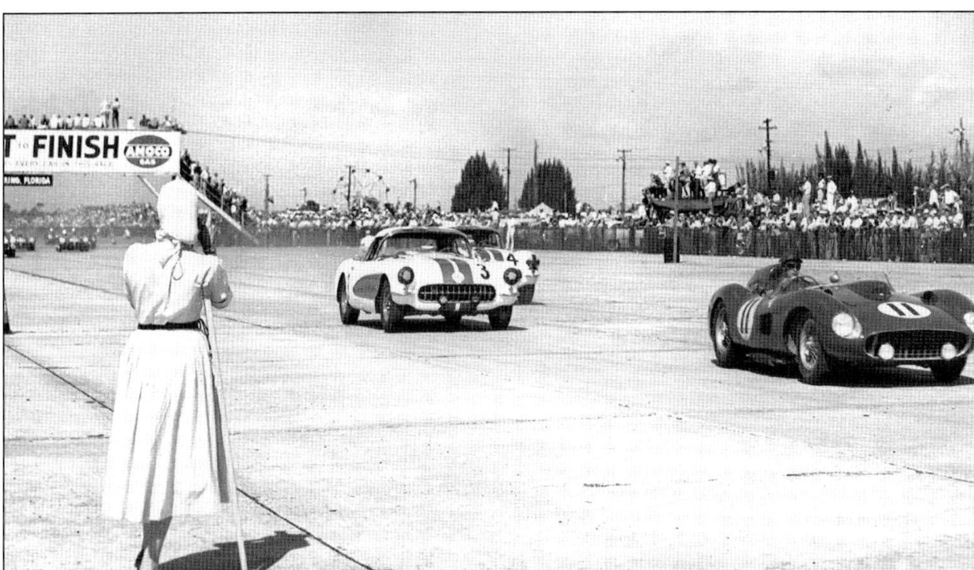

The Amoco Trophy in 1957 was awarded to Maserati drivers Jean Behra and 1956 winner Juan Manuel Fangio. Argentinian Fangio was one of racing's most successful drivers, winning five Formula One world championships during his legendary career. His nephew Juan Manuel Fangio II posted Sebring victories in 1996 and 1997. Fans were able to get a trackside view of the 1957 action. (Photograph by Jess Woods, courtesy Sebring Historical Society.)

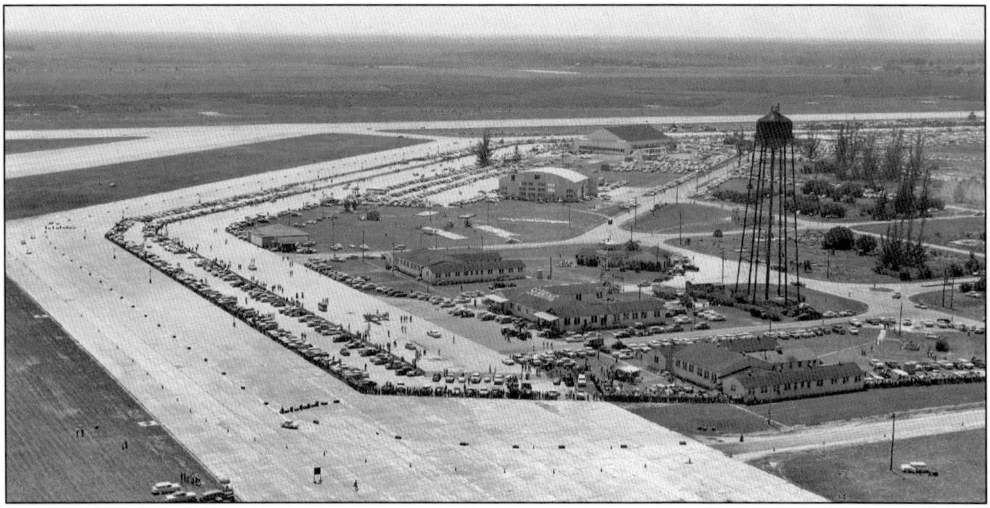

This aerial view during the 1957 race shows Tower Turn and the Second Ramp Bend. The circuit remained virtually unchanged from 1952 to 1982 except for the elimination of Webster Turn prior to the 1967 race. A tragic 1966 crash in that corner resulted in the deaths of four race spectators and prompted stricter spectator safety controls. The track is presently 3.7 miles in length. (Photograph by Jess Woods, courtesy Sebring Historical Society.)

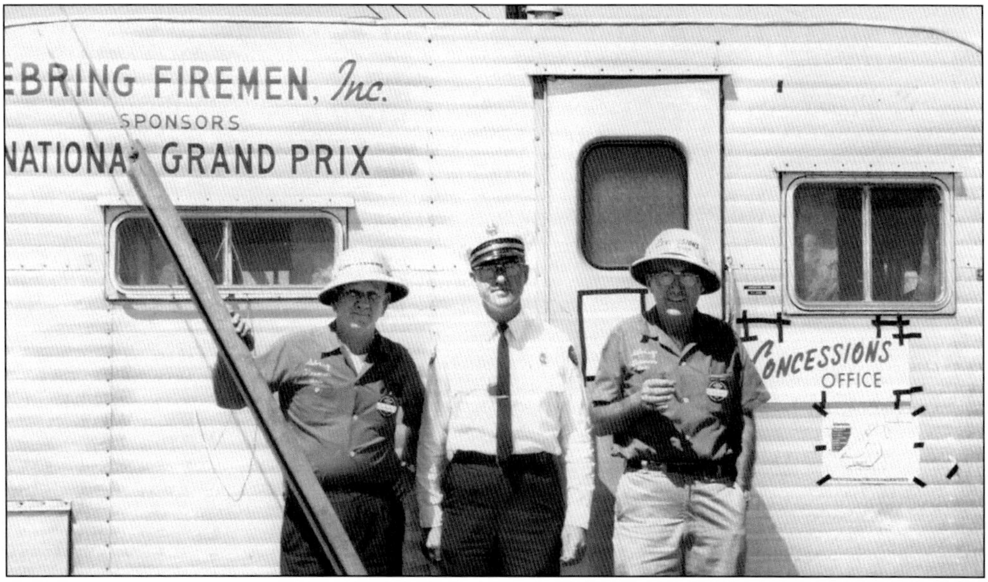

The Sebring Firemen Race Committee was instrumental in establishing the airport as a raceway site, and they assisted in all manner of support. In 1963, Miles Baker (at right) was in charge of race concessions; he was accompanied by P. G. Gearing and Thurmond Haywood. Baker was one of the city's longest-term residents, having arrived as a youngster with his family when Sebring was settled in 1911. (Courtesy Sebring Historical Society.)

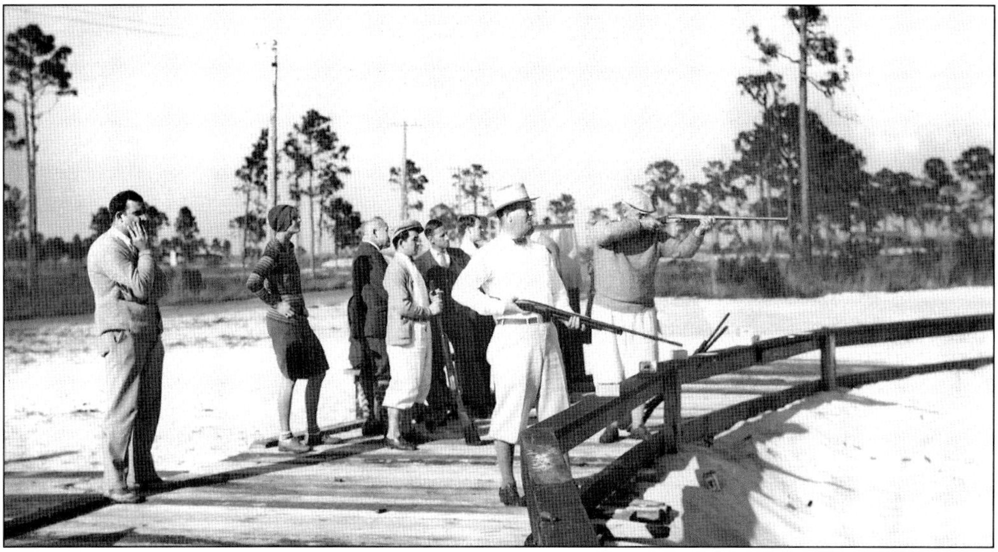

Rex Beach (far right) is joined by other members of a skeet-shooting party, an event particularly popular among winter residents. Quail hunting, bird dog field trials, fishing, foot races around the Circle, tennis, pitching horseshoes, and boat races were other outdoor leisure activities. The two-lane bowling alley on the Circle gave bowlers three attempts to dislodge five suspended paddles. (Courtesy Sebring Historical Society.)

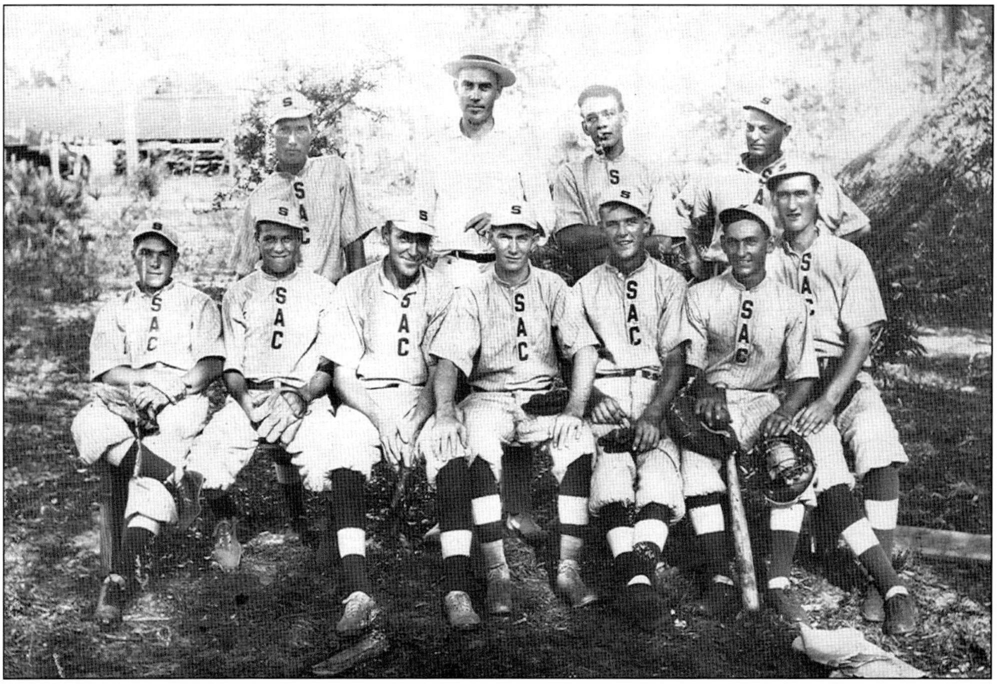

The Sebring Athletic Club baseball team is shown in about 1914. Baseball was the most popular team sport with the entire town turning out for Thursday afternoon games. The March 29, 1917, *Sebring White Way* reported on a game between local youngsters and their older counterparts—the "Neverwassers" versus the "Hasbeens." The spirited contest was called for darkness after the seventh inning: a 6-6 tie. (Courtesy Sebring Historical Society.)

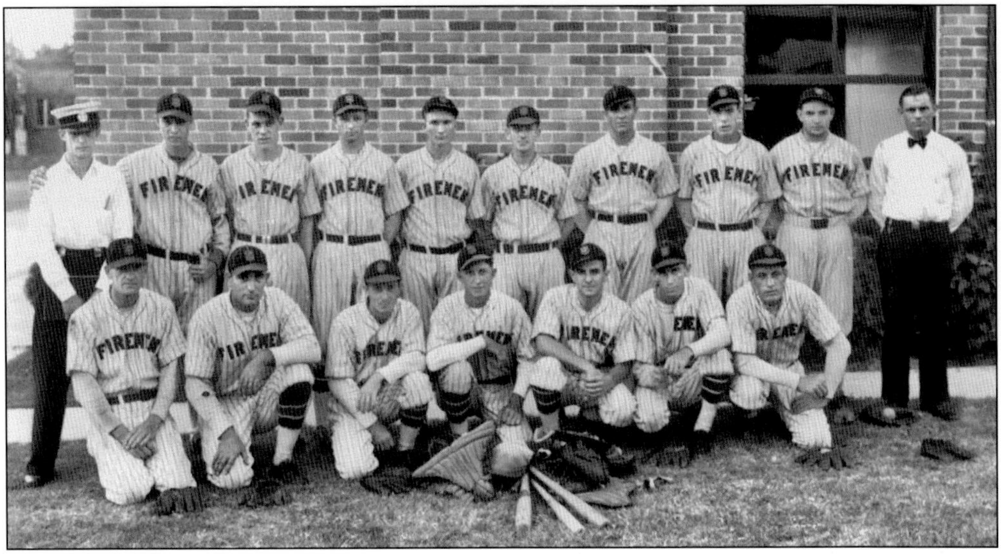

The Sebring fire department fielded a competitive baseball team in the 1930s Orange Belt League. This team included, from left to right, (first row) Zeke Etheridge, Tom Dimberline, Joe Long, Hoyt Ewing, Walter Ivings, Doug Estes, and George Hicks; (second row) Joe Lighthiser, Ralph Morgan, Bill Mackay, E. W. "Ebb" Gallaher, Fred Wheeler, P. G. Gearing, Jack Parker, Hal Long, Tommy Whitehouse, and Allen C. Altvater. (Courtesy Allen C. Altvater III, from the Allen C. Altvater Collection.)

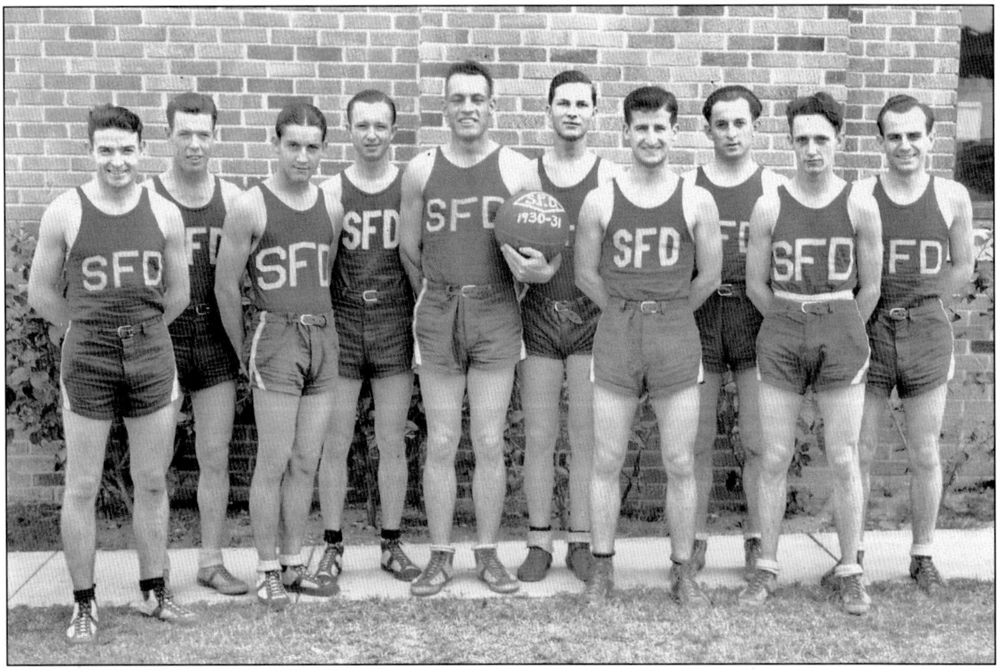

The Sebring fire department formed its first basketball team in 1927, competing against area college and fire department teams. The 1930–1931 team was coached by George Hicks, an all-state center from Southern College in Lakeland, and included (from left to right) Tommy Whitehouse, Harold W. "Hal" Long, Max Long, E. W. "Ebb" Gallaher, coach Hicks, Gowdy Adams, Bobby Butts, Mel Starr, Joe J. Lighthiser, and Walter Ivings. (Courtesy Sebring Historical Society.)

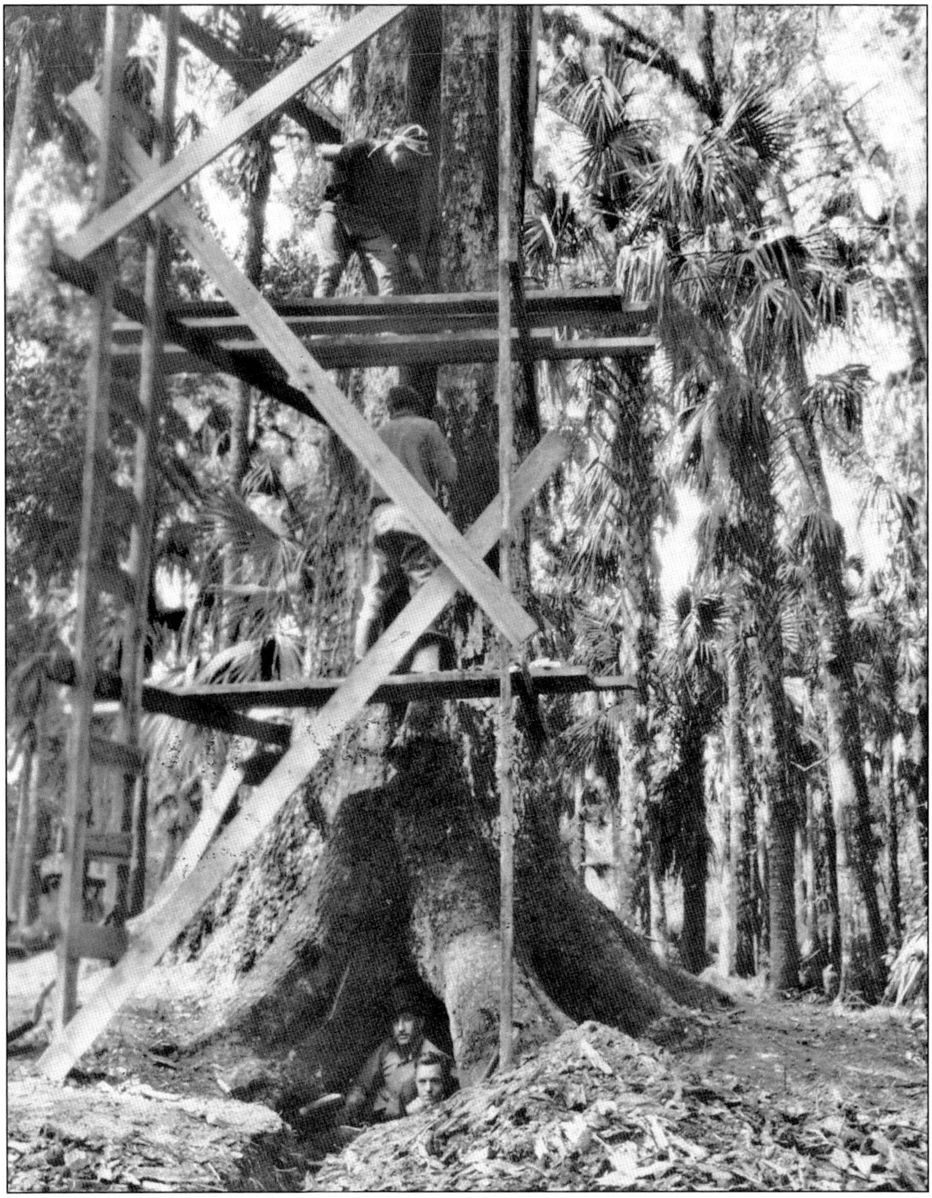

Highlands Hammock State Park is located on the west side of Lake Jackson, four miles from Sebring. Formerly known as Hooker Hammock, the land was purchased by the Tropical Florida Parks Association with significant financial backing from John A. Roebling II, his wife, Margaret Shippen Roebling, and enthusiastic support from the populace. The park opened in 1931, and on November 31, 1935, Highlands Hammock became Florida's first state park. The Roebling's son Donald became interested in the work of preserving the natural live oak and cabbage palm forest, and donated $5,000 to prolong the lives of three enormous oaks. One was dedicated to the memory of Margaret Roebling, who died in October 1930. According to information in the Sebring Historical Society collection, "the operators removed the decayed wood in the center of the trees. . . . Disinfectants were applied to discourage further decay and then the tree's cavity was filled with concrete and reinforced with steel bars. A total of 1,581 bags of cement, 2,762 cubic feet of sand, and 5,527 cubic feet of gravel was used." (Courtesy Sebring Historical Society.)

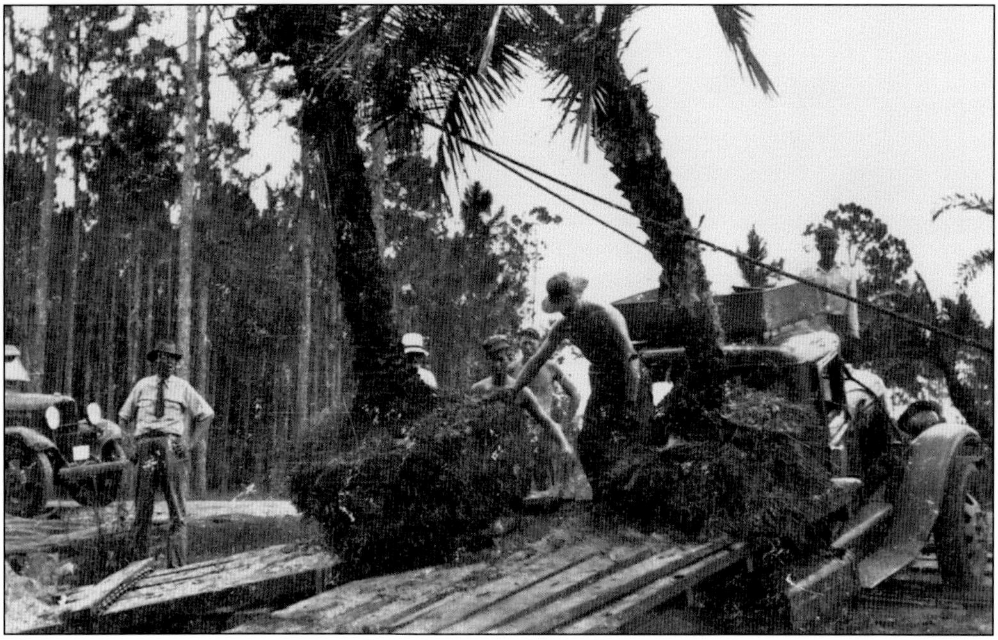

The Civilian Conservation Corps (CCC) was established in 1933, and between 1934 and 1942, approximately 230 young men helped develop Highlands Hammock. The CCC provided these men "training by doing" opportunities, which served the country and taught valuable skills to workers rebounding from the Depression. Many CCC projects at Highlands Hammock are still in use, and the park hosts an annual CCC festival and reunion. (Courtesy Sebring Historical Society.)

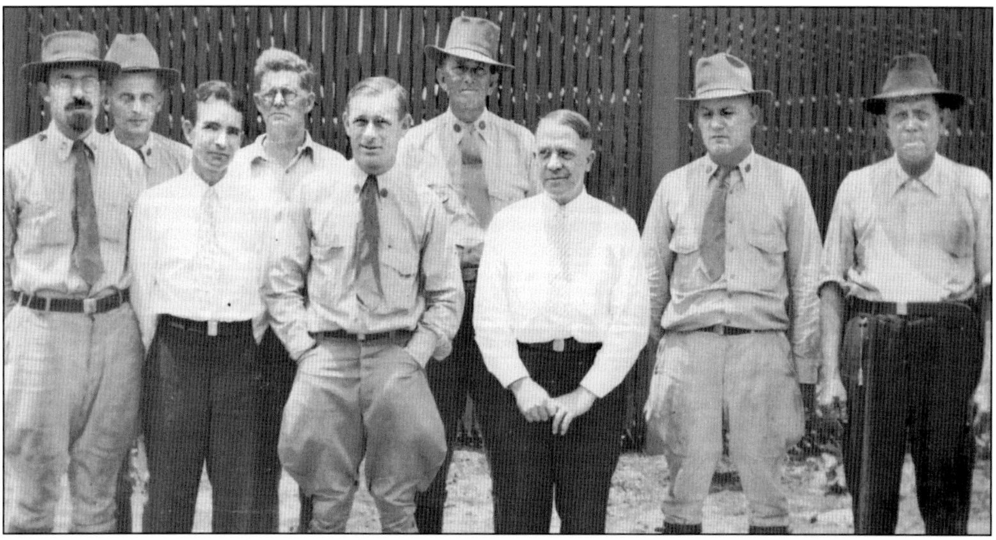

At Highlands Hammock State Park in about 1936, the Civilian Conservation Corps supervisory personnel included, from left to right, botanist James McFarlin, engineer Robert Mann, clerk Fred Ley, mechanic J. P. Lighthiser, superintendent Allen C. Altvater, foreman William Norris, architect Wilbur Cornell, foreman Lamont Wolff, and blacksmith Tom Bass. Personnel not shown were foreman George Hicks and landscape designer Clara I. Thomas. (Courtesy Allen C. Altvater III, from the Allen C. Altvater Collection.)

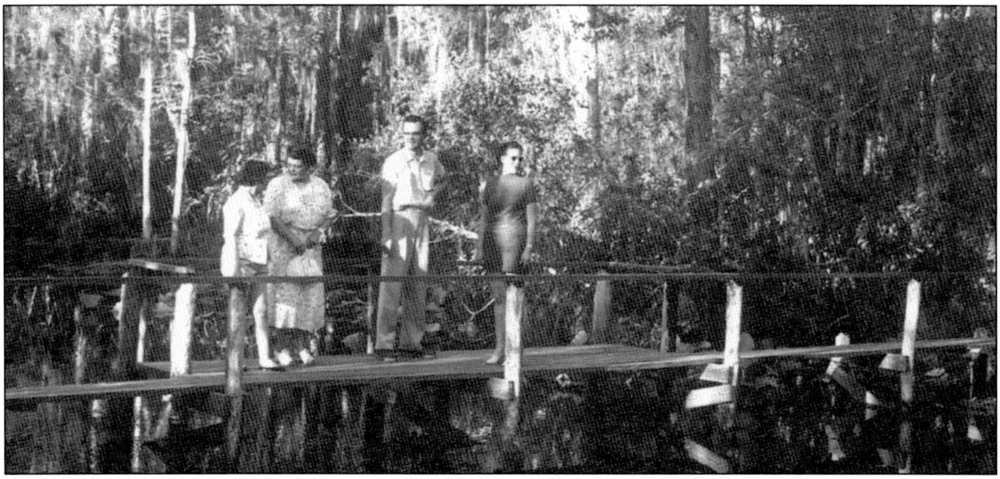

Among the park's 9,000 acres is an old-growth cypress swamp, navigable across an elevated boardwalk trail called the catwalk. The catwalk is seen here in about 1938 where it crosses Charlie Bowlegs Creek. Pictured from left to right are Mary Altvater, Mrs. Irving Zuelks, Dave Gallaher, and Cordelle (Zuelks) Gallaher. Among the other trails are the Young Hammock, Ancient Hammock, Fern Garden, Wild Orange Grove, and Allen Altvater trails. (Courtesy Sebring Historical Society.)

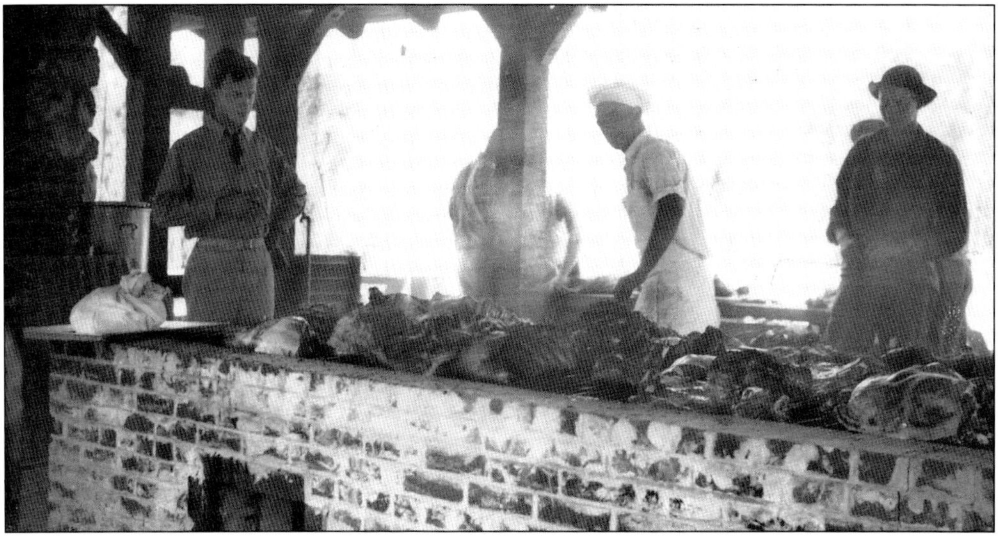

This April 5, 1940, Highlands Hammock photograph depicts what appears to be a CCC barbecue. This pavilion, still in use, and the nearby picnic grounds were popular destinations for families and local civic and social groups. Highlands Hammock is home to Florida's Civilian Conservation Corps Museum, opened in November 1994 and renovated for a rededication in 2003. (Courtesy Sebring Historical Society.)

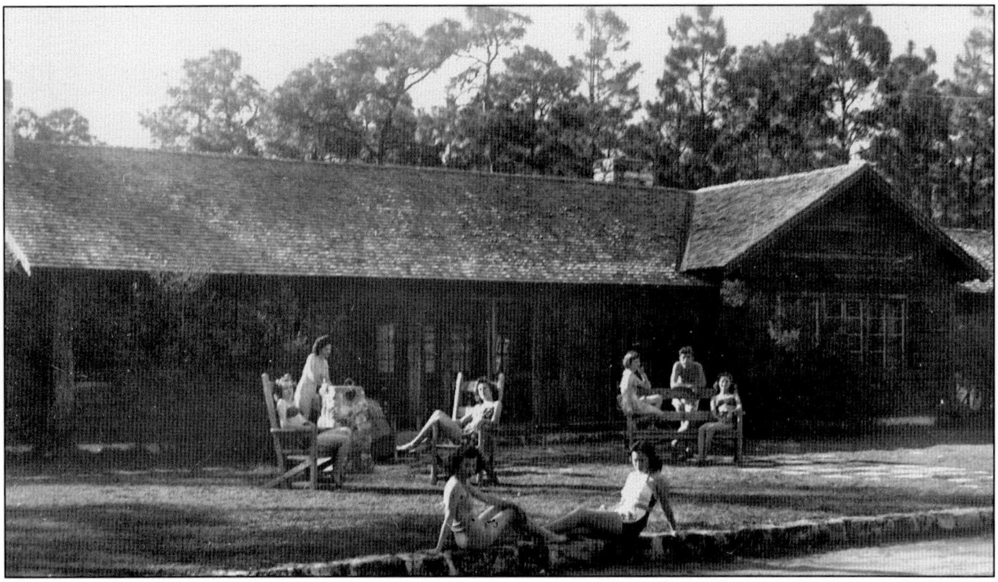

The Hammock Inn was one of the first structures at Highlands Hammock. It has served as a meeting and banquet hall, and is still the park restaurant. Within easy bicycle-riding range of the city, the park was a safe haven for local youngsters who spent lazy summer days riding the wooded roads and trails, hiking along the catwalk, and playing ball in the old orange grove. (Courtesy Sebring Historical Society.)

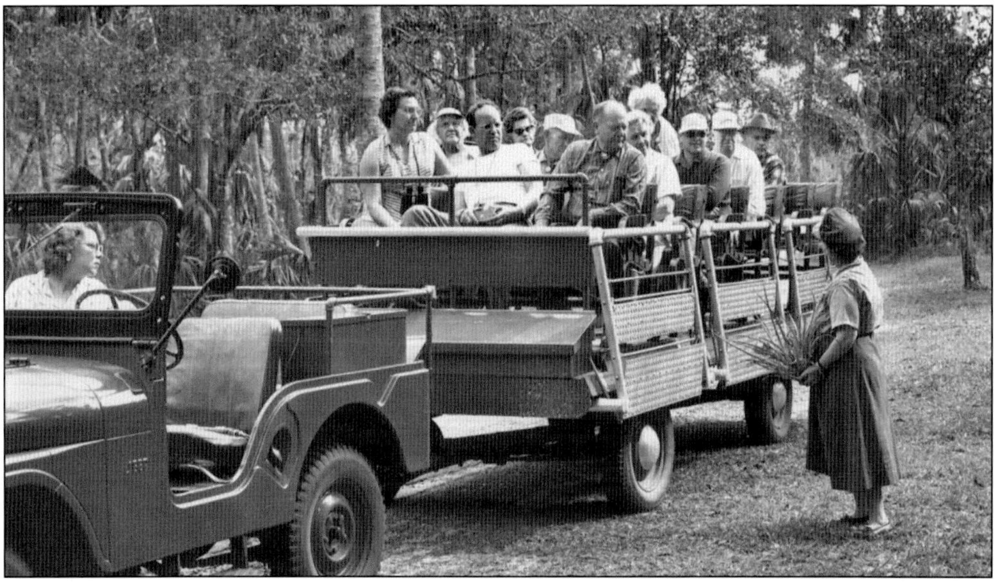

Carol Beck's park tram tour provided a narrated glimpse of early Hammock settlers, development of the park, and the natural setting. Tourists passed close to the amphitheater, the site of fashionable Sunday-afternoon religious and political gatherings prior to World War II. The amphitheater has also hosted band concerts and other civic and cultural events. (Courtesy Sebring Historical Society.)

Eight

TOURISM

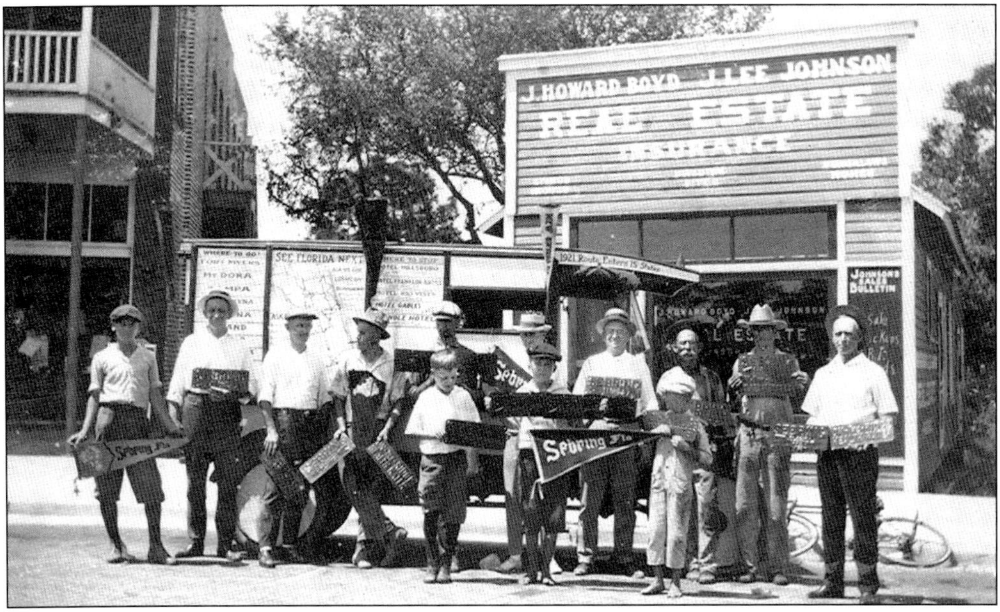

Enthusiastic promoters stood on the Circle in 1921 holding pennants and signs proclaiming Sebring's location and advantage: "On the Ridge. Health Water." The J. Howard Boyd and J. Lee Johnson Real Estate and Insurance agency advertised citrus groves, building lots, and bungalows. The remodeled real estate office was formerly the Sebring Confectionary adjacent to the Zeall Building at the corner of South Center Avenue and Circle Drive. (Courtesy Sebring Historical Society.)

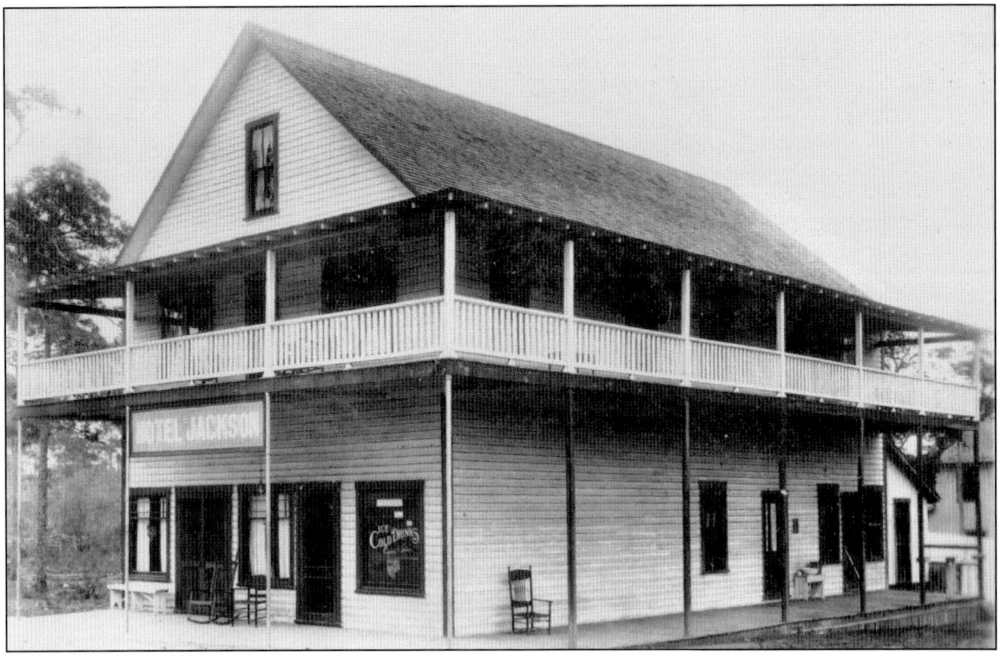

Hotel Jackson offered the first full-scale downtown accommodations when it opened in 1912 at the corner of the Circle and South Commerce Avenue as W. G. Cason's Hotel; this photograph likely dates from late 1913. The two-story pine hotel burned in Sebring's first major fire in 1914. It was replaced by another building that closely resembled this one just off the Circle on South Commerce Avenue at Wall Street. (Courtesy Sebring Historical Society.)

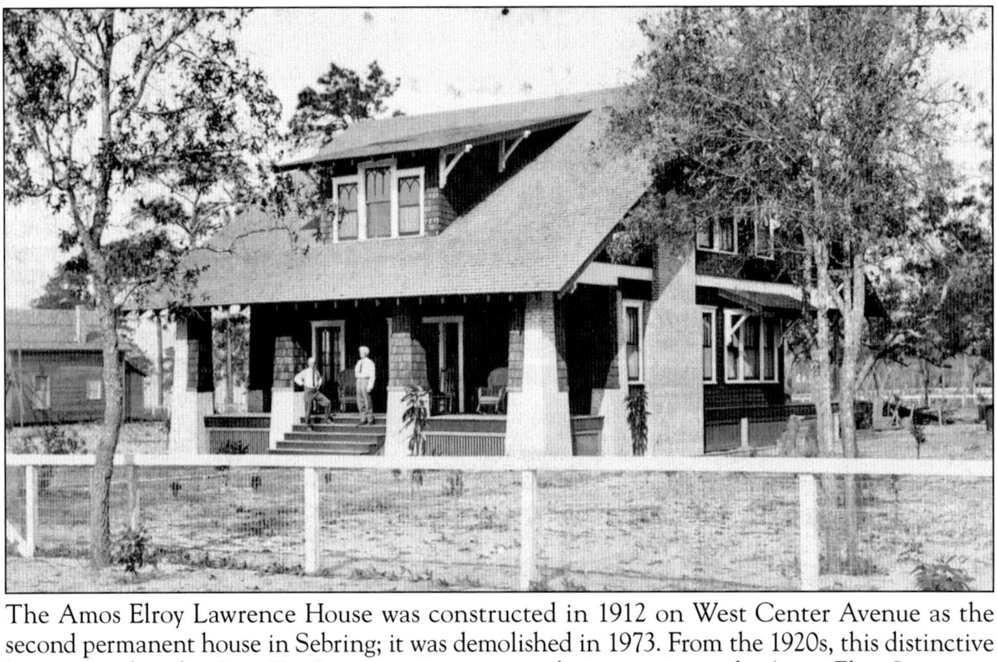

The Amos Elroy Lawrence House was constructed in 1912 on West Center Avenue as the second permanent house in Sebring; it was demolished in 1973. From the 1920s, this distinctive home served as the Grey Top Inn, catering to an exclusive tourist trade. Amos Elroy Lawrence (1862–1932) was a member of the Pittsburg Party and served as mayor, county judge, and city and county attorney during his distinguished career. (Courtesy Sebring Historical Society.)

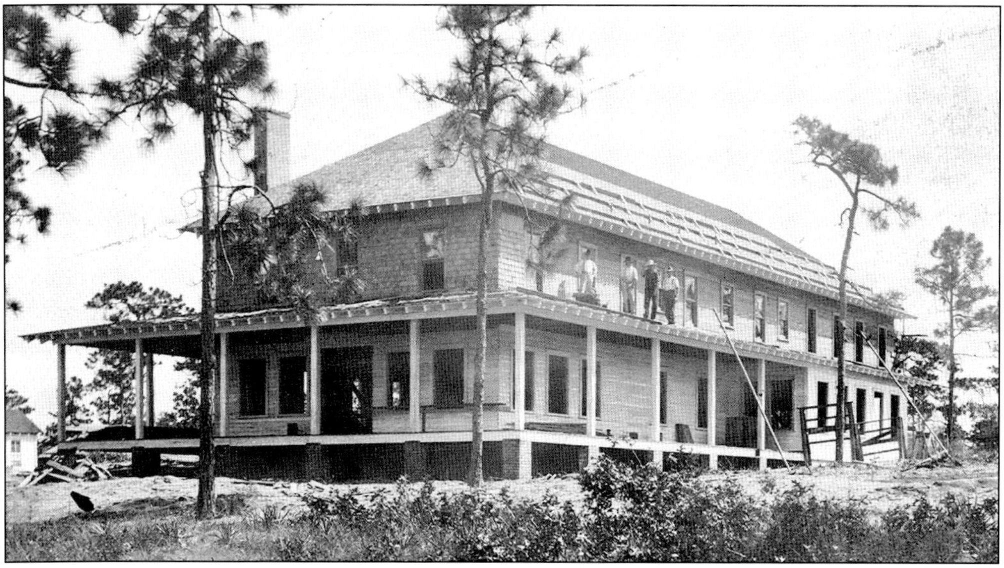

The Arrowhead Hotel was the earliest large tourist hotel and was built by George Sebring in 1912 on Lakeview Drive. The Chamberlain cottage (see page 19) may be seen at far left. For a time it was the home of hotelier Frank B. Chamberlain, and it became a tool and paint house for the hotel. Bill and Nettie Amy of Asbury Park, New Jersey, managed the Arrowhead. (Courtesy Sebring Historical Society.)

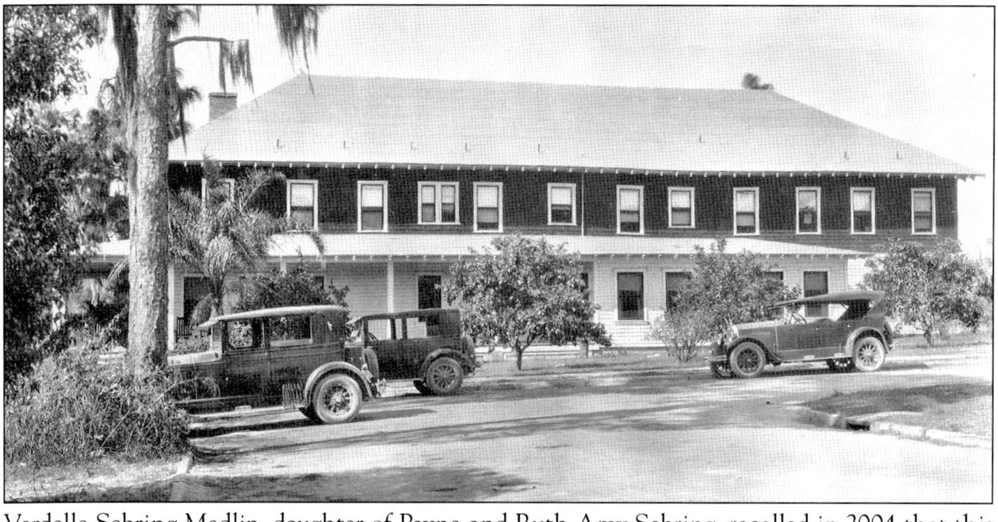

Verdelle Sebring Medlin, daughter of Payne and Ruth Amy Sebring, recalled in 2004 that this hotel "was named the Arrowhead for the numerous Indian arrowheads that were found in and around the lake." Bill and Nettie Amy were Verdelle's maternal grandparents. The hotel was sold during the late 1920s, renamed the Pennsylvania Hotel, and was demolished in the 1960s to make way for the Edgewater Arms condominium. (Photograph by Woodward, courtesy Sebring Historical Society.)

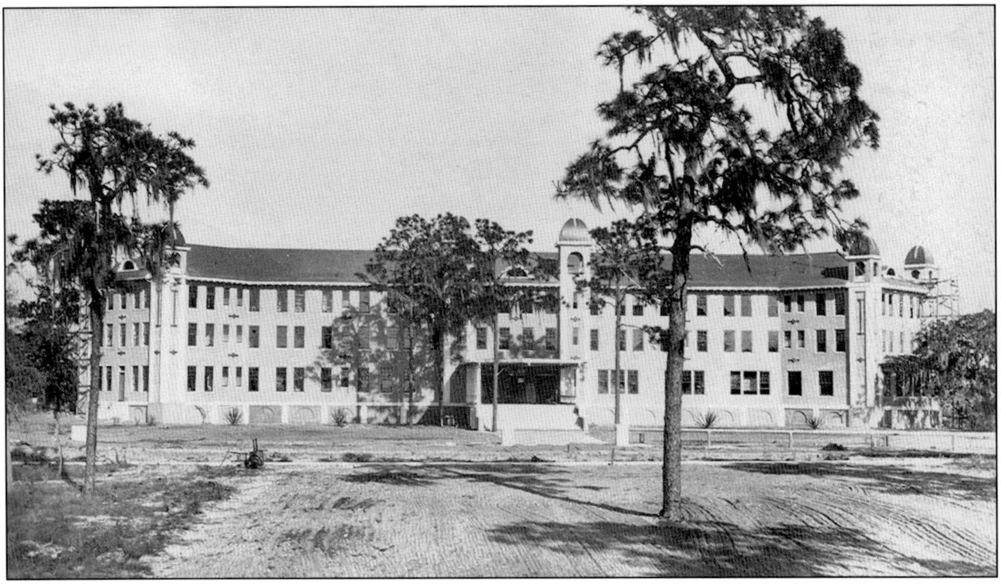

Constructed by George E. Sebring and contractor B. A. Cope a scant four years after his community was founded, the sweeping Mediterranean Revival–style Kenilworth Lodge has enjoyed a lasting reputation as the city's finest hostelry. Located on Lakeview Drive SE within easy walking distance of the Circle, the Kenilworth originally catered to northerners escaping harsh winters and was only open for several months each year. (Courtesy Sebring Historical Society.)

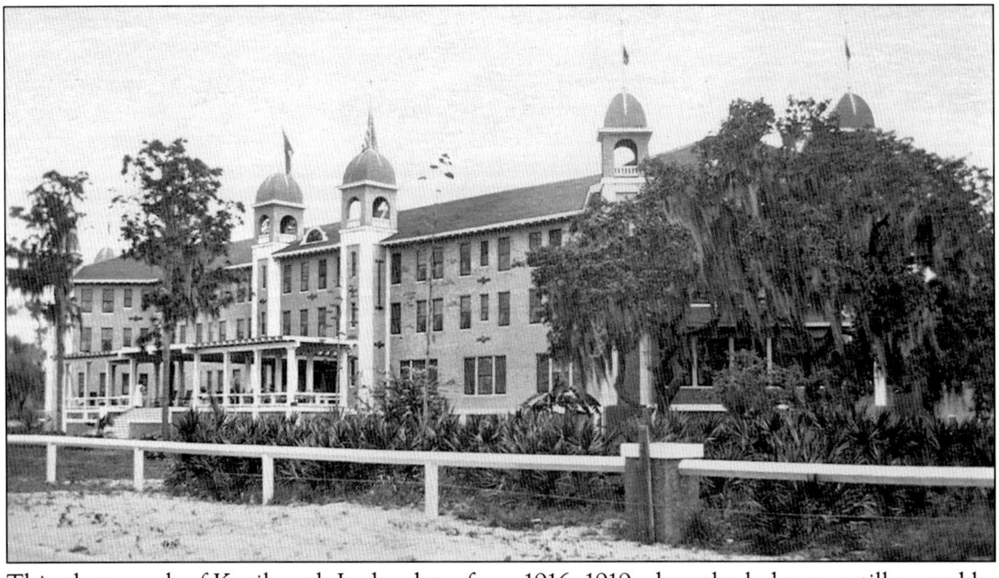

This photograph of Kenilworth Lodge dates from 1916–1919 when the lodge was still owned by George E. Sebring. Later visitors arriving by train were greeted by cars from Kenilworth Lodge and were taken to the 320-acre site, where they enjoyed an 18-hole golf course, a terraced garden and orange grove, and recreation on Lake Jackson. (Courtesy Sebring Historical Society.)

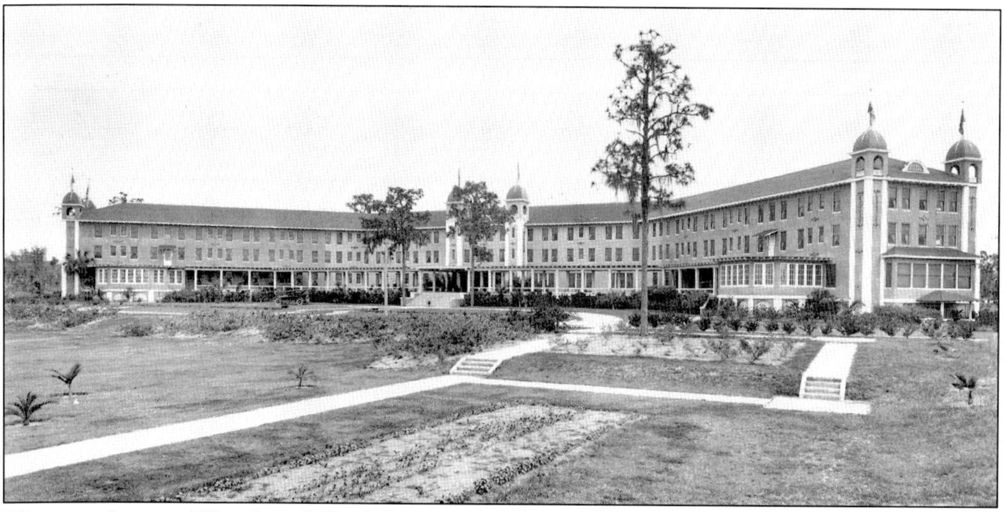

The popularity of Kenilworth Lodge necessitated an expansion in 1919. The north and south wings were added to the central building, and a large porch—since removed—was added to the west side. Nearly all of the rooms had private baths, save for a half-dozen family suites with shared baths. This image is from April 1926. (Photograph by Burgert Brothers Tampa, courtesy Sebring Historical Society.)

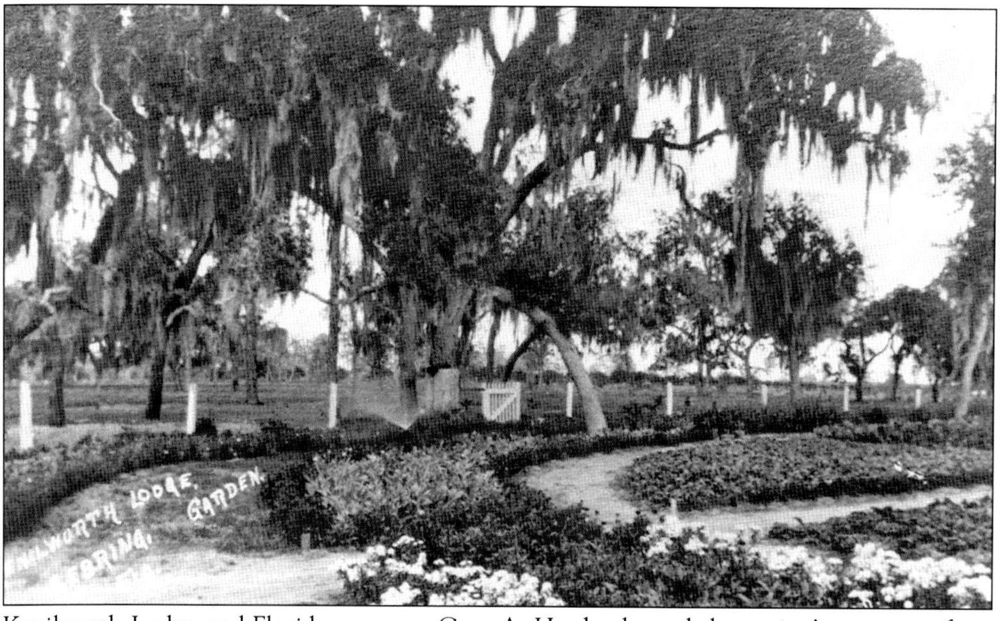

Kenilworth Lodge and Florida governor Cary A. Hardee hosted the nation's governors for a portion of the national Governors' Conference in November 1924, which included a tour of the state. They were welcomed to Sebring by event host Ira Rigdon and John E. Connelly, president of Kenilworth Lodge. Kenilworth Lodge was placed on the National Register of Historic Places in 2000. (Photograph by Field, courtesy Sebring Historical Society.)

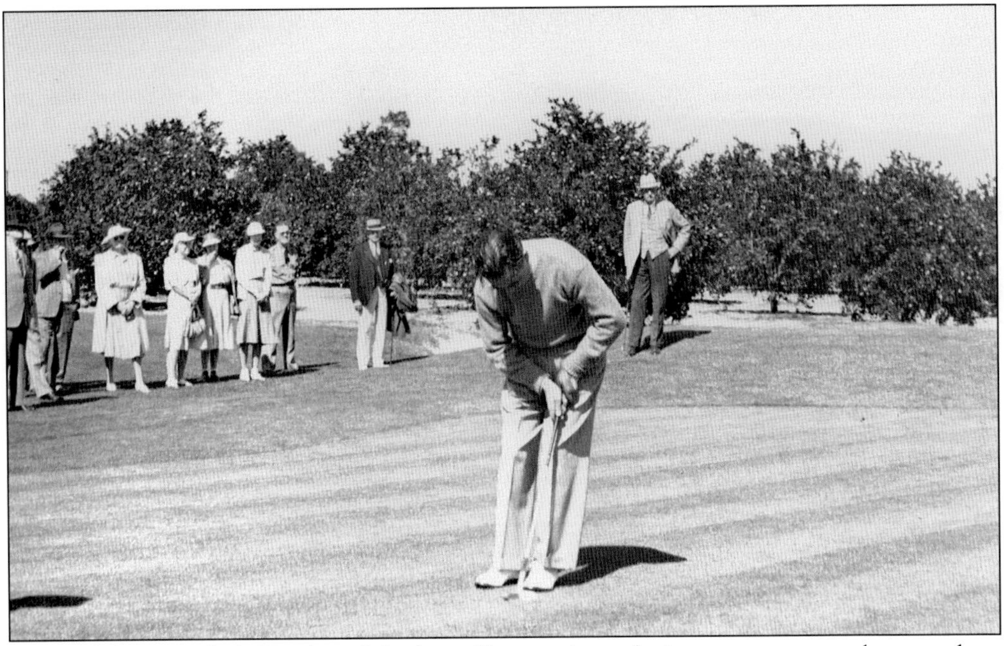

The undulating 18-hole Kenilworth Lodge golf course hosted winter tournament play as early as the 1920s. The December 6, 1924, New York *Sun* lauded the 6,300-yard course, reporting that national open champion Cyril Walker and club pro James Maiden were representing the lodge in league play. This photograph likely dates from the 1940s and shows how close the course was to the lodge orange groves. (Courtesy Sebring Historical Society.)

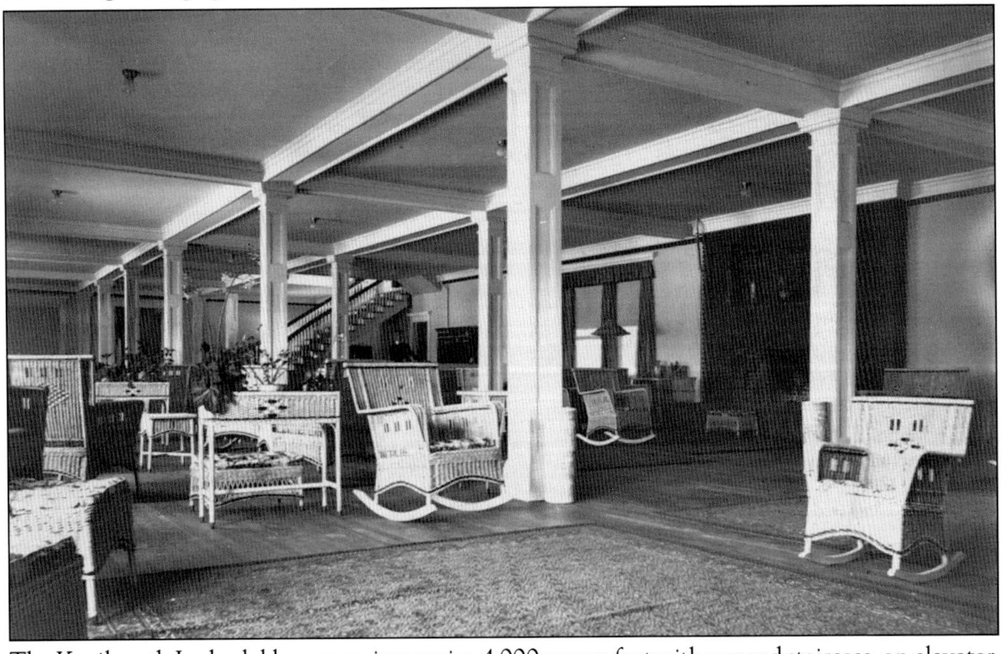

The Kenilworth Lodge lobby was an impressive 4,000 square feet with a grand staircase, an elevator, a large fireplace, and wicker furniture throughout. The lodge's covered pier on Lake Jackson was visible from the front porch. Since 1995, the Kenilworth has been owned by Mark and Madge Stewart, who first leased the lodge in 1987. (Courtesy Sebring Historical Society.)

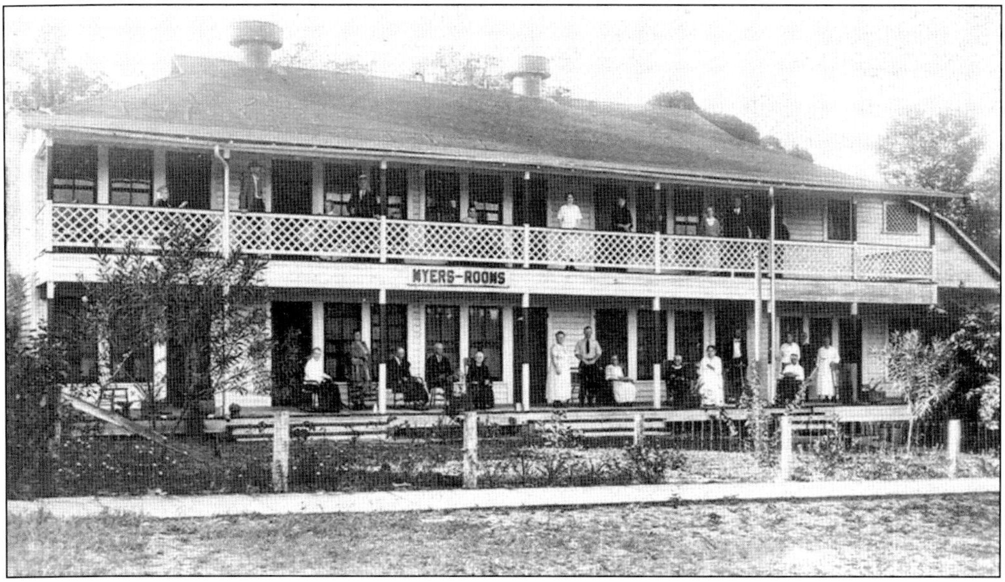

Myers Rooms was built in 1919 at the corner of North Pine Street and Pomegranate Avenue. It served as a boarding house for winter visitors, later became the Pinehurst Apartments, and was demolished in 1995. In 1980, longtime teacher Esther Ritter recalled that when she arrived in Sebring in 1923, accommodations were scarce and expensive; luckily a local home housed unmarried female teachers. (Courtesy Sebring Historical Society.)

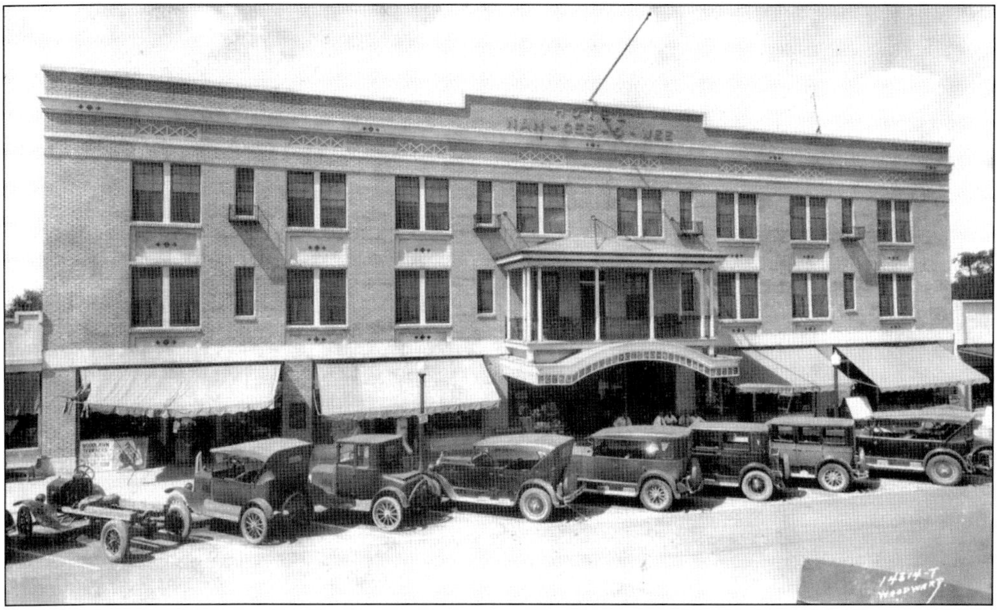

The Nan-Ces-O-Wee Hotel was constructed by George Sebring in 1923 at a cost of more than $100,000. Located on North Ridgewood Drive adjacent to the George Sebring Building (1923), the Nan-Ces-O-Wee included 60 hotel rooms upstairs and five street-level storefronts. The year-round hotel advertised "American Plan" room rates of $5 and under, and proclaimed "No sunshine, no charge for rooms." (Photograph by Woodward, courtesy Sebring Historical Society.)

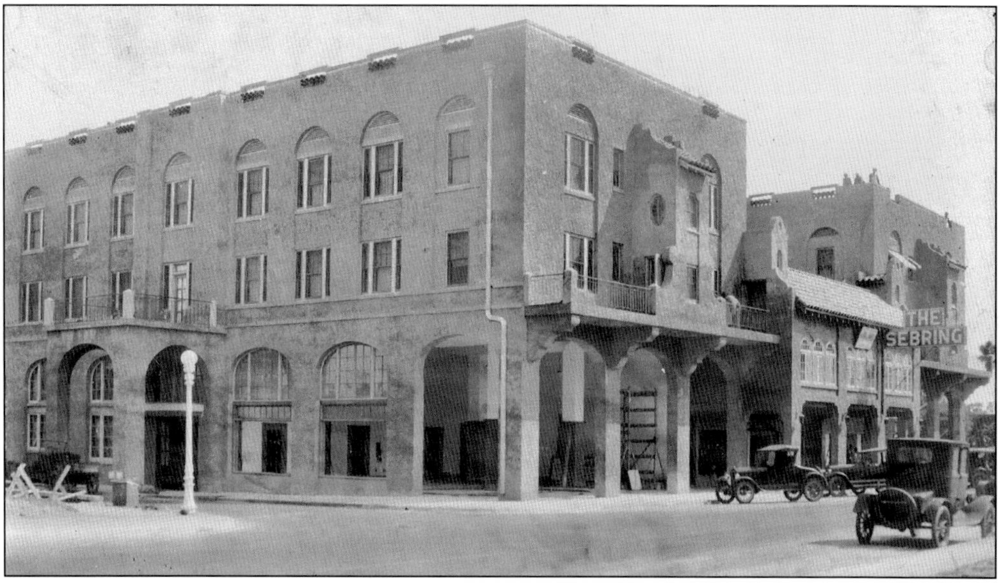

The Sebring Hotel was constructed by H. Orvel Sebring in 1925 at the corner of Oak Avenue and South Ridgewood Drive. The hotel served as a social center for decades until it became the Palms Nursing Home in 1961. In 1984, Jack Hancock remembered that the Sebring Hotel was a popular meeting spot for soldiers from Hendricks Field and their girlfriends. The Sebring Hotel was demolished in 1985. (Courtesy Sebring Historical Society.)

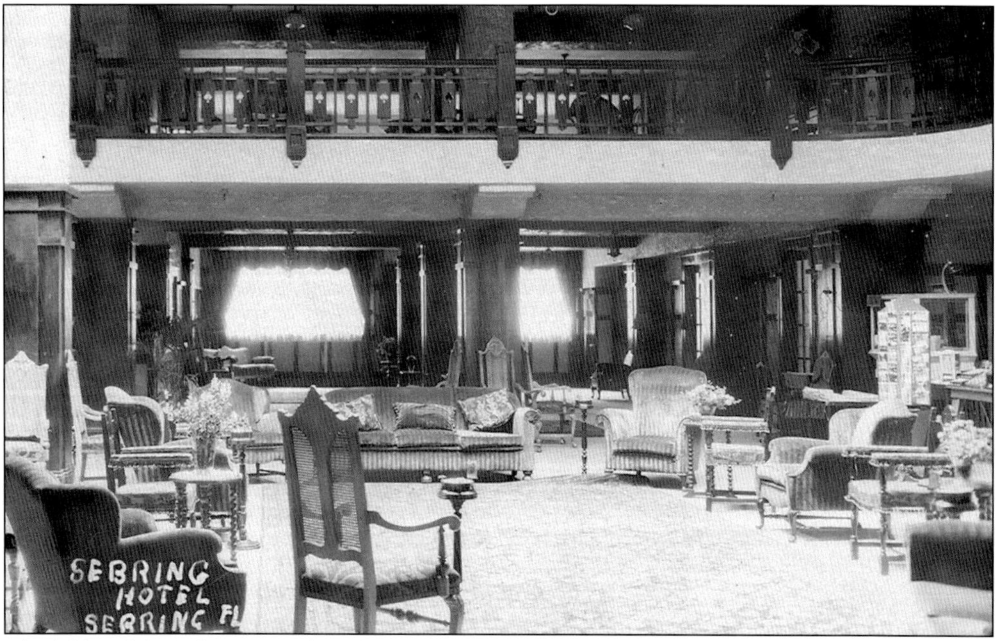

The lobby of the Sebring Hotel was handsomely appointed and featured a pipe organ located on the mezzanine level adjacent to the central staircase that was used during Sunday afternoon concerts. Longtime Sebring resident Martha Hammond recalled in 1984 that musical accompaniment during dinners was provided by a three-piece orchestra. This photograph shows the lobby and mezzanine shortly after construction. (Courtesy Sebring Historical Society.)

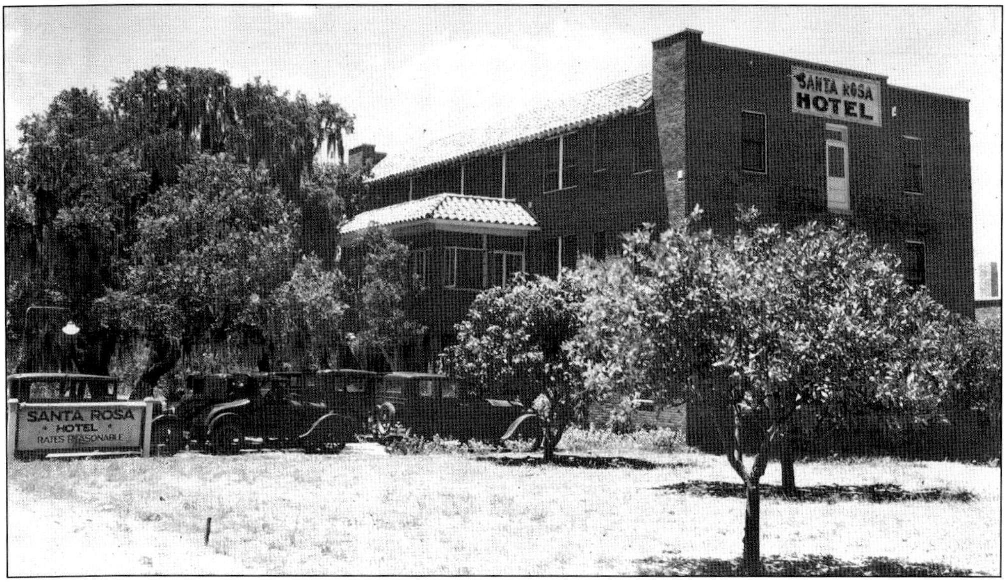

The 30-room brick Santa Rosa Hotel was constructed on North Ridgewood Drive in 1923 by pioneer resident Aaron Withers. He was the town's first marshal and first fire chief, and served as president of citrus company Withers and Harshman. In 1935, the Santa Rosa was purchased by Martin and Mary McGee; after Martin's death in 1948, Mary managed the hotel until the 1980s. (Courtesy Sebring Historical Society.)

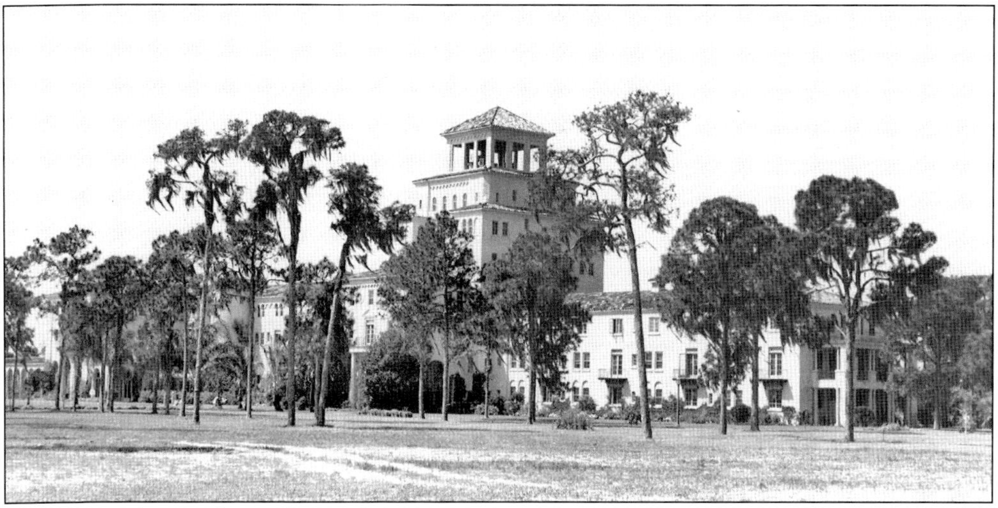

The spectacular Harder Hall opened to great acclaim in 1928 with 200 guest rooms in a three-story, Spanish-style edifice with a seven-story central tower, adjoining a golf course with homes planned for the 2,000-acre property. The hotel remained open during the Depression but sat vacant for many years until a series of renovation attempts between the 1980s and 2007. The city assumed ownership of Harder Hall in July 2007. (Courtesy Sebring Historical Society.)

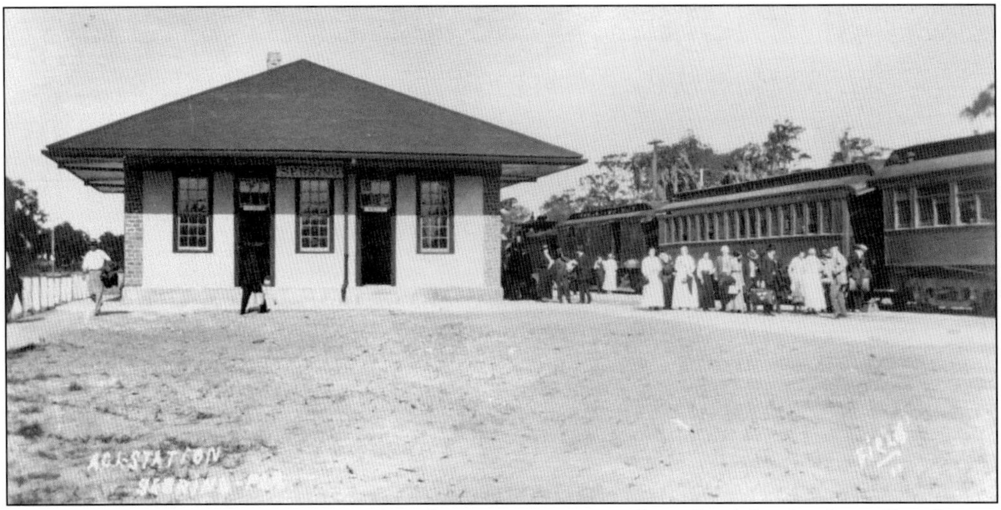

The second Atlantic Coast Line Railroad station was situated north of the Circle on Eucalyptus Street. Constructed in 1917 to replace the first station at the end of North Commerce Avenue, this station remained in use until the 1960s. It was demolished when the Sebring Parkway was constructed along a portion of the old ACL right-of-way. This photograph dates from about 1919. (Photograph by Field, courtesy Sebring Historical Society.)

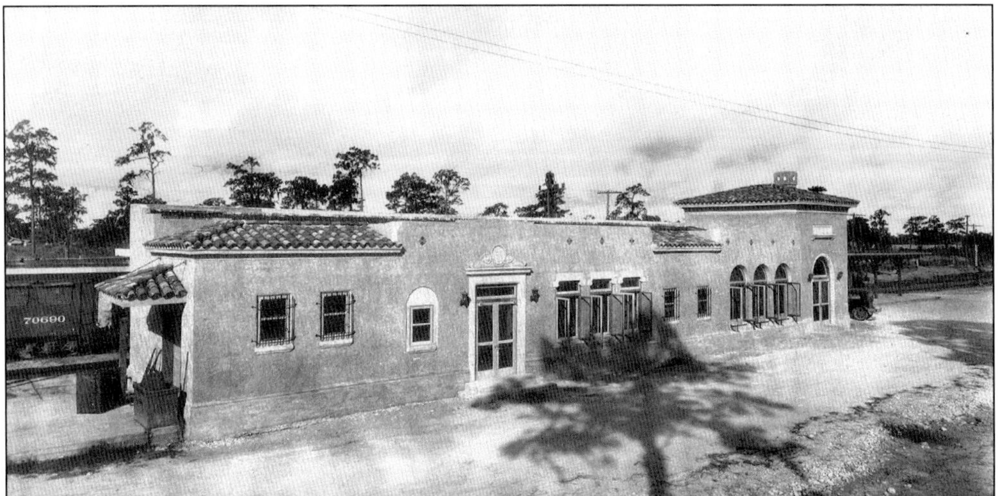

The Seaboard Airline Railroad station was constructed in 1924 as Sebring's third station, a year before this photograph was taken. The *Sebring White Way* reported on June 20, 1924, that $30,000 was required to purchase right-of-way land for the tracks so that the station could be located within the city. The 850 residents raised the required capital in just 30 days, a remarkable feat. (Photograph by Woodward, courtesy Sebring Historical Society.)

BIBLIOGRAPHY

Altvater, Allen C. *Sebring Air Terminal, Sebring, Florida: Book One*. Lake Placid, FL: The Garage Print Shop, 2005.

———. *Story of the Sebring Firemen*, 2nd ed. Lake Placid, FL: The Garage Print Shop, 2007.

Heartland Heritage. Sebring, FL: Sebring Historical Society, 1983.

The Historian. (Various dates.)

Olausen, Stephen A. *Sebring, City on the Circle: A Guide to the City's Historic Architecture*. St. Augustine, FL: Southern Heritage Press, 1993.

Savage, Julia A. *The A.M.E. Church Review*. 31 (4): 1915, 378–381.

Sebring Historical Society. *The Newcomb and Baker Collections*. Sebring, FL: Sebring Historical Society, 1976.

Sebring Historical Society. *The Seventy-Five Years of Sebring: 1912–1987: History and Official Program, October 11–18, 1987*. Sebring, FL: Sebring Historical Society, 1987.

Sebring Semi-Centennial Committee. *The Fifty Years of Sebring, 1912–1962: History and Official Program, Semi-Centennial Celebration, October 8–13, 1962*. Sebring, FL: Sebring Semi-Centennial Committee, 1962.

Sebring White Way. Various dates.

Twice Told Tales. Sebring, FL: Sebring Historical Society, 1986.

Ulmann, Alec. *The Sebring Story*. Philadelphia: Chilton Book Company, 1969.

Walker, Robert J. *The Way Things Were: Short Stories of Past Experiences*. Bloomington, IN: 1st Books Library, 2002.

The Way it Was in Early Sebring History. Sebring, FL: Sebring Historical Society, 1982.

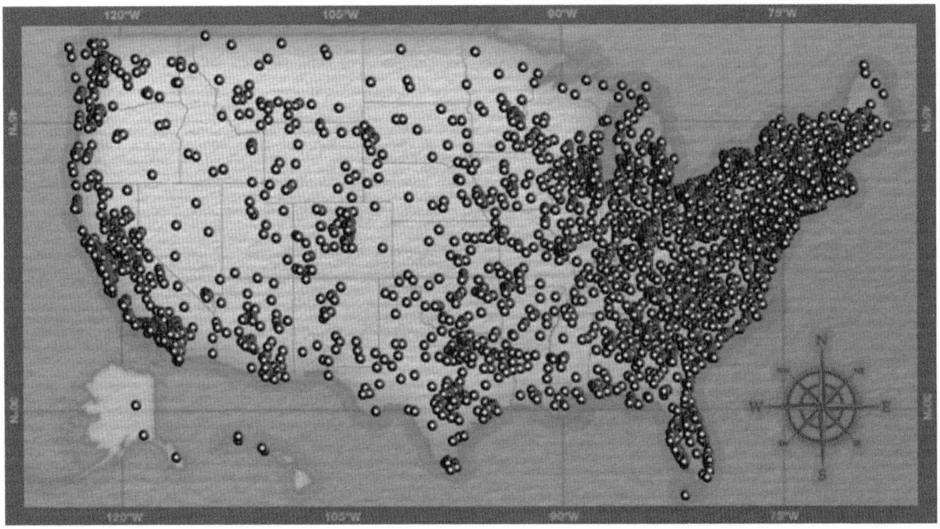

Consistent with our mission to preserve history on a local level, this book was printed in South Carolina on American-made paper and manufactured entirely in the United States. Products carrying the accredited Forest Stewardship Council (FSC) label are printed on 100 percent FSC-certified paper.

MADE IN THE USA